Unity and Diversity in Language Use

Selected papers from the
Annual Meeting of the British Association for Applied Linguistics
held at the University of Reading, September 2001

Edited by

Kristyan Spelman Miller &
Paul Thompson

Advisory Board: Srikant Sarangi, Celia Roberts and Gunther Kress

BRITISH ASSOCIATION FOR APPLIED LINGUISTICS

in association with

continuum
LONDON • NEW YORK
www.continuumbooks.com

Continuum

The Tower Building, 11 York Road, London SE1 7NX
Lexington Avenue, New York, NY 10017-6503

First published 2002 © Kristyan Spelman Miller, Paul Thompson and
contributors 2002

British Library Cataloguing in Publication Data

A catalogue record for this book is available from the British Library.

ISBN 0-8264-6106-9 (paperback)

Library of Congress Cataloging-in-Publication Data
British Association for Applied Linguistics. Meeting (34th : 2001 :
University of Reading)
    Unity and diversity in language use: selected papers from the
Annual Meeting of the British Association for Applied Linguistics, held
at the University of Reading, September, 2001/edited by Kristyan
Spelman Miller & Paul Thompson.
      p. cm. – (British studies in applied linguistics ; 16)
    Includes bibliographical references and index.
    ISBN 0-8264-6106-9 (pb.)
Applied linguistics—Congresses. I. Spelman Miller, Kristyan. II.
Thompson, Paul. III. Title IV. Series.
P129 .B75 2001
418—dc21

2002073743

Typeset by Paul Thompson

Printed and bound in Great Britain by
Biddles Ltd, *www.biddles.co.uk*

Contents

1 Introduction

KRISTYAN SPELMAN MILLER AND PAUL THOMPSON

University of Reading

Conference titles are often intentionally open-ended or ambiguous. A brief glance at recent themes of annual conferences of the *British Association for Applied Linguistics* reveals such teasing titles as *Evolving models of language, Change and continuity in Applied Linguistics, Language across boundaries, Change and language.* Through their use of ambiguity and contrast, such titles invite broad discussion and interpretation within the general domains of language, education, and society.

In choosing the theme for the 34th Annual BAAL Conference held in September 2001 at the University of Reading, we have, of course, been influenced by such tradition. In a manner which echoes the balance and elegance of other titles, we have selected a pair of contrasting terms, unity and diversity. The tension between these two concepts both parallels earlier themes, in particular those of evolution, change and continuity, and prompts explicit focus on the range of concerns within Applied Linguistics and the wider socio-political context of language use at the beginning of the 21st Century. Discussion is invited, at a number of levels, of major issues of standardisation and diversification, of globalisation and localisation, of generality and particularity, and of the opposing forces of centralisation and fragmentation. The theme 'Unity and diversity in language use', therefore, appeals in the broadest sense to those concerned with the investigation of language use – researchers, teachers, policy makers, testers, learners, communicators in multifarious contexts – whose concerns and interests set the agenda for the conference.

This collection can only represent a small subset of the many lively and creative papers, posters, and colloquia presented at Reading. We have chosen to organise the thirteen papers selected here not within strict sub-themes, but according to a thread of connectivity, which visits such topics as multilingualism, genre, computer-mediated comm-unication, interaction styles, research stances, and variation in language learning and teaching. We begin and end with papers from two of our plenary speakers (Kramsch and Seidlhofer) and position our third plenary paper, the Pit Corder Memorial Lecture by Johnson, appropriately we feel, at the centre of the sequence of contributions.

We have chosen to open our collection with Kramsch's challenging discussion of dimensions of second and foreign language learning. The reality of multilingualism and multiculturalism around the world suggests that we should look again at our conceptualisation of second and foreign language learning and teaching. Kramsch points out that both SLA and FL traditions, while coming from different disciplinary origins – the social sciences and the humanities - 'have considered "the language learner" as a generic entity, whose goals and needs are assumed to match those of the institutions that teach them'. With the setting of such large-scale goals, Kramsch persuasively argues, insufficient account is taken of the subjective dimensions of language learning – notions of the learner's identity and personal history, of the learner's voice and language choice. Through illustration of a multilingual subject's writing and reflections, we witness the complex relations of voices, identities and stances, reflected in choices from within her language repertoire, and come closer to an understanding of her position as a language user 'at the confluence of various cultural experiences'. Such a broadening of focus beyond the social and functional dimensions of language learning to incorporate 'the totality of the language learning experience' clearly sets up the theme of the tension between, and potential symbiosis of, the particular and the generic.

The notion of 'generic' is brought under scrutiny from another perspective in the paper by Edge and Wharton. Here, the authors explore the extent to which notions of genre, identified in terms of 'communicative and formal unity ... toward a common social purpose', may, at the same time, tolerate and accommodate diversity. Within the context of Master's students making the shift from producing course assignments to writing articles for publication, the individual responses of writers are discussed, highlighting tensions between originality and conventionality, framework and constraint. The authors demonstrate how such issues may be productively built into a pedagogy which explores not only the choices available to writers of particular genres but also the implications of these choices.

The theme of forms of organisation in written text is picked up in Galloway's paper with reference to school-age and university writers in Australia. With the goal of identifying developmental patterns of language choice associated with perceived coherence, the author examines the characteristics of persuasive texts rated for coherence by untrained readers. Diversity in the range of patterns observed, although more marked as writers develop, is apparent even in the younger writers, and explanations for this variety are explored in relation to pedagogic practice.

While the two previous papers have sought to elaborate details of diversity in the realisation of very familiar written genres, Simpson's timely discussion of computer-mediated communication (CMC) invites us to examine the emergence of a more recent phenomenon, text-based synchronous communication (in this case, internet relay chat and instant messaging). Analysis of such discourse reveals, on the one hand, the merging of spoken and written characteristics and, on the other, the development of features specific to this type of real-time, and highly interactive, text-based communication. In particular, Simpson highlights medium-generated features of turn-taking and exchange structure and the representation of the prosodics and paralanguage of face-to-face discourse in text, as participants attempt to increase interactivity. In his conclusion, the author points to the 'mutual relationship between the technology and the broader social contexts within which the technology exists'. Once again, the theme of system constraints and human interaction with these constraints provides the backdrop to this discussion.

The following two papers (Gillen and Sime) further develop the topic of multi-modality, but in other contexts. Gillen's study of two eleven-year-old boys engaged in collaborative activity using a computer raises important issues concerning the complexity of observational data and methodological approaches to their analysis. The challenge for the researcher to interweave data from different modalities (in this case, speech, actions, and activity on the screen) reflects larger issues concerning the research process within a multi-modal context. In exploring the complexity of language use at this specific, local level, 'the ways in which visual and vocal conduct feature in the *in situ* accomplishment of particular social actions and activities' (Heath 1997: 198, cited in Gillen), Gillen's paper sits well with Sime's discussion, which follows, of gesture within the interactive context of the language classroom. Heath's quotation resonates here, too, in establishing the goal of Sime's paper: to investigate the complementary roles of language and gesture in constructing meaning. The importance of gesture in mediating learning reminds us, too, of Kramsch's earlier discussion of the significance of the individual learning experience in conceptualising and understanding language learning. The learner's perception and interpretation of the teacher's gestures within the classroom is of central importance in such an account, and Sime's clear illustration of instances of gesture use and student understanding further underlines the theme of variety, and of individuality.

The multi-faceted nature of communication is reflected in Roberts and Sarangi's discussion of interactional performance within the specific context of medical student-patient interaction. At one level, we encounter diversity in the sense of a variety of interactive styles: from the empathetic, 'tuneful' moves of candidates who successfully integrate 'authority and solidarity', to less involved, retractive styles, where candidates distance themselves emotionally from their patients. At a further level, interaction is also explored in this paper between the researchers and the professional medical community in which this study is situated. The authors' honest reflection on the process of communicating their findings to practitioners from a different profession points to broader issues concerning researcher role and stance, which are developed next within this collection.

The relationship between the researcher and the substance of the research is addressed in several papers. With respect to qualitative research, Holliday focuses on the processes of research writing - 'the impossibility and the possibility of qualitative researchers writing about other people' – and, in particular, the representation of the researcher's voice as distinct from the voices of those researched. Holliday argues from a progressivist position for the 'management of subjectivity', balancing consistency and accountability on the one hand, and responsiveness to the diversity of individual research settings on the other. In this discussion, notions of rigour and reflexivity, of systematic unity and multiplicity are seen as complementary rather than as contrasting terms.

The powerful metaphor of woods and trees, employed by Johnson in the Pit Corder Memorial lecture, provides the basis for the pivotal discussion of the shifts in focus within applied linguistic practice, research and policy-making over recent years. Johnson suggests that the tendency to concentrate on diversity and particularity – the trees – may obscure from vision the larger picture of 'the wood'. Oppositions which are established and maintained through the characterisation of paradigm positions, for example between positivist and interpretivist research stances, between product and process, between decontextualisation and contextualisation, fail to acknowledge the potential productivity of a duality of vision. Reflecting on Brumfit's (2001) discussion of uniqueness and universality, Johnson argues that 'whatever *dissimilarities* occur (between activities, experiences, ideas, entities), there are *similarities* that can be perceived, universalities that need noting'. Critical notions expressed here are those of complementarity, combination and integration.

The specifics of a language learning context, that of Hispanic immigrant mothers learning English in the United States, are explored by Duran in the following paper. The close investigation of input to the adults' second language learning process through interaction with their children in two different informal contexts (while engaged in homework activity and in conversation at mealtimes) reveals rich interaction opportunities in terms of quantity and quality of language. The potential benefits of this type of interaction for language learning are then discussed within the broader social, educational and literacy contexts. In a similar way, the report by Meara and Schur of an investigation into word association provides a further example of how the specific may raise issues of broader (and more general) significance. In this paper, an experiment is reported into the comparison between computer-generated random networks and word networks produced by native and non-native subjects. Differences between the speaker groups and also between the random and learner networks allow the authors to propose the use of the random data as a baseline against which native and non-native performance may be measured. Central to such a proposal, and to the underlying question of the potential of comparing the totally random with observed similarities within diversity, are the notions of norm and of deviance, issues which will be revisited from a different, broader perspective in the closing paper (Seidlhofer).

The imposition of unity within language and learning is forcefully challenged by Cook. In his discussion of language teaching, learning, and use, Cook argues that undue emphasis has been placed on 'real' activity in a way which does not fully acknowledge or value the scope of the 'human capacity for humour, deceit and the creation of imaginative realities'. The notion of artifice, underlying our natural ability to assume and move between multiple identities, has already been alluded to by Kramsch in her discussion of the subjective dimension of language learning. Here, Cook underlines the significance of the individual language user's engagement with the language, and calls, within the language teaching context, for freedom from authoritarianism to explore and enjoy multiple identities.

The closing paper in our collection (Seidlhofer) widens our discussion of unity and diversity to the socio-political context, by prompting a reconceptualisation of the role and status of Global English. In this provocative paper, Seidlhofer raises arguments against a deficit view of English as a Lingua Franca, 'in which variation is perceived as deviation from ENL [English as a native language] norms', and unity (or uniformity) is imposed through the definition of targets in exclusively native-speaker terms. Given the sociopolitical and socioeconomic reality of global language use, Seidlhofer questions the appropriateness of the 'English' being taught and learnt, and, in the absence of a 'coherent and comprehensive lingua franca model', calls for the establishment of a descriptive base as a first step in the process of reconceptualisation. Responding to Kachru's earlier insistence (cited in Seidlhofer) that 'the unprecedented functional range and social penetration globally acquired by English demands fresh theoretical and descriptive perspectives' (1996: 906), Seidlhofer outlines the aims and scope of such a descriptive base, realised through the development of a large-scale corpus, the *Vienna-Oxford International Corpus of English* (*VOICE*). This move, grounded as it is in the need for change, offers a progressive and constructive end to these conference proceedings. More subtly, however, through reference to Latin, former lingua franca of the Western World, the paper also demonstrates the co-existence of change with continuity, of diversity with unity.

References

Brumfit, C.J. (2001) *Individual Freedom in Language Teaching*. Oxford: Oxford University Press.

Heath, C. (1997) The analysis of activities in face-to-face interaction using video. In D. Silverman (ed) *Qualitative Research: theory, method and practice*. London: Sage.

Kachru, B. (1996) English as a lingua franca. In Goebl, H., Nelde, P., Star, Z. & Wölck, W. (eds) *Kontaktlinguistik. Contact linguistics. Linguistique de contact*. Vol 1. Berlin: De Gruyter.

1 Beyond the second vs. foreign language dichotomy: The subjective dimensions of language learning

CLAIRE KRAMSCH

University of California at Berkeley

Introduction

The differences between second language learning and foreign language study, forcefully stressed by VanPatten, Dvorak & Lee fifteen years ago (1987:2-3), have become blurred with the spread of communicative language teaching in schooled language instruction. In their desire to make language teaching and learning more relevant to learners' communicative needs and more effective on the market of linguistic exchanges, both foreign language (FL) and second language (SL) teachers have focused on enhancing the communicative competence of language learners. But the communicative turn in FL study has not necessarily homogenized the educational philosophies of SL and FL teaching, which remain attached to two different traditions, that of the social sciences (SL teaching) and that of the humanities (FL teaching). Both traditions have considered "the language learner" as a generic entity, whose goals and needs are assumed to match those of the institutions that teach them.

Now that the needs of language learners have become more diversified and unpredictable in multilingual and multicultural contact situations, second language acquisition (SLA) researchers have started to look beyond the social sciences to aspects of language learning that are best approached from a humanities perspective. Humanistic dimensions of language acquisition have become the object of a great deal of attention, e.g., the aesthetic and expressive functions of language acquisition (Cook 2000, Lam 2000, Sullivan 2000, Pavlenko 2001, Hanauer 2001), its social semiotic potential (Kramsch 2000), its phenomenological underpinnings (Kramsch forthcoming a), its symbolic value (Pavlenko & Lantolf 2000). These aspects of language acquisition have often been claimed by educational systems to be one of the objectives of foreign language study (see section 2 below), but they are now seen as relevant to the teaching of both foreign and second languages. How can SLA and humanistic education research benefit from each other's experience to understand the more subjective aspects of language learning?

In this paper, I first define the terms SLA vs. FL education in their historical contexts. I then compare the findings of SLA research to-date and the stated national objectives of FL education in three different countries. Finally, I reflect on the ways in which SL and FL research can help each other understand the subjective dimensions of language acquisition in multilingual contexts of use.

Two disciplinary traditions

Despite many common methodological aspects, SL and FL research have grown out of two different disciplinary traditions. SL research, born of the needs to teach English around the world in the wake of WWII (Pennycook 1994), and to teach other European languages within the European Community (e.g., Trim et al. 1980, Council of Europe 1996) has been mainly psycholinguistic and functional in nature. It has sought to explain and facilitate the acquisition of national languages to adult workers and immigrants to industrialized countries; both teachers and learners are only loosely affiliated with national academic institutions; learner motivation is mostly pragmatic; the focus is on the development of communicative competence, taking as a model native speaker behavior, and the eventual socialization into a target language community that is not necessarily coextensive with any particular national society (see, for instance, *English as a Second Language, Francais Langue etrangere, Deutsch als Fremdsprache*).

By contrast, FL research has traditionally been humanistic and educational in nature. It has sought to facilitate the pedagogy of national languages to adolescent learners in institutional settings. Its goals are subordinated to the general educational goals pursued by the respective national school systems at academically sanctioned institutions. Student motivation is, as in all academic subjects, driven by the desire to succeed academically; the focus is on the development of linguistic and cognitive competencies, social and cultural awareness, moral and civic virtue, and critical literacy skills. FL teaching has taken its model, not from the native speaker, but from the standardized grammar and spelling of the nationally recognized formal register of academic prose, and, at the advanced levels, the analytical and interpretive reading skills of the literary and cultural critic. Foreign language learning as a school subject is typically expected to earn students the 'profit of distinction' (Bourdieu 1991) reserved for a country's well-educated citizenry, it is not meant to socialize them into another kind of community of practice (however, see below).

As a consequence, both traditions have tended to scorn each other. FL learning has been scorned by some SL researchers (e.g., VanPatten, Dvorak & Lee 1987:2) as incapable of imparting neither 'enjoyable' nor 'valuable', i.e., usable, skills. In turn, communicative language teaching has been criticized by humanists for its lack of intellectual rigor (Sanders 1982:319ff). More recently, the application of SL pedagogy to the FL context has proved problematic for the teaching of L2 English, for example in Sri Lanka (Canagarajah 1999), South Africa (Chick 1996), Hong Kong (Lin 1999), Vietnam (Sullivan 2000), and Turkey (Clachar 2000).

Of course, the distinction between SL and FL has not always been as clear-cut as I have described it above. In the '70s, SL and FL educators across Europe joined efforts to develop a common communicative core curriculum for the teaching of various national languages within the European Union (see, e.g., Trim et al. 1980 and the various *Threshold Levels*: van Ek 1976, Coste et al 1976, Baldegger et al. 1980) and those efforts are sustained to this day (see Council of Europe 1996). However, such a curriculum was adopted mostly for the teaching of second languages within a global, professional, European framework, not for the teaching of these languages as foreign languages within state educational systems (e.g., German in French schools, or French in German schools). As I show in the next section, the educational objectives of local educational systems are rather different from those of larger, global frameworks. Furthermore, in the particular case of English, many educational systems (e.g., in Hungary, Bulgaria, Greece) use methodologies and pedagogical materials developed in English-speaking countries and based on a global (anglosaxon) native speaker norm of communicative competence, not on the local educational objectives common to all subjects taught within a given school system.

SL vs. FL educational objectives

It is enlightening to compare the stated findings from SLA research with the stated objectives of language teaching at US American, French, and German schools.

The differences in tone, genre, and discourse style reflect deep cultural differences about the value attributed to language acquisition and its place in general education.

Findings from SLA research

The results of 25 years of SLA research were summarized recently by Lightbown (2000) in the ten research generalizations below:

1. Adults and adolescents can 'acquire' a second language
2. The learner creates a systematic interlanguage which is often characterized by the same systematic errors as the child learning the same language as the first language, as well as others which appear to be based on the learner's own native language.
3. There are predictable sequences in L2 acquisition such that certain structures have to be acquired before others can be integrated.
4. Practice does not make perfect
5. Knowing a language rule does not mean one will be able to use it in communicative interaction.
6. Isolated explicit error correction is usually ineffective in changing language behavior
7. For most adult learners, acquisition stops before the learner has achieved native-like mastery of the target language.
8. One cannot achieve native-like (or near native-like) command of a second language in one hour a day.
9. The learner's task is enormous because language is enormously complex.
10. A learner's ability to understand language in a meaningful context exceeds his/her ability to comprehend decontextualized language and to produce language of comparable complexity and accuracy.

This statement of research findings is based on a rigorous study of "what second language learners say or write or show that they understand, how they judge the grammaticality of sentences and how they reveal in other ways how their knowledge of the L2 is developing" (Lightbown forthcoming). It is intent on informing language teachers, parents and school administrators of the 'scientific facts' about SLA, and on countering prevalent teaching practices and popular beliefs about language learning, thus staving off unrealistic expectations. The tone is cautionary and authoritative, it has the ring of scientific truth. Underlying each of these truths is a well-researched dichotomy that refers to some of the canonical concepts in SLA:

1. Acquisition vs. learning
2. L2 vs. L1 acquisition
3. Systematicity/predictability vs. randomness/arbitrariness
4. Repetitive practice vs. meaningful communicative practice

5.   Knowing vs. using the language
6.   Isolated focus on forms vs. systematic focus on meaning
7.   Fossilization vs. native speaker mastery
8.   Instruction vs. acquisition
9/10. Decontextualized vs. contextualized language use

These findings have contributed not only to improving teaching practice (especially of English as a second or a foreign language), but also to building second/foreign language acquisition as a valid, scientifically respected field of research. The educational goals implied by these findings are: the ability to achieve native-like behaviour, to use language accurately and appropriately in communicative interactions, and to have realistic expectations about the outcomes of language instruction.

But SLA research is not the only source of inspiration for languages teachers and school administrators. In the teaching of foreign languages other than English, other, more ideological, goals can be found as well. In the following section, I examine the avowed goals of foreign language education in the U.S, Germany, and France

Foreign language education in the United States

In the 1996 *National Standards in Foreign Language Education* project, the goals of foreign language learning in the United States are expressed in the forms of "assumptions" or beliefs expressed in the indicative. These indicatives, unlike those used in the SLA research findings, are performatives, that rely on the perlocutionary effect of the "five C" icons: communication, cultures, connections, comparisons, communities.

> *Communication* ... is at the heart of second language study ... Through the study of other languages, students gain a knowledge and understanding of the *cultures* that use that language ... Learning languages provides *connections* to additional bodies of knowledge that are unavailable to monolingual English speakers. Through *comparisons* and contrasts with the language studied, students develop greater insight into their own language and culture and realize that multiple ways of viewing the world exist. Together, these elements enable the student of languages to participate in multilingual *communities* at home and around the world in a variety of contexts, and in culturally appropriate ways. (p.27)

Each of these icons is programmatically broken down. Thus, for example:

Competence in more than one language and culture enables people to:

Communicate with other people in other cultures in a variety of settings

Look beyond their customary borders

Develop insight into their own language and culture

Act with greater awareness of self, of other cultures, and their own relationship to those cultures

Gain direct access to additional bodies of knowledge, and

Participate more fully in the global community and marketplace.

(*National Standards* "Statement of Philosophy" 1996:7)

The Standards then itemize "what students of foreign languages should know and be able to do at the end of high school", including "recognize the distinctive viewpoints that are only available through the foreign language and its cultures", and "show evidence of becoming life-long learners by using the language for personal enjoyment and enrichment." (*National Standards* 1996:23)

Lightbown's SLA research findings (in particular numbers 4, 5, 8, 10) are echoed here, but we find added to them a concern with understanding other cultures, with acquiring metalinguistic and metacultural knowledge, and with gaining different perspectives and viewpoints, as well as personal enjoyment and enrichment. FL study is embedded within an educational philosophy that strives to develop the adolescent individual as a whole. Unlike the SLA statement, the tone is here exhortatory and programmatic, as befits National Standards addressed to school boards and curriculum developers. The discourse is correspondingly ideological. Phrases like "life-long learners", "variety of settings and topics", "global community and market place" index a pluralistic, multicultural, marketized discourse that fits with the overall goals of American education.

The educational goals underlying these Standards are linguistic, cognitive, social and cultural, but no mention is made of approximating the native speaker. The implicit linguistic norm is the national standard L2 grammar and vocabulary. The implicit cognitive, social and cultural norms of behavior for "gaining knowledge", "acquiring information", "developing insights" and "participating in multilingual communities" are, one must assume, the learner's own, not those of any NS community. While most SLA research emphasizes the *acquisition* of standard linguistic forms and meanings, the US National Standards seem to put the emphasis on their *communicative use*, but it is not clear which social and cultural conventions regulate that use.

We find a similar state of affairs with foreign language instruction in Germany, albeit with different educational priorities, which I emphasize in the text.

Foreign language education in Hessen, Germany

At the Junior High School level, the goals of foreign language instruction in the state of Hessen are as follows:

> Language helps people to orient themselves in the world, it enables them to understand and communicate human experience, it is the means for personal and *esthetic creativity.* (*Rahmenplan Sekundarstufe I* 1996:5, my emphasis. my trsl.)

This preamble leads to four goals of foreign language instruction:

> [Foreign language instruction] must awaken a *constructive curiosity* in the students and *foster their willingness* to immerse themselves into the daily life and culture of other countries and communicate with speakers of other languages . . . [it must] include ways of raising students' interests, pleasure and creativity, and of giving them the space to discover, explore and find answers by themselves.

> it must give them multifarious and authentic insights in the realities of life in other countries. . . Students should discover anew aspects of their own culture, . . establish a distance to their own views and beliefs and question their own society. . .[and] approach foreign cultures with empathy, tolerance, and a critical perspective.

> It must enable students to meet their communicative needs . . .

> It must foster those values and behaviors that strengthen *the will and the ability to communicate* and to behave in a responsible manner, e.g.: desire to understand and communicate with speakers of other languages, *courage to stand up for one's convictions, willingness to take responsibility for self and others*, and to act both *cooperatively and autonomously (selbstverantwortlich).* (ibidem p.5, my emphasis, my trsl.)

At the high school level, the tone is somewhat more abstract.

By preparing learners for the realities of the 21st century, foreign language education contributes eminently to the character development of our students and to their education in *social responsibility*. ... It enables them to encounter people from other cultures with empathy and to shape interpersonal relations along *principles of respect and tolerance, justice and solidarity*. It should give *them insights into Christian and humanistic traditions,* to behave according to *moral principles and to respect religious and cultural values*. Foreign language teaching thus makes a unique contribution to general education ...Knowledge of a foreign language fosters cultural and *intercultural competence* .... (*Rahmenplan Gymnasiale Oberstufe* 1998:3-4, my emphasis, my trsl.)

Among the skills to be developed through the study of spoken and written texts, the German guidelines include the ability to seek out and use information critically, to develop skills of perception, sensibility and self-expression, to work together for the social good, and *to settle conflicts reasonably and peacefully, but also to accept dissent and conflict.*" (ibidem 1998: 4, my emphasis, my trsl.)

Unlike the performative indicatives of the American standards, based on the secular belief in the good of a pluralistic society, the German guidelines use mostly injunctions and apodictic statements marked by modals (should, must) to express the moral obligation of educators to help school pupils become responsible citizens in a democratic society – the historical legacy of WWII.

The norms of language learning, in these German guidelines, are primarily moral and cognitive, social and political, and only secondarily linguistic. The native speaker is viewed as "the Other, the Foreign" and foreign language learning as "a primary component of the learners' search for their own identity as well as their growing openness to [that] Other." (*Rahmenplan Gymnasiale Oberstufe* 1998:3). FL learning in Germany serves the general educational goals of the local state eager to promote the democratic ideal of an enlightened, informed, and open-minded citizenry, that is willing and able to view itself and others critically within the 18th century spirit of tolerance and respect, and that upholds the classic humanistic values of rational debate, aesthetic fulfillment, and moral virtue. As in the US Standards, there is little concern here with an approximation to any NS norm of language use.

Foreign language education in France

Unlike Germany and the US, that have decentralized educational systems, France has one National Ministry of Education that issues binding national standards for all schools. Here are excerpts from the most recent guidelines, in which I have italicized the statements that differ from both the German and the US American.

> At the junior high school (collége) and the high school (lycée) levels, foreign language instruction has a triple objective: communicative, cultural and linguistic. . . As instrument of communication, *as linguistic sign*, and as the cultural expression of the countries where the language is spoken, a modern foreign language is also *the means and the object of a specifically linguistic reflexion*. (Ministere de l'Education Nationale 2000a, my emphasis, my trsl.).

More specifically, at the junior high school level:

> Learning a foreign language . . . gives students *access to other linguistic usages, other ways of thought*, and other values. To learn a foreign language is to learn to respect the Other in his difference, it is *to acquire a sense of the relative* and the spirit of tolerance. These values are all the more necessary to-day as school communities tend to become increasingly multicultural.
>
> The learning of a foreign language involves a progressive reflexion on the nature and functioning of language proper. This language awareness includes also an awareness of French.
>
> It contributes to the development of the students' intellectual capacities and fosters their autonomy in self-expression (l'autonomie d'expression).
>
> Finally, the use of new technologies . . . and of their interactive potential offers an additional incentive to learn a foreign language, while enhancing the autonomy of the foreign language learner (*l'autonomie de l'eleve*). (Ministere de l'Education Nationale 2000a:14 my emphasis, my trsl.)

The high school level guidelines reinforce the standards applied at the junior level by aiming at:

> the consolidation, extension and deepening of FL comprehension skills and skills of autonomous personal expression in the spoken and written modalities

an increasingly nuanced study of texts of increasing complexity,
deepening of a *reasoned understanding of culture*

the deepening of a metalinguistic reflexion on the target language
and on language in general. (Ministere de l'Education Nationale
2000b:19, my emphasis, my trsl.)

Like the US American Standards, the French guidelines read like a
Declaration of Human Rights, that state philosophical truths about
language study. They offer a complex blend of linguistic, cognitive,
moral and esthetic norms. As in the two other cases, no mention is made
of native speaker norms of use, or of NS communicative styles. Unlike
the American and German standards, the focus is primarily on the
linguistic code and linguistic relativity, on rationality and intellectual
reflexion. The goal here is not "intercultural competence", but, rather,
the French Enlightenment view of the ideal citizen of 1789. The French
and German calls for student *autonomy* are similar and yet historically
rather different from the autonomy called for by American
psycholinguists. 'Autonomy' in psycholinguistics means freedom from
institutional constraints, i.e., individual choice and cognitive
responsibility; for example, van Lier defines 'autonomy' as self-
regulation and control in the decision about what to learn, and how and
when to learn it (1996:12).(1) In the German guidelines, 'autonomy'
(*Selbstverantwortung)* indexes moral courage and ethical responsibility,
while in the French document 'autonomy' (*autonomie)* suggests
freedom from the pressure to conform to the dominant discourse of the
community.

The discursive relativity of second/foreign language learning and teaching

A comparison of the educational implications of mainstream SLA
research with the stated educational goals of the three educational
systems discussed above shows that the teaching of second/foreign
languages is validated and legitimized by different powerful discourses.
These discourses express the economic, social, and political interests of
the various institutions that benefit from language teaching and
learning.. They differ in their disciplinary roots, their conception of the
"language learner", and their educational objectives.

From a disciplinary perspective, SLA research wields the powerful
discourse of the social sciences – linguistics, psycho- and sociolinguistics It is interested in the way children and adults around the
world learn and acquire second/foreign languages, especially English.
Its main focus is on the spoken skills, functional communicative

competence, and oral fluency. Foreign language education, by contrast, speaks the discourse of educational psychology and the humanities, i.e., literary and cultural studies. It is oriented mostly towards adolescents who learn foreign languages as part of their general education. Its discourse has the authority of national educational systems that prepare citizens for their civic, moral and intellectual responsibilities. Its main focus has traditionally been on the development of literacy skills, both in L1 and in L2 (Kramsch 2000).

Language learners, in the discourse of SLA research, are "non-native speakers" who strive to "achieve native (or near native) mastery of the target language" and to use their skills in "communicative interaction" with native (or other non-native) speakers in "meaningful contexts". The norm against which their "interlanguage" is measured is the native speaker's use of the target language. Meaningful contexts of use are contrasted with "decontextualized" uses of the language, as in classroom drills or nonsense sentences invented to illustrate grammatical paradigms (Cook 2000).

By contrast, in foreign language education, learners are "students", citizens of nation-states who are encouraged to "look beyond their customary (national) borders" and to better understand "their own language and culture", and their relationship to other "cultures". In the U.S, these goals are combined with a view of language as a mode of action (e.g., communicating, connecting, comparing, building communities) and with the desire for American youngsters to play an active role on the global political and commercial scene. In Germany, they are linked to the need to uphold the basis for a critically-minded, socially responsible and politically participatory citizenry in a social democracy, imbued with Christian principles of religious tolerance and cultural and religious freedom. In France, self and other-understanding are coupled with the traditional humanistic study of language as a mode of thought and reasoning, and as a gateway to a student's "intellectual" development. The study of both L1 and L2 is not only an instrumental skill, but a moral and aesthetic imperative.

In neither of these educational systems' guidelines is there any mention of native speaker norm. Since very few students will end up going to the target country or using the target language in any functional way, the focus of instruction is on the acquisition of the standard, written, forms of the language and on the ability to analyze and interpret L2 texts from the standard literary canon. Both skills are prestigious symbols of a high level of education, rather than everyday instrumentalities.

With regard to their educational objectives, both SLA research and foreign language education ascribe to learners those goals that serve the needs and interests of the institutions – corporations, nation-states, disciplines, or social institutions. These institutions offer them the benefits that come from knowing one or several languages other than one's mother tongue: social prestige, better employment, financial rewards. The prototypical learner in both cases is viewed as a monolingual, monocultural individual learning one L2 in natural or schooled settings. But the last ten years have seen an increase in the number of L2 learners who are neither monolingual nor monocultural, and who will not owe their allegiance or happiness to any particular institution. The typical learner of German at a Texas university in the US, for instance, is a Nigerian with a Canadian passport and a prior knowledge of French and two or more African languages. Nor are languages and cultures as standardized and homogeneous as they once seemed to be. "French" culture is also the culture of Portuguese or Algerian immigrants, of Muslims, Christians and Jews. Nowadays, many learners acquire an L4 on the background of a variously mastered L2 or L3, and with resonances of variously internalized hybrid cultures of displacement and immigration. As the subject position of the language learner has become more complex and changing, the subjective aspects of language study have become the focus of increased attention on the part of educators and researchers alike.

The subjective dimensions of language learning

It is clear that learning another language is not like learning math or word processing. Especially in adolescence, it is likely to involve not only the linguistic and cognitive capacities of the learner as an individual, but her social, historical, emotional, cultural, moral sense of self as a subject.

The foreign language guidelines discussed above take into consideration to varying degrees language learners' subjective needs. The need for learners to develop a "greater awareness of self" (US, France), to "orient themselves in the world", to "search for their own identity" and to acquire a "growing openness to the Other" (Germany); the need to develop their "interests, pleasure and esthetic creativity" (Germany), their "autonomous personal expression" (France); the need to "acquire a sense of the relative" and to engage in a "metalinguistic reflexion on language" (France), are all evidence that learning a language engages one's sense of self and one's place in the world.

Concurrently, SLA research has started to explore aspects of second and foreign language acquisition that have to do with the social identity of the language learner (Lantolf and Genung forthcoming, Norton 2000), and with learners' affective make-up and identification with the

Other (Schumann 1997). Pavlenko (2001) and Pavlenko & Lantolf (2000) have used as data ethnographic accounts and literary testimonies of language learners, and have applied the methods of the social sciences to analyze and interpret these data. They have found that the presentation and representation of self, especially in literary autobiographical narratives, may require other, more literary, tools of analysis (Wortham 2001, Kramsch & Lam 1999), and an understanding of language relativity (Kramsch forthcoming c).

SL research has become interested in the more subtle causes of miscommunication in cross-cultural encounters such as projected and perceived identity, status, role, or choice of voice (Kramsch forthcoming d). For example, Kramsch & Thorne (2001) describe the clash of identities that occurred in e-mail exchanges between American undergraduate students in a second semester French class in the US, and French high school students of English at a French lycée. In the absence of any face-to-face acquaintance with each other, French and American identities were exclusively mediated by the genre of the exchange. For the Americans, the e-mail medium provided an informal, private, orate, individual mode of communication, focused on exchange of information and friendly chatter; for the French, it afforded a formal, public, literate presentation of self as French nationals engaged in an international exchange of views. The social notion of communicative competence was insufficient to explain the breakdown in communication. Both parties used language (the Americans wrote in French, the French wrote in English) in relatively accurate and appropriate ways, yet by ignoring the historical aspects of their respective discourses, they could not understand why they each resonated differently to each other's messages.

The notion of genre, that, as both a social and an historical construct, constrains individuals' utterances (Bakhtin 1986, Bazerman 1994, Berkenkotter and Huckin 1995), can help understand how the social and the individual intersect in cross-cultural communication. Furthermore, the emotionally charged tone of this exchange showed that learners' identification with an historical genre tradition is more than an educational or social habit; it is, in Bourdieu's terms, a 'habitus' that shapes one's self-esteem and colors the esteem one has of others. It draws the contours of one's perception of self in relation to others, i.e., one's position as a subject.

To further explore the historical and subjective dimensions of "the multilingual subject" (Kramsch forthcoming b), I gave in fall 2000 an undergraduate freshmen seminar at UC Berkeley on "Language and Identity", that was attended by fifteen first semester students, fresh from high school. Half of them were US born of immigrant parents, half were born and schooled abroad and were recent immigrants to the US. All of them knew one or several languages besides English. English was, for all of them, a second or a foreign language. The students read a variety of autobiographical and semi-autobiographical works by bilingual authors writing in a language that was not their native language, including Elias Canetti's chronological narrative *The Tongue Set Free* (1977), Eva Hoffman's highly reflexive prose in *Lost in Translation* (1989), and Christine Brooke-Rose's experimental multilingual novel *Between* (1968). As a class assignment, I gave the students to write a one-page essay on "what it means to know several languages". They could choose the style, the format, and the language(s) that best expressed their relationship to their various languages. They were later interviewed and asked to comment on their essays. I examine below the essay of one student, Zoe, and her comments.

Zoe, 19, was born and raised in the CSSR of Czech parents. Her mother tongue is Czech, she learned English, French and German in her Czech high school. She came to the US at age 18 and is now learning Japanese at Berkeley. For Zoe, "each language has somewhat of a different resonance": Czech resonates with "love and family", French with romance, play and banter, English with professional fluency. But what she mostly enjoys is the multiple physical relation she entertains to all of them: "speaking English", "dipping" into French, "slipping" into German. Zoe's text is a reflexive dialogue between the Czech narrator and her Czech boyfriend on both sides of the Atlantic. It attempts to capture the highs and lows of their multilingual love affair through ample use of intertextuality (Kristeva 1974) and heteroglossia (Bakhtin 1986).

1   Cherie, I love you.
2   Nádherná solidarita založená na nedorozumení. [1]
3   A musty old apartment. Smells like cat. I think I love you. Here,
        have the keys.
4   I'd like you to be able to come and go as you please.
5   Lásko miluju te, jses neskvelejsí bytost, kterou jsem kdy
        poznal. [2] I LOVE YOU BABY. And the feeling is
        gone...replaced by musty old cat smell and keys to come and go
        as I please. Why do you say it? Do you feel that I can only
        understand I love you? Proc mi nerikás kocicko, lásko, zlato
        pod' na to, at' to stojí za to.*usmev* [3] Even a simple du bist
        mein Alles [4] no matter how mangled. Anything that doesn't
        conjure up cats. And marriage proposals. And a feeling that,
        well, if you don't rob the state, you rob your own family.

Koneckoncu, kdo neokrádá stát okrádá vlastní rodinu. [5] Oh wait, that didn't go as well as it should you ever feel the need for a friend, appelez-moi. [6]
My bonnie is over the ocean, my bonnie is over the sea and we're like little kids again. Only well then we don't know each other and nothing's a problem until you make it one. Well and if I wasn't leaving on that jet plane and you weren't l'autre et ainsi l'enfer, on aurait pu avoir quelquechose de magnifique.[7] Instead, it's all about I love you baby, and apartments that smell like cats and which I can never leave. And I sit here typing away, as if I really care about all those strangers calling me liebchen, kocicko, drahousku, kote, [8] but see at least they don't tell me they love me ... Tak to budes moje ceská milenka, jo? No jasne, a budeme se mít strasne rádi, jo? No jasne, milácku. Dobrou. Nebála byses
v noci ve vezi? [9]

1. (Czech) Beautiful solidarity founded on misunderstanding
2. (Czech) Darling I love you, you are the best person I have ever met
3. (Czech) You don't say, love, dearest, let's do it, so it's worth while. Smile.
4. (German) you are my everything
5. (Czech) After all, he who does not rob the state, robs his own family
6. (French) call me (formal 2d P)
7. (French) [if you weren't] the other and thus hell, we could have had something magnificent
8. (German) darling, (Czech) dearest, honey, little cat
9. (Czech) so you want to be my Czech lover? By all means, we will love each other, right? Of course love. Good. Would you be afraid to spend the night in a tower?

Zoe's essay literally showcases the complex discursive position of the multilingual subject, i.e., various positionings of self and other, in increasing degrees of distantiation and artfulness. The text starts with a dialogue of intimacy and closeness between the self and her Czech boyfriend in the playful cohabitation of French, English and Czech (lines 1-5). At the boyfriend's abrupt switch from "I love you" to "I LOVE YOU BABY", the multilingual dialogue unravels. English takes over in lines 6-7, Czech remains only a memory of intimacy (line 8); even German would be better than this all-pervasive English (line 9). The narrator becomes more distant as she ventriloquates in English a popular Czech saying dating from the Communist era in the CSSR (line 10). When the original Czech saying appears in line 11, it has the effect of a bombshell. The boyfriend is insulted, and the narrator resorts to a citational utterance ("should you ever feel the need for a friend") and a French formal formula ("appelez-moi") to distance herself from the damage done (line 11-12). In the next 5 lines, English becomes the language of sadness, loss, and nostalgia, while the playfulness indexed by French and the tenderness indexed by Czech are rallied, as if to ease the pain (lines 13-19). The last three lines of the text provide a final ironical twist. As Zoe explains in her interview, these are direct quotes from an exchange she had with an unknown Czech interlocutor on the Internet.

Research in literary and cultural theory (Bakhtin 1986; Kristeva 1974, 1980, 1988; Bhabha 1994) and poetics (Hymes 1996, Friedrich 1986, Becker 2000) can help us understand how the multilingual subject exploits the semiotic resources of code, stance, and subject position to enact the paradox of multilingualism. The narrator and the boyfriend, and, somewhat marginally, the anonymous Internet correspondent take on various identities, depending on the language they speak and how that language is positioned vis-à-vis the others (Ivanic 1998). We have, for example, an autobiographical-discoursal I/you as in "*Cherie I love you...I think I love you... Lasko miluju te*"; a narratorial I that evaluates, comments on the events as in "*And I sit here typing away, as if I really care...*"; a personal/impersonal you used for generic statements, sayings, slogans and the like as in "*if you don't rob the state, you rob your own family*"; a paradigmatic I/you that displays a sentence rather than performs it as in "*I LOVE YOU BABY*", whose value is not in its referential meaning, but in its illustration of English language use; a parodistic I, that repeats in ironic indirect discourse a phrase of affection said earlier, as in "*and keys to come and go as I please*" . Through various grammatical, lexical, and pragmatic choices, the multilingual author shows what it means to speak, think, and feel across various languages. The same linguistic features (e.g., *I, you, we, I love you, miluju te, keys to come and go as I/you please, Du bist mein alles*) are used to index both closeness and distance, intimacy and alienation, and to maintain this ambivalence throughout, depending on the physical and emotional resonances that Zoe's various languages have for her. In the subsequent interview, she comments:

> English is the language I use on the whole the most, I have the widest vocabulary in English. It is the language that I can best manipulate to suit my views but I don't consider a language mine until I can actually feel I own the words, and I don't, in English. I

'm not very grammatically proficient at French to say the least but I can express myself in a good enough manner and I feel confident enough about my French that I can say yes I own that language, although I don't always get the subjunctive right and the spelling and all that, but I do feel that I own the words to the extent that I can make them say what I want to say.

Being able to say things in more languages changes your relationship to each specific one ... If I didn't speak English and I didn't speak French and I didn't speak German, it would never occur to me that I could have words that are linked to specific emotions that are untranslatable into other languages. I see this sometimes with my boyfriend, because although he is multilingual he does not have the experience of necessarily living in these different languages and so it's harder for him to relate.

For most multilingual people I think that language becomes at the same time much less consequential and much more consequential. Language is much more of a mutable thing. I think people who have different languages come to value maybe the specific meanings and the specific experiences that are associated with those languages much more. [For some people], language is just maybe a facility or a tool, but there's the meaning that's hidden behind the words. That meaning is associated with experience, whether it's the experience of flipping flashcards or reading a book or speaking to someone. Those experiences are part of someone's linguistic identity, they vary with languages and with the knowledge of a language.

The subjective feelings expressed in this testimony are only starting to be investigated in SLA research: speaking like a near-native speaker yet not feeling that one "owns" one's words; the relative resonances that various second/foreign languages have amongst each other for the multilingual learner; the feeling of linguistic arbitrariness (language as a "mutable thing") that has been observed in bilingual children but not researched in adolescent and adult learners; the affective link between language learning experiences and personal identity. These dimensions of language acquisition and use are different from feelings of linguistic adequacy or inadequacy, sociopragmatic appropriateness or inappropriateness in the here-and-now of verbal encounters with native speakers or in tests of academic performance. They are associated with personal memories and imaginings, perceptions of sounds and shapes, preferences and interests, that are highly emotional and idiosyncratic and not always constrained by social norms of use. As Rampton noted, these aspects of language learning are often associated with a "preoccupation with fragmentation, contingency, marginality, transition, indeterminacy, ambivalence, and hybridity" (1997:330) that is typical of our post-modern times. "Being neither on the inside nor on the outside, being affiliated but not fully belonging, is said to be a normal condition" (ibidem). It is rather different from the stable, monolingual learner trying to approximate a stable L2 native speaker norm.

Conclusion

Both SLA and foreign language education research have viewed language learning from the perspective of a generic learner whose goals are subservient to the larger goals of scientific, national, or global institutions. The learner's bi- or multilingual subjectivity and his/her biography at the confluence of various cultural experiences have not been taken enough into consideration. The subjective aspects of language acquisition introduce a necessary historical dimension to what has been, up to now, mostly linguistically and socially oriented research. To investigate that historical dimension, language learning research will need to include methods of analysis that draw on work done in literary and cultural theory, semiotics and poetics. It will have to focus on the development of a learner's voice, on the notion of paradigmatic and syntagmatic choice, as well as on the learner's choice of code, register and audience, and the crafting of a multilingual, multicultural identity. Such a focus can bring together second language learning and foreign language study in an effort to take into account the totality of the language learning experience, and not just its social and functional dimensions.

Note:

1   For a review of the concept of autonomy in language learning, see Wenden 2001.

References:

Bakhtin, M. (1986) *Speech Genres and Other Late Essays*. Trsl.by C. Emerson and M. Holquist. Austin: U of Texas Press.
Baldegger, M., M. Mueller, G. Schneider. (1980) *Kontaktschwelle Deutsch als Fremdsprache*. Muenchen: Langenscheidt.
Bazerman, C. (1994) Systems of genres and the enactment of social intentions. In A. Freedman and P. Medway (eds.) *Genre and the New Rhetoric*. London: Taylor and Francis, 79-101.

Becker, A.L. (2000) *Beyond Translation. Essays toward a Modern Philology.* Ann Arbor: University of Michigan Press.

Berkenkotter, C, and T. Huckin. (1995) *Genre Knowledge in Disciplinary Communication: Cognition, Culture, Power.* Hillsdale, NJ: Erlbaum.

Bhabha, H.(1994) *The Location of Culture.* London: Routledge.

Bourdieu, P. (1991) *Language and Symbolic Power.* Ed. and Intr. J.B. Thompson. Trsl. Bino Raymond and M. Adamson. Cambridge, MA: Harvard University Press.

Canagarajah, S. (1999) *Resisting Linguistic Imperialism in English Teaching.* Oxford: Oxford University Press.

Chick, K. (1996) Safe talk: Collusion in apartheid education. In H. Coleman (ed.) *Society and the Language Classroom.* Cambridge: Cambridge University Press, 21-39.

Clachar, A. (2000) Opposition and accommodation: An examination of Turkish teachers' attitudes toward Western approaches to the teaching of 'writing'. *Research in the Teaching of English* 35: 66-100.

Cook, G. (2000) *Language Play, Language Learning.* Oxford: Oxford U Press.

Cook, G. (2001) 'The philosopher pulled the lower jaw of the hen'. Ludicrous invented sentences in language teaching. *Applied Linguistics* 22/3: 366-87.

Coste, D. Courtillon, V. Ferenzi, M. Martins-Baltar, E. Papo, CREDIF and E. Roulet. (1976) *Un niveau-seuil.* Strasbourg: Council of Europe.

Council of Europe. (1996) *Modern Languages: Learning, Teaching, Assessment. A Common European Framework of Reference.* Draft 2 of the Framework proposal. Strasbourg: Council for Cultural Co-operation. Education Committee.

Friedrich, P. (1986) *The Language Parallax. Linguistic Relativism and Poetic Indeterminacy.* Austin, TX: U of Texas Press.

Hanauer, D. (2001) The task of poetry reading and second language learning. *Applied Linguistics* 23/1: 295-323.

Hymes, D. (1996) *Ethnography, Linguistics, Narrative Inequality.* Toward an *Understanding of Voice.* London: Taylor & Francis.

Ivanic, R. (1998) *Writing and identity. The discoursal construction of identity in academic writing.* Amsterdam: John Benjamins.

Kramsch, C. (2000) Social discursive constructions of self in L2 learning. In J. Lantolf (ed.),pp. 133-54.

Kramsch, C. (2000) Second language acquisition, applied linguistics, and the teaching of foreign languages. *The Modern Language Journal* 84/3: 311-26.

Kramsch, C. (Forthcoming a) Introduction. How can we tell the dancer from the dance? In. C. Kramsch (ed.).

Kramsch, C. (Forthcoming b) The multilingual subject. In I. De Florio-Hansen and A. Hu (eds.). *Mehrsprachigkeit und multikulturelle Identitaetsentwicklung.* Tuebingen: Stauffenburg Verlag

Kramsch, C. (Forthcoming c) Language, thought, and culture. In A. Davies and C. Elder (Eds.) *The Handbook of Applied Linguistics.* Oxford: Blackwell.

Kramsch, C. (Forthcoming d) Identity, role, and voice in cross-cultural (mis)communication. In J. House, G. Kasper and S. Ross (ed.) *Misunderstanding in social life.* London: Longman.

Kramsch, C. (ed.) (Forthcoming) *Language Acquisition and Language Socialization. Ecological Perspectives*. London: Continuum

Kramsch, C. and E.W.S. Lam. (1999) Textual identities. The importance of being non-native. In G. Braine (ed.) *Non-Native Educators in English Language Teaching*. Mahwah, NJ: Erlbaum, 57-72

Kramsch, C. and S. Thorne. (2001) Foreign language learning as global communicative practice. In D.Block and D.Cameron (eds.) *Language Learning and Teaching in the Age of Globalization*. London: Routledge.

Kristeva, J. (1974) *Revolution in Poetic Language*. Trsl.Margaret Waller, Introduction L. Roudiez. New York: Columbia U. Press

Kristeva, J. (1980) *Desire in Language: A Semiotic Approach to Literature and Art*. Ed. L. Roudiez, trsl. A. Jardine, T. Gora and L. Roudiez. Oxford: Blackwell.

Kristeva, J. (1991) *Strangers to Ourselves*. Trsl.by L. Roudiez. New York: Columbia U Press.

Lam, E. (2000) Second language literacy and the design of the self. A case study of a teenager writing on the Internet. *TESOL Quarterly* 34/3: 457-82.

Lantolf, J. (2000) *Sociocultural theory and second language learning*. Oxford: Oxford University Press

Lantolf, J. and P. Genung. (Forthcoming) 'I'd rather switch than fight': An activity theoretic study of power, success and failure in a foreign language classroom. In C. Kramsch (ed.).

Lightbown, P. (2000) Classroom SLA research and second language teaching. *Applied Linguistics* 21/4: 431-62.

Lin, A. (1999) Doing-English-lessons in the reproduction or transformation of social worlds? *TESOL Quarterly* 33/3: 393-412.

Ministere de l'Education Nationale. (2000a) Les langues vivantes au college. In: *Anglais LV1-LV2. Enseigner au college. Programmes et accompagnement*. Paris: Centre National de Documentation pedagogique.

Ministere de l'Education Nationale. (2000b) Dispositions communes a l'ensemble des langues vivantes (Arrete du 14 mars (1986). Langues vivantes dans la renovation des lycees (Circulaire no.94-194 du 1er juillet 1994). In: *Anglais LV1-LV2. Renovation pedagogique des lycees. Programmes et accompagnement*. Paris:Le Centre National de Documentation Pedagogique.

National Standards in Foreign Language Education project. (1996) *Standards for Foreign Language Learning. Preparing for the 21st Century*. Yonkers, NY: ACTFL.

Norton, B. (2000) *Identity and Language Learning*. London: Longman.

Pavlenko, A. (2001) Language learning memoirs as a gendered genre. *Applied Linguistics* 22/2: 213-40.

Pavlenko, A. and J. Lantolf. (2000) Second language learning as participation and the (re) construction of selves. In Lantolf, J. (ed.) 155-78.

Pennycook, A. (1994) *The cultural politics of English as an International Language*. London: Longman.

Rahmenplan Neue Sprachen. (1996) Sekundarstufe I. Wiesbaden: Hessisches Kultusministerium.

Rahmenplan Neue Sprachen. (1998) Gymnasiale Oberstufe. Aufgabenfeld I.2. Wiesbaden: Hessisches Kultusministerium.

Rampton, B. (1997) Second language research in late modernity: A response to Firth and Wagner. *The Modern Language Journal* 81/3: 329-33.

Sanders, R. (1982) Review of Neuner et al. Deutsch Aktiv 1979, 1989, and Ubungstypologie zum kommunikativen Deutschunterricht 1981. *Die Unterrichtspraxis* 15/2: 318-22.

Schumann, J. (1997) *Neurobiology of Affect in Language.* Oxford: Blackwell.

Sullivan, P. (2000) Playfulness and mediation in communicative language teaching in a Vietnamese classroom. In J. Lantolf (ed.), 115-32.

Trim, J., R. Richterich, J. van Ek and D. Wilkins. (1980) *Systems development in adult language learning.* Oxford: Pergamon.

Van Ek, J. (1976) *The Threshold Level for Modern Language Learning in Schools.* London: Longman.

Van Lier, L. (1996) *Interaction in the Language Curriculum Awareness, Autonomy & Authenticity.* London: Longman.

VanPatten, B., T. Dvorak and J. Lee (Eds.) (1987).*Foreign Language Learning. A Research Perspective.* Rowley, MA: Newbury House.

Wenden, A. (2001) Learner development in language learning. *Applied Linguistics* 23/1: 32-55.

Wortham, S. (2001) *Narratives in Action. A strategy for research and analysis.* New York: Teachers College Press.

2 Genre teaching: the struggle for diversity in unity

JULIAN EDGE & SUE WHARTON

Aston University

Introduction

In this paper we discuss some recent developments of a continuing action research project in pedagogic linguistics that began in a teacher education context in Istanbul shortly after the publication of Michael Hoey's (1983) *On the Surface of Discourse*. The earliest published evidence of the work is Edge (1985) and the most recent is Wharton (2001). At some stage during that period, certainly influenced by Swales (1990), we came to describe this work as *genre teaching*.

A genre can exist only if a sense of communicative and formal unity can be demonstrated toward a common social purpose. At the same time, and particularly important in terms of a pedagogic linguistics, this unity should not be seen as a monolithic entity, but as a sociolinguistic phenomenon that exists as a functional grouping of individual diversity. As we consider the relationship between unity and diversity in genre teaching, the reflexive relationships that spring to mind as parallels are those between society and the individual, between the schema and the datum, between assimilation and accommodation: we see a genre as a framework which is rigid enough to suggest form and imply meaning, but also flexible enough to tolerate variety, to develop according to that variety, and also radically to transform itself should the need arise.

The professional environment from which we report here involves current participants on a distance-taught master's course in TESOL. These highly motivated teachers are graduates, frequently with additional TESOL qualifications, and always with at least three years' teaching experience. Having selected an aspect of their professional context to investigate (linguistic or pedagogic depending on the module they are studying), and having designed and carried out a small-scale research project, these participants write up their research in the form of an assignment for evaluation. In some instances, the writers will want to go on to transform this assignment into an article for publication. Making this shift from assignment to article is our focus in this paper.

Before proceeding to the detail of our approach, we will provide some additional contextual information, as well as some points of principle which we regard as axiomatic for our present purposes. We present the points under three sub-headings: textual, pedagogic and ideological. This is not to suggest, of course, that these issues can actually be disentangled in such simplistic terms.

Textual

1   Hoey's work on semantic patterning in text (here specifically the Problem/Solution pattern, Situation-Problem-Response-Evaluation in its original, canonical form, (Hoey 1983, but see also Hoey 2001) is extremely useful in the analysis of article-length writing in TESOL. In terms of psychological schema, and often of textual realisation, the simplest form of an article in *English Teaching Professional*, or *ELT Journal*, for example, will be:

S   This where I work, both literally and in terms of an area of ELT.

P   This is the aspect of my work on which I intend to focus (frequently problematic).

R   This is my preferred response, my centrally important statement.

E   Here are some outcomes of this response that lead me to see it as successful.

In the development of our work, we have found it useful to identify a fifth category, Basis for Response (**BR**), in which writers argue the case for the R that they propose.

2   As well as having functional relationships with each other (as above) such elements as S-P-R-BR-E can be seen as having functional relationships in terms of the communication between writer and reader. Canonically speaking again, for example, we can see S and P serving to establish common ground with the reader in preparation for the writer's R.

3   From both perspectives, R is the essential part of the article, the purpose for writing, the point of motivation and relevance for the other elements.

4   It is well acknowledged that the creation of newness and the claim for newness are two of the main purposes that motivate the desire to publish. The argument has many nuances: Bazerman (1988), Hyland

(1999), Kaufer & Geisler (1989), Myers (1990), Ivanic & Simpson (1992), Swales (1993) Mitchell (1994), Skelton (1997) have all discussed it from different perspectives. For us, a key point is that novelty creation be seen as a purpose of academic *writing* as well as of academic *writers*. The genres themselves carry an expectation of emergent originality which is projected onto those who seek to write in them. We have argued elsewhere (Edge & Wharton 2001) that genres themselves may have goals, and that texts written in such genres will be understood as attempting to realise these. Once again, the unity is created and continued by the individual diversity that constitutes and develops it.

The particular case of the TESOL article genre is interesting in that its readership is very wide, so that Myers' (1989) notions of esoteric and exoteric audience are particularly relevant. Authors need to position themselves simultaneously as expert and as community member. As a community member, they must correctly judge and represent the issues which are of concern to the community. As an expert, they must be able to say something new to both exoteric *and* esoteric audiences, working at the level of the latter without losing sight of the concerns of the former.

Pedagogic

5   Our course participants are already familiar with the canonical SPRE pattern and have been encouraged to consider its use in the development of their research assignments. During an on-line discussion of its usefulness, the following comment was made, capturing the assessment of several of those taking part:

> The best thing about SPRE, I found, is that it provides us with a template of sorts (redefined helpfully in the Foundation Module so that P becomes something more relevant to the nature of our research). We all have the instinct that our writings should have a beginning, a middle and an end, with some kind of logical inter-connectedness. Without the SPRE, I think we would have to rely (but how well?) on our own intuitions of what is satisfyingly argued, constructed and complete, without any objective benchmarks to evaluate our argumentative structure. Yes, SPRE is a constraint, as has been mentioned in the discussion, but a constraint that has the positive connotations of 'discipline.'

6   Given this familiarity with SPRE, the essential move that our writers must make as they transform assignments to articles is with regard to the way they structure their relationship with their readers. By

the nature of the genres themselves, assignments construct their authors as novices, while articles construct their authors as experts (Wharton 1999).

For a less experienced writer, the notion that the genre itself can construct its author as an expert may be threatening. There is a requirement for originality and conventionality, for unity and diversity, which may feel like a paradox. An MSc participant comments:

> I 'use' SPRE as a post-writing checking tool... I'm not really sure though if I'm using it or if it's using me

One of the goals of our genre teaching is to demystify this seeming paradox, attempting to help writers integrate with the genre to the point where:

> expressing one's individuality and affirming one's membership of the elite become effectively identical (Womack 1993 p47).

7   There is a supportive fit between the action-research orientation of the degree program itself and the SPRE approach to genre teaching that we take. This does not go unnoticed by our course participants:

> I can see very clearly how SPRE is a very suitable template for doing action research. After all, the capital S in the acronym takes us right into the heart of things, where action research begins, with our own particular situation.

> I find SPRE very effective when it comes to preparing my assignment proposals. It disciplines my thinking, driving me sometimes to sheer despair when it comes to classifying my ideas. On the other hand, the constraint this system imposes is very productive for the shaping of my research.

Ideological

8   Increased awareness and the consequent exercising of informed choice are key elements in the empowerment of the individual and, as such, key purposes in all educational endeavours:

> What I found strange was that after having done A-levels, a degree in history, and even part of an MBA and various TEFL qualifications, nobody had ever talked to me about SPRE, IMRO, or any other discourse patterns. The TDA module was thus an eye-opener in terms of how to write. This is something that you would have thought should be mentioned to all undergraduates NS and NNS alike but (in my experience) isn't. Now I am very conscious

of using SPRE, IMRO, or whatever in my writing.

9 The teaching of established genres (and indeed languages) of power is ideologically sound insofar that it makes available to learners ways of extending their repertoires of communication and development towards their own purposes. This requires a pedagogy based on aware choice (and not simply the copying of models) in which individual diversity is encouraged in interplay with generic unity.

Against this contextual and conceptual background, we shall now narrow the focus of our paper considerably in order to exemplify ways in which the use of a pedagogically appropriate genre analysis can enable novice authors of ELT-related articles to recognise not only the choices available to them as they negotiate their way into their target discourse community, but also the significance of those choices with regard to:

- the nature of their contribution
- the style of their contribution
- the research tradition according to which they justify their contribution.

A pedagogic genre analysis

Diversity in unity: a textual perspective

We will now introduce the genre analytical model which enables us to demonstrate some of those choices and their significance. For the purposes of this paper, we will examine just one element in the model: the R element which is seen as carrying the main contribution of the text. We will examine some of the many options which our research indicates are available to writers for the realisation of this element, consistent with the requirements of the genre. The categories which we will put forward are based on research originally carried out on a corpus consisting of all the standard articles published in *ELT Journal* in 1994 plus a certain number from 1995. In this paper, we illustrate our comments with reference to articles published in the April 2000 issue. Claims that we make should be seen as arising from and relating to this corpus, with more general claims awaiting further research.

Types of R

Perhaps in any discourse analysed using the problem-solution pattern, the most obvious interpretation of R is as actions, or procedures: an active 'solution' to a 'problem' in the everyday sense of those words.

The 94/95 corpus of *ELT Journal* articles does indeed contain a number of R sections which fit this idea. These are methodology articles: those whose contribution is the suggestion of a concrete teaching idea. This was the type of article which gave rise to Edge's (1986, 1989) original characterisation of TESOL texts in terms of the SPRE pattern (See type 1, below).

However, there are also a number of articles which do not seem to centre on descriptions of actions or procedures. In order to describe these articles in terms of the SPRE pattern, we looked for what appeared to be their main contribution and interpreted this as R. This process allowed us to discern a pattern in the 'types' of R that appeared in the corpus.

These types of R may be described as follows:

1   **Action-type** Rs which detail a course of action or a procedure. Their force or illocutionary point is to invite the reader to consider taking a similar course of action in appropriate circumstances.

2   **Rationale-type** Rs which explain and detail the reasons for a course of action or approach. The course of action/ approach is usually the author's own, and the force or illocutionary point is also to invite the reader to consider taking a similar course of action in appropriate circumstances.

3   **Analysis-type** Rs which interpret, explore and try to explain a state of affairs: often a state of affairs which is considered problematic. They aim to increase our understanding, without necessarily advocating action. Their force or illocutionary point is to try to persuade readers of the validity of their perspective.

4   **Evaluation-type** Rs in which authors evaluate work other than their own. The evaluation 'target' is usually the specific work of (an)other person(s), but may also be a well-known approach or technique, such as role-play activities. Their force or illocutionary point is also to try to convince readers of the validity of their perspective.

It is important to remember that these different types of R all share the same pragmatic function within the text and the genre. They all carry the author's suggestion or main contribution.

At this point we would like to provide some examples of these different types of R. Because of constraints of length it is only possible to provide very brief extracts. The extracts are contextualised by the author's own words about the purpose of the article, taken from the abstract. We trust that the extracts are long enough to give a "flavour" of the different types of R.

i   An example of an action type R:
(From an article which "describes the implementation of a 'cyclic', practical model-based syllabus on a short pre-service training course").

On both courses, trainees were exposed to models from the first day. Typically, a 45-60 minute model lesson was followed by analysis which took different forms (for example, trainees noted down the things that had struck them and then compared notes, or they were instructed to take notes under certain headings supplied by the trainer, or given a set of questions to answer about the lesson, etc.).

Retrospective timetabling
No timetable was given for the first week of the course, the underlying rationale being that trainees would be freer to notice a greater variety of teaching principles and/or techniques if their preconceptions were not bound by labels such as 'A listening lesson' or 'A vocabulary lesson'. For inexperienced trainees, the first week is often that with the greatest learning curve. A homework task for the end of the first week of each course consisted of trainees filling in a blank timetable with two things they felt they had learned on each day of the previous week, an activity which Hunt calls 'a retrospective timetable' (1996: 37).

Source: Hockly N 2000 "Modelling and 'cognitive apprenticeship' in teacher education" ELTJ 54/2: 118-125.

This brief extract is part of a longer section which explains in some detail what happened on the courses in question. The procedures are described in sufficient detail to allow readers to recreate something similar if they wished. There is an implication that similar procedures could indeed help others in appropriate circumstances to achieve a worthwhile goal. In this extract, note how an element of rationale is introduced in order to back up the procedural suggestions.

ii   An example of a rationale type R:
(from an article which "considers the value of relating music and language in the EFL classroom.")

Music and memory

Singing is an easy way of memorising something. Most of us can probably remember having learnt the multiplication tables with a specific tune. Melody seems to act as a path or a cue to evoke the precise information we are trying to retrieve.

Tim Murphey (1990) defines the 'song-stuck-in-my-head' phenomenon as a melodic Din, as an (in)voluntary musical and verbal rehearsal. Murphey also hypothesizes that the Din could be initiated by subvocal rehearsal. So, for example, we are able to rehear mentally the voice and words of a person with whom we have had an argument. Similarly, while reading the notes taken in a lecture, we will probably rehear the lecturer's voice, while at the same time we can mentally visualise the place from which s/he was talking and even her/his gestures or body movements.

Music seems to leave a particularly deep trace in our memories; this could be due to the fact that it is related to affective and unconscious factors. It could also be related to the hypothesis that it is less-energy-demanding because musical perception starts before birth.

Source: Fonseca Mora C 2000 "Foreign language acquisition and melody singing" ELTJ 54/2: 146-152

In isolation, this extract looks as if it could be a long BR section: giving the reasons for a specific classroom technique involving music that the writer has described or will describe in detail. But in fact the article never does elaborate specific techniques in detail: its main point, its contribution, is a discussion of reasons for the principle of inclusion of music. "Music and memory" is one of several angles taken in the overall argument that music in language teaching is a good thing. The article can therefore be categorized as having a rationale-type R, whose force is to ask readers to consider taking a similar approach if they are in appropriate circumstances.

iii   An example of an analysis type R:

(from an article which proposes "a rating scale as a practical means of addressing the difficult task of assessing both the level of a particular communicative performance in a small group and the general ability to perform in small group conversations over time" and argues "that theoretical difficulties of designing and using rating scales for this purposes, while requiring serious consideration, are out-weighed by practical advantages".

Problems of task implementation

An attempt to set up realistic conditions of performance is an important feature of construct validity, but we should never forget that a task only simulates real-life communication. The problem of extrapolation is hence inextricably linked to task design and implementation, as task type and task familiarity always have an influence on performance which cannot be measured. Task familiarity is potentially the biggest concern in assessing performance, as it is difficult to decide how familiar students should be allowed to become with tasks. A totally unfamiliar task type is unlikely to produce typical performance, but high familiarity may easily help exam-wise students to perform above the level they can be expected to achieve in real life. Practice in the classroom must in any case never involve rehearsal of assessed task activities. In this project, no more than basic familiarity with the actual assessment task types was allowed. Students had frequent practice in the skills of small group interaction, using a very wide variety of tasks, but were not over-trained in the actual assessment tasks; only one practice session in the lesson preceding each assessment used a similar task format. Assessment tasks always involved a three-way exchange of information, followed by a discussion using this information to try to come to some kind of agreement or decision in the group.

(Source: Nunn R 2000 "Designing rating scales for small group interaction" ELTJ 54/2: 169-178)

Looking at the first lines of this extract in isolation, one might assume that they form part of the P section of their article and are intended to make way for a response which will attempt to resolve some of the issues mentioned. The last lines (from "In this project") look like what Hoey (2001 p129) terms a recommended response. In fact these interpretations are not appropriate: this extract comes towards the end of the article, *after* a section in which specific task rating scales are proposed. The extract is from a long (2.5 page) section entitled "Problems of using rating scales for small group interaction" whose purpose seems to be to increase readers' awareness and understanding of the kinds of difficulties that can occur and the reasons for them. The article can therefore be categorized as having two Rs: an action type, in which the scales are proposed, and an analysis type, which is the one quoted from here.

iv   An example of an evaluation type R:
(From an article which "analyses the strengths and weaknesses of product, process and genre approaches to writing in terms of their view of writing and how they see the development of writing" and "argues that the three approaches are complementary, and identifies an approach which is informed by each of them".)

The weaknesses of product approaches are that process skills, such as planning a text, are given a relatively small role, and that the knowledge and skills that learners bring to the classroom are undervalued. Their strengths are that they recognise the need for learners to be given linguistic knowledge about texts, and they understand that imitation is one way in which people learn.

The disadvantages of process approaches are that they often regard all writing as being produced by the same set of processes; that they give insufficient importance to the kind of texts writers produce and why such texts are produced; and that they offer learners insufficient input, particularly in terms of linguistic knowledge, to write successfully. The main advantages are that they understand the importance of the skills involved in writing, and recognize that what learners bring to the writing classroom contributes to the development of writing ability.

[A similar paragraph evaluating genre approaches follows].

Source: Badger R & White G 2000 "A process genre approach to teaching writing" ELTJ 54/2: 153-160

The extract is clearly evaluative. It does not look like the E section of an article, partly because the evaluation is very balanced but more importantly because the object of evaluation is not the writer's own work. It *could* be a series of negatively evaluated Rs, discussed and then discarded to make room for the writer's own proposal. An alternative proposal is indeed forthcoming in the article, (the "approach which is informed by each of them" of the abstract) but it takes up rather less space than the evaluation of the three "standard" approaches. The evaluation of well known approaches in this article is not 'merely' to make space for the writer's own contribution, but is *itself* part of the main contribution of the article. The article can therefore be categorized as having *both* an evaluation type R *and* an action type R, with the evaluation type being the more important.

The notion that an article may have two Rs is an important one. In the 94/95 corpus we found a number of articles which combined two different types of R section, though none which combined more than two. Sometimes each of the types had equal weight (measured in terms of how long they were), but more often one type seemed to be a 'main' R and the other type a 'secondary' R. By far the most frequent combination was of analysis type with action type (See example iii above).

The decision to label the options discussed above as different types of R perhaps needs some justification in the light of Hoey's (2001) discussion of "other culturally popular patterns" (ch 8) in which he argues the existence of patterns (*goal-achievement, opportunity-taking, desire arousal - fulfillment, gap in knowledge - filling*) which are closely related but not identical to the canonical problem-solution pattern. Although a discussion of the extent to which TESOL articles may be usefully described for our purposes in terms of one of Hoey's alternative patterns is beyond the scope of this paper, some comment seems appropriate.

On the one hand, preliminary research suggests that our categories are relatively independent of pattern type at this level of detail. In *ELT Journal* April 2000, for example, two articles that are arguably categorisable as *goal/achievement* are Waters & Vilches "Integrating teacher learning: the school-based follow up development activity" and Badger & White "A process genre approach to teaching writing" (quoted from above). Of these, we categorise the first as having an action type R and the second an evaluation type R. In this sense, it seems that the two category systems work in parallel. On the other hand, it is intuitively attractive explicitly to extend the range of organisational choice available to emergent writers to include such differing nuances as *opportunity-taking, gap-filling* and perhaps, even, in a world where passionate scholarship is also demanded of us, of *arousal-fulfillment*.

As things stand, then, our categories of R are fuzzy, and there are places where they blend in to each other. It is therefore important to remember that this is a writer-oriented, pedagogic model: its essential purpose is to assist a writer to gain a sense of the contribution they want to make and to ensure that all sections of their text work together towards that goal. If a writer can identify their own text with one or more of these categories, they will have a powerful way of keeping their text on task.

Managing the contribution

Whatever the type of R, the purpose of this element in this genre remains the same: to be the main contribution. We have so far given examples of types of R which tend to recur. This is one textual perspective on diversity in unity. Yet diversity is not only a question of what type of Response is present, it is also a question of how the contribution, as expressed in that Response, is managed.

In this next section we will propose a continuum for the realisation of the R element, and also attempt to show how choices along it relate to issues of discourse community positioning. The continuum posited is relevant for all four types of R.

Realisations of R can be seen as occurring on a continuum whose poles are

Demonstrate <----------> speculate

Realisations nearer to the demonstrate end of the continuum tend to be strongly linked to a context, be based on a specific writer experience, to take a relatively narrow focus and look at it in detail. Realisations nearer to the speculate end tend to be more abstract, to be deduced from general principles and/or from the writer's state-of-the-art knowledge, and not to be linked to a particular context. In terms of formal features, more speculate Rs are more likely to include modals, hedging expressions, and indefinite nominal groups. Demonstrate Rs are more likely to refer directly to data, and to have a 'staged' structure. They quite often use the past tense.[1]

It is possible to see the ends of the demonstrate<-->speculate continuum as representing two different approaches to knowledge-building in the discipline. A very demonstrate R is a contribution which relies on its context-specificity and its detail to allow the reader to judge its value to them. A very speculate R is one which relies on the generality of underlying principles to ensure its value to the reader. This distinction may be a culture-shift issue in our profession: one could argue that a speculate R still relates to the theory-application discourse that has been part of our profession for a long time, and that a demonstrate R links to ideas on the nature of situated research which have emerged more recently, and partly in response to the questionable efficacy of a theory/application discourse. This change is discussed by e.g. Clarke 1994, Edge 2001, Nunan 1991. In this sense, choices along the continuum for R are a matter of positioning oneself in the discourse community with reference to the type of warrant that one claims for the statements that one makes (Edge & Richards 1998).

Let us now go back to the extracts we looked at as examples of different types of R, and see where they might be interpreted as falling on the demonstrate <--> speculate continuum.

The first extract, an example of an action type R, falls nearer to the demonstrate end of the continuum. It is strongly tied to a particular context and to a lived experience of the writers, and it is detailed at the level of procedure. Its force of suggestion for similar action is via the writers' detailing of their own experience.

The second extract, an example of a rationale type R, is nearer to the speculate end of the continuum. The argument is based on general principles about the relationships between music and memory. These principles are expressed with reference to other research, and the relevance to language teaching is not at this stage made explicit.

The third extract, the analysis type R, seems to combine both speculate and demonstrate features. The first part of the extract is more speculate, concerning itself with discussion of the general issue of extrapolation and construct validity. This narrows down to the issues of task familiarity, and then – with a definite shift towards the demonstrate end of the continuum – the extract discusses how this particular issue has been approached in the project from which the article arises.

The final extract, an example of an evaluation type R, is again nearer to the speculate end of the continuum. It evaluates the three approaches to writing at a fairly abstract level, it is not, for example, analyzing data from particular coursebooks. The evaluation parameter is state of the art knowledge about what is desirable in the teaching of writing, rather than e.g. knowledge of the constraints of a particular context.

The examples of analysis given here use only a part of our model of the TESOL article genre. In the larger model, the kind of diversity that we have demonstrated here for realisation and management of the R element of the SPRE pattern is demonstrated for other elements of the pattern too. The model we present is, then, a model of some of the choices available to writers in this genre and of some of the implications of these choices. It offers a systemic view of textual and indeed experiential reality, in which all choices interact and there are no isolable or guaranteed correspondences between, for example, particular writer options and particular perlocutionary effects.

Diversity in unity: pedagogic and ideological perspectives

This is a project in genre teaching, not only in genre description. The question arises, then, of how the insights of the descriptive strand should best be shared with writers and aspiring writers. It is a key question since we regard the pedagogy, no less than the description, as an opportunity to model and to explore the unity and diversity which we are claiming as characteristics both of the target genre itself and of the relationships between genre and writer.

We have developed a set of self-access materials, based on the model partially described in this paper, whose aim is to assist interested MSc participants to reformulate a course assignment as an article to submit for publication. Users of the materials are invited to examine their existing text in the light of the descriptive model. The model is illustrated by extracts from the TESOL literature which exemplify the tendencies described.

The use of extracts from TESOL literature brings participants face to face with the diversity of SPRE realisation in the genre. One of our participants comments:

> ... in my experience, text structure rarely follows a simple S then P then R then E pattern: for example, we typically find blocks eliminated, or fused, or repeated, or cycling patterns, or hierarchical patterns, etc. etc.

With reference to his pedagogy, he adds:

> ... [this has] got me wondering whether I could develop activities involving recognition of SPRE functions, without worrying about order.

Our own pedagogy concentrates very much on unity in terms of purpose at the level of element and function, and diversity or choice in actual realisation.

Clearly related to the above is the argument that the materials are intended to elucidate an existing text, rather than to prescribe the nature of any future text. In the context of assignment writing, one participant comments:

> ... it's more a case of noticing afterwards 'Hey this fits the SPRE pattern' rather than setting out with the explicit goal of writing an assignment that fits the pattern. In that sense I don't find SPRE at all constraining, but I do find it liberating in the sense it can give me confidence that the assignment I've just written is well-structured.

The self-access materials aim to encourage a process of reflection at a deeper level, using SPRE to consider perspectives beyond the structural. It is hoped that users will gain a deeper understanding of the choices they are currently making in their own writing, and will be able to use this understanding to revise the writing if they so wish.

The materials attempt to position the individual voice of the writer at the centre of the process of textual revision. They require that the users make contextually appropriate decisions about the levels of claims they wish to make and how they wish to situate themselves *vis a vis* the community as a whole. They encourage writers to think consciously about the relationship that is created in text between the persona of the author and the situations, actions, people and ideas that the author writes about, as well as about the relationship with cited sources and with the constructed readership.

The materials respond to a goal which their users have, and this gives what might be termed 'task authenticity'. Work done with these materials is not a rehearsal for article writing, but is part of the process of article writing; it is carried out at the moment when the user chooses to work towards that goal.

The materials examine features of the target genre from the perspective of purpose. The examples in the materials demonstrate options which can help to realise certain goals. They do not, then, constitute a course of instruction in rhetorical strategies: formal features are presented as arising out of community standards, rather than themselves constituting community standards. For this reason users are not asked to imitate forms, but rather to consider the extent to which the forms they are already using support their own communicative goals. Any decision to modify the text will then be for a consciously articulated reason which relates to the user's purposes.

We argued earlier in this paper that writers in the TESOL article genre must present themselves both as experts and as community members. We would argue that our self access materials encourage experiential as well as textual development of both these personae. Their aim is to constitute a tool by which people increase their awareness of the choices they can make and of the responsibilities which are associated with the choices.

Our commitment is to genre teaching which is questioning, purpose-driven and non-monolithic. We set out to affirm the diversity within generic unity and – mindful of post-modern positions on the intertextuality of writing practices and the illusory character of individual novelty – equally to affirm the unity which underlies diversity. We attempt to demonstrate our commitment by the textual model used, and to realise it in experience via the pedagogic inter-action.

Acknowledgements

We would like to thank all MSc TESOL participants who contributed to the on-line discussion of the usefulness of SPRE, and particularly Jonathan Clifton, Danyal Freeman, Stephan Hegglin, James Hobbs, Guy Norman and Raymond Sheehan for allowing their comments to be included in the paper.

Notes

1 There is more to be said (and discovered) about the formal realisation of this and all the functional categories we are dealing with here (see Wharton

1999), but such a discussion would go beyond the focus of the present paper.

References

Bazerman C. (1988) *Shaping written knowledge* Madison, Wisconsin: University of Wisconsin Press.

Clarke M. (1994) The dysfunctions of the theory/practice discourse *TESOL Quarterly* 29/1: 9-26.

Edge J. (1985) Do TEFL articles solve problems? *English Language Teaching Journal* 39: 153-157.

Edge J. (1986) *Towards a professional reading strategy for EFL teacher trainees* Unpublished PhD thesis University of Birmingham UK.

Edge J. (1989) Ablocutionary value: on the application of language teaching to linguistics *Applied Linguistics* 10/4: 407-417.

Edge J. & K. Richards (1998) May I see your warrant, please?: justifying outcomes in qualitative research *Applied Linguistics* 19/3: 334-356.

Edge J. (2001) Attitude and access: building a new teaching/learning community in TESOL. In J. Edge (ed) *Action research* Alexandria, VA: TESOL Inc.

Edge J. & S. Wharton (2001) Patterns of text in teacher education. In Scott M. & Thompson G. (eds) *The Patterns of Text* Amsterdam: Benjamins.

Gosden H. (1992) Research writing and NNS: from the editors *Journal of Second Language Writing* 1/2: 123-139.

Hoey M. (1983) *On the surface of discourse* London: George Allen Unwin.

Hoey M. (2001) *Textual interaction: an introduction to written discourse analysis* London: Routledge.

Hyland K. (1999) Disciplinary discourses: writer stance in research articles. In Hyland K. & Candlin C. *Writing: texts, processes, practices.* Harlow: Addison Wesley/Longman.

Ivanic R. & Simpson J. (1992) Who's who in academic writing? In Fairclough N. (ed) *Critical language awareness* London: Longman.

Kaufer D. & Geisler C. (1989) Novelty in academic writing *Written Communication* 8: 286-311.

Kaufer D. & Geisler C. (1991) A scheme for representing academic argument. *The Journal of Advanced Composition* 11: 107-122.

Mitchell S. (1994) *The teaching and learning of argument in higher education: final report* Hull: University of Hull School for Education/ Centre for Studies in Rhetoric.

Myers G. (1989) The pragmatics of politeness in scientific articles *Applied Linguistics* 10: 1-35.

Myers G. (1990) *Writing Biology: texts in the social construction of scientific knowledge* Madison, Wisconsin: University of Wisconsin Press.

Myers G. (1992b) 'In this paper we report...': speech acts and scientific facts *Journal of Pragmatics* 17: 295-313.

Nunan D. (1991) *Language Teaching Methodology* Cambridge: Cam-bridge University Press.

38 UNITY AND DIVERSITY IN LANGUAGE USE

Sionis C. (1995) Communication strategies in the writing of scientific research articles by non-native users of English *English for Specific Purposes* 14/2: 99-113.

Skelton J. (1997) The representation of truth in academic medical writing *Applied Linguistics* 18/2: 121-140.

Swales J. (1990) *Genre analysis: English in academic and research settings* Cambridge: Cambridge University Press.

Swales J. (1993) Genre and engagement *Revue Belge* 71/3: 689-698.

Wharton S. (1999) *From postgraduate student to published writer: discourse variation and development in TESOL.* Unpublished PhD thesis, Aston university.

Wharton S. (2001) Writing from a context: course assignments and professional development. Paper at Writing Development in Higher Education, University of Leicester, 24-25 April 2001.

Womack P. (1993) What are essays for? *English in Education* 27/2: 42-49.

3 Organisation in school and university students' persuasive texts

ANN GALLOWAY

Macquarie University, Sydney, Australia

Introduction

This paper presents some of the findings from research investigating aspects of children's later language development. The study is using written language data to investigate the development of the use of some of the features of language that contribute to readers perceiving persuasive texts as coherent.

Coherence is a global property of texts, and is ultimately achieved in the mind of the reader through interaction with the text on the page; it is not resident in the text itself (e.g., Brown & Yule, 1983; Cook, 1989; Givon, 1992). There are various ways of using language that have been identified as being helpful to readers in achieving coherence, such as thematic unity; consistency or continuity of referents, temporality, locality, and structure; the use of cataphora; and the use of a principled basis of text organisation (e.g., see Bamberg, 1983; Gernsbacher, 1997; Givon, 1995; Lawe Davies, 1998; Van Dijk, 1977). If writers employ these features appropriately, it increases the probability that readers will perceive the resulting text as coherent. It is therefore of interest to discover the progress that young language users are making in the use of these features which assist readers in processing text. This paper presents an overview of the results from the investigation of the developmental patterns in using one of the features that has been found to contribute to coherence – the use of a principled form of text organisation.

Background to the study

The participants in this study were 9-15 year-old (Grade 4-10) school students and undergraduate university students (see Table 1). The students came from a mix of socioeconomic backgrounds. The school students attended co-educational, non-government sector schools in the metropolitan area of Perth, Western Australia. The undergraduate students ranged in age from 18 years (school-leaver level tertiary entry) to 50 years (mature-age/alternative route tertiary entry), and were studying in various disciplines at Western Australian universities. The majority of the female tertiary students were studying in humanities disciplines, while the majority of males were in science disciplines.

Age group	Age range	Participants	Total texts
Primary:			
Grades 4/5	9-10 years	48	96
Grades 6/7	11-12 years	48	96
Secondary:			
Grades 9/10	13-15 years	40	80
Tertiary:			
Undergraduate	18-50 years	24	48
Total		160	320

Table 1: Participants

All participants wrote on the same two everyday topics in the context of writing a letter to a school newsletter. The writing prompts were:

Jobs
Do you think children should be paid for helping with jobs at home, or should they help around the house without being paid? Write a letter to the school newsletter and give your opinion about this matter. Try to convince your readers that you are right.

Television
A parent has written to the school newsletter, suggesting that children should only be allowed to watch TV at weekends and on holidays. What do you think? Should children be allowed to watch TV only at weekends and during school holidays? Write a letter to the school newsletter and give your opinion about this matter. Try to convince your readers that you are right.

The order of the presentation of these tasks was counterbalanced within and across age groups. The tasks required a persuasive text to be written. Formal teaching of this type of writing generally does not take place in Western Australian schools until the latter part of Grade 6 (second last year of primary school), and sometimes not until Grade 7. So, at the time of the data collections, few of the primary school students had received much, if any, formal instruction in writing the type of texts required by these tasks. The secondary students had had at least two years' formal teaching of that type of writing.

The purpose of the present study was to identify developmental patterns in using features of language that contribute to persuasive texts being perceived as coherent. This study adopted a reader-based approach to identifying these features, an approach similar to that used by Lawe Davies (1998) in her study of coherence in tertiary student writing. In the present study, each text was read by six untrained raters, representative of the variety of people who read school newsletters: teachers, parents and other family members, and interested community members. Each reader was asked to select the texts which, in his or her opinion, represented a readable, well-structured, coherent response to the topic. A rating score was then assigned to each text, based on the number of readers who had selected it as meeting those criteria. The highest rating possible was 5, given to texts accepted by five or six of the six readers [H-rated texts], and the lowest was 0, texts accepted by none of the readers [L-rated texts].

The group of H-rated texts (n = 19), that is, those on which there was general consensus that they were coherent, were analysed to identify the characteristics of language use that appeared to have contributed to coherence. The importance of those features was con-firmed by comparing the results with those from a similar analysis of the L-rated texts (n = 50). This process identified a variety of features that needed to be present if the texts were to be perceived as coherent. These features included characteristics of form, content, organisation and sentence-level comprehensibility. Subsequently, all the texts in the sample (n = 320) were analysed to identify the developmental patterns in the use of each of the features.

Text organisation

The tasks in this study required that a letter be written, so the texts were considered to have both external and internal form. The external form of a letter consists of salutation, body and closure sections, while the internal form (or internal rhetorical structure) refers to the form of the body section of the letter (see Figure 1), which is made up of three main sections: introduction, which establishes the topic and generally gives the writer's opinion on the issue under discussion; development, which sets forward the writer's reasons for his or her position on the topic; and conclusion.

SALUTATION (Dear Editor)	
BODY Introduction	
Development	
Conclusion	
CLOSURE (Yours sincerely)	

Figure 1: Text form

It is the organisation of the development section of the body of the letter which is the focus of this paper.

The analysis of features that readers expect in a coherent persuasive text indicated that it was important that the development section of a text be organised on some principled basis. There was no evidence that any one pattern of organisation was favoured over others.[1] Nine different organisational patterns were evident in the texts in this study, although in some cases only three or four examples of a particular pattern occurred across the whole sample (n = 320). The characteristics of the main patterns of organisation will be outlined first, and then an overview provided of some of the developmental changes that occur, using three of the patterns of organisation as exemplars.

Characteristics of organisational patterns

Logical

The most common form of organisation was Logical form, characterised by the use of a logic marker to introduce reasons for the position being taken, for example:

[1]   Dear editor   children should not be Paid at home becas they make some mess too and the adult would have more money for bill's and for yummy food.   [9M13AR1] [2]

Most commonly the logic marker employed in the Logical form of organisation was the causal adverb *because*, plus one or more additive connectives, as in [1] above, although other forms such as resultative and conditional adverbials, for example, *so (that)* and *if (then)*, were also quite widely used.

Inferential

The next most frequently occurring form of organisation was the Inferential form, characterised by the absence of overt marking of the semantic relationships between different sections of text, for example:

[2]   To the school newsletter,
I strongly disaggree with the suggestion that highschool students should only watch T.V. on weekends and school holidays. [because] T.V. is not all bad. [and because] Some programs are educational. [so] You can learn a lot from such shows. [therefore] I think that highschool students should be allowed to watch TV ...
In conclusion, TV is a source of relaxation, entertainment, education, and simple pleasure in life. Don't take this away from us.   [14F4BR5 - extracts]

Topical

In the Topical form of organisation, key noun phrases or short clauses, which occurred first in the text introduction, were used at the front of successive units of text to develop a new section of the argu-ment, as the superscripted sections in the following example indicate:
[3]   I agree and disagree with the statement 'High School Students are not allowed to watch T.V. on school days.' For four reasons [1]It would improve study habits and grades, [2]The students would not have enough time to relax and enjoy viewing, [3] Students can learn ideas and get their own views on what is going on and [4]T.V is sometimes garbage and not stimulating.
If students didn't watch T.V. on school days [1]they would have more time to study and would improve their work. For example ...
Students and young people alike all like a time to relax and [2]T.V. is the best way to relax and enjoy this time. After a hard day it school ...
                         [15M2AR3 - extracts]
In these data, a Topical form of organisation was frequently introduced with a short cataphoric statement, such as *for several reasons*, or, as in the example above, the specification of the number of reasons to be given: *for four reasons*.

Sequential

Sequential organisation may be realised linguistically in several forms, but most commonly in the data in the present study Sequential organisation was marked by the use of enumeration, for example:
[4]   Dear Editor,
        I am writting to reply to a letter sent in by another parent. That perant's arguments were good and he made his point very clear, but I disagree with him. Children should be allowed to watch T.V on weekdays not only weekends and holidays. Some of the resons why are:
1. Some programs are educational ...
2. It keeps them entertained....

3. It keeps them out of trouble.

4. Kids can get ideas from T.V. It can ...

5. It keeps them informed with whats happening in the rest of the world....

But Childrens T.V time should be limeted. ....

Thank you for taking time to read this letter,

    A Concerned Perant.   [11F20AR5 - extracts]

Other forms that appeared in these data included the use of dot points, and the use of sequential or additive connectives, usually preceded by a cataphoric statement such as *here are some reasons*, or, as bolded in the above example, *Some of the resons why are.*

Problem-solution

The Problem-solution pattern is marked by the use of lexis that has connotations of a difficulty or problem and how it could be overcome, for example:

[5]   Dear Madam/Sir

In reading the suggestion by a parent in the school newsletter, that high school students should only be allowed to watch TV at weekends and on holidays, I have to say that I totally agree with them. Problem If parents have been complaining about the low marks their children have been getting, Solution why not take this suggestion up and cut out TV on weekdays. Outcomes The children will have nothing to do ... they will remember that home work thats due tomorrow, and that Science test on Friday...   [15F5AR4 - extracts]

In the above example, the problem section of the text is introduced by *parents have been complaining*, and then a solution proposed, the means of overcoming the difficulty presented, *take this suggestion up and cut out TV on weekdays*. In some cases, as in example [5] above, the outcomes or benefits that would accrue to the reader from the application of the solution were also indicated, here, that children would remember to do their homework and study for tests, from which the reader is to infer that, if this occurred, marks would improve.

The Logical, Inferential, Topical, Sequential and Problem-solution patterns of organisation were the most commonly-used in these data. In addition, there were several other forms, which occurred in very low numbers, for example, the use of rhetorical strategies, and of narrative. These low occurrence patterns of organisation were grouped together for more reliable analysis.

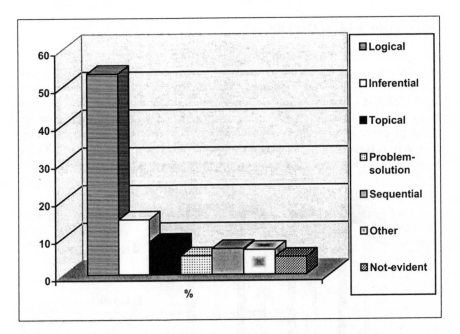

Figure 2: Forms of organisation

Form	Texts	
	n	%
Logical	171	53.4
Inferential	47	14.7
Topical	28	8.7
Problem-solution	16	5.0
Sequential	22	6.9
Other	21	6.6
Not Evident	15	4.7
Total	320	100.0

Table 2: Forms of organisation

Of all the forms of organisation identified in these data, Logical form was the most common, with 53.4% of all the texts in the sample using some form of logic marker as their organising principle; a further 40.7% of texts used one of Inferential, Topical, Sequential, or Problem-solution forms; while the remaining 5.9% of texts were almost equally divided between the categories of Other (very low occurrence forms) and Not evident (no reasons given for the position taken), as Figure 2 shows.

Developmental patterns

The general trend of development was the use of an increasing diversity of patterns of organisation as students got older. Within each of these forms of organisation, changes in use with increasing age were identified. At primary school level, Logical form was the most common form of organisation, with other forms increasingly being used as children grew older, especially once they moved into secondary school, probably reflecting the influence of formal teaching. Figure 3 and Table 3 provide an overview of the developmental patterns.

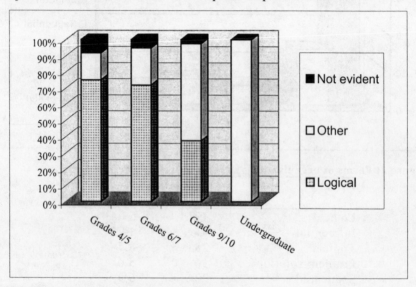

Figure 3 Developmental Patterns: Overview

Age group	Texts n	Logical %	Other %	Nil %	Total %
Grades 4/5	96	75.0	16.7	8.3	100.0
Grades 6/7	96	71.9	22.9	5.2	100.0
Grades 9/10	80	37.5	60.0	2.5	100.0
Undergraduate	48	-	100.0	-	100.0
Total	320	53.4	41.9	4.7	100.0

Table 3 Developmental patterns: Overview

Another general developmental trend, although outside the scope of this paper to discuss in detail, is the change with age in the way logic markers were used. Rather than logic markers being the dominant organising principle in texts of more mature writers, other, usually more complex, patterns of organisation were employed. However, within these other forms of organisation, logic markers were often employed as the basis of organisation of some sections of the text (e.g, see example [16], below). A wider variety of linguistic means was also used to express relations, such as reason/cause, earlier encoded by logic markers (e.g., use of non-finite clauses).

Although forms of organisation other than Logical were not common until secondary school, all forms of organisation were present even in texts written by the youngest students, as Figure 4 and Table 4 indicate.

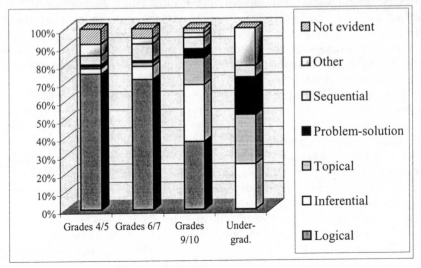

Figure 4 Developmental Patterns: Detailed

Age group	Grades 4/5	Grades 6/7	Grades 9/10	Undergraduate	
Texts n	96	96	80	48	320
Logical %	75	71.9	37.5	-	53.4
Inferential %	3.1	7.3	31.3	25	14.7
Topical %	1	2.1	15	27.1	8.8
Problem Solution %	1	1	5	20.8	5
Sequential %	5.2	9.4	6.3	6.3	6.9
Other %	6.3	3.1	2.5	20.8	6.6
Not evident %	8.3	5.2	2.5	0	4.7
Total %	100	100	100	100	100

Table 4 Developmental patterns: Detailed

The fact that all forms of organisation were present even in texts of the youngest writers is interesting and worthy of further investigation, because low numbers of occurrences do not necessarily mean 'not significant' in terms of what they may indicate about linguistic development (cf, Perera, 1984). In addition to the quantitative changes that are evidenced by the statistics in Table 3, there were qualitative changes occurring *within* organisational patterns, especially during the primary school years. The quantitative results alone do not adequately reflect all that was going on in terms of the development of these discourse level linguistic skills. Similar types of changes occurred within each organisational pattern, so three categories of organisation will be used as illustrative of the changes that take place in text organisation as children mature.

The first example of qualitative change within a form of organisation is the Logical category. In that category, there was a shift from reliance almost exclusively on reason/cause adverbials (usually the very common *because*) coupled with one or more additive connectives to give a string of reasons (the generic *I think X because Y and Z*), for example, text [7], to the use of a wider variety of other types of adverbials, such as purposive/resultative *so (that),* and conditional/concessive *if...(then)*, as in texts [8] and [9]:

[7]   Dear editor   children should not be Paid at home becas they make some mess too and the adult would have more money for bill's and for yummy food.

[9M13AR1]

[8]　Dear Editor,
I object to the suggestion that children should only be allowed to watch T.V. on the weekends and the school holidays. I think that children should be allowed to watch T.V. anytime they want otherwise they might get bored, get in other people's way or something like that. I find that if children do not watch T.V. they complain a lot and have lots of tantrums.　　　　　　　　　[10M2AR5]

[9]　to School Newsletter,
　　　I am writing to express my opinion on the issue of Highschool Students being paid for helping with Jobs around the home. I believe that a teenager should be paid as it will teach them a sence of responsibility when it comes to money. They will learn how to manage their money so they do not spend it all at once. It will also teach them For when they have a Full time Job and are earning a constant income so they do not spend all their money at once but learn to budget.....
　　　　　　　　[15F13AR2 - extract]

Within Logical form, there was also a move away from the use of additive connectives, especially *and*, to the use of other structural means to add ideas to the discourse. The most common additive connective in the texts of less mature writers was *and*, which frequently seemed to function as a marker of continuation in some of these texts, as well as a means of adding ideas, for example:

[10]　Dear Editor,
　　　I think that kids shouldn't need to be paid because they live there and they should contribute... And their parents buy toys, food... and so I think that kids should not be paid because all they need is... And that is why kids should not be paid for doing chores and other stuff.
　　　THE END　　　　　　　　[11M10AR1]

One structural change that occurred early was a move away from the use of *and* to join a series of sentences to the use of separate sentences. A second was that, where additive connectives were employed, forms other than *and* began to be used, initially usually *also* or *plus,* and later others such as *further*. For example:

[11]　Dear Editor,
I think kids should be paid for helping with jobs. because if they're paid they wont always be asking their parents for money to by stuff. Another reason is that they can learn how to manage money and use it wisely. They can also learn about the value of money and they will learn how to add and subtract money. Plus they will learn about place value. in learning about how to manage money they will be able to save up for

special things that they want, instead of always asking for a load of money all at once.
These are some of the many reasons why kids should get paid.

[10M19AR4]

As children matured, texts became longer, not only because the older children had greater facility with the mechanics of writing, or had a greater number of reasons to offer in support of their position on the issue, but also because they elaborated more on the reasons that they gave in support of their position. Whereas younger students, especially at Grade 4 level (9-year-olds), simply gave a string of reasons, introduced by logic markers (as in [7], above), older students provided greater elaboration, as, for example, in [9] above, *It will also teach them ... so they do not spend all their money at once but learn to budget.*

Another example of qualitative changes within a form of organisation was in the Sequential category. As already indicated, enumeration was the most common realisation of Sequential organisation in these data at primary school level. It is quite possible that, in using enumeration, children were drawing on existing linguistic knowledge, perhaps of writing procedural texts, to help them deal with organising the less familiar persuasive text form. However, by secondary school level, students were moving from reliance on enumeration as the basis of organisation of reasons within the sequential form of organisation (texts [12] and [13], below) to other, more integrated forms of organisation such as the use of sequential connectives (texts [14] and [15], below), or additive forms, such as *one reason..., another reason....*

[12]   Dear Editor
I think kids should be able to watch TV on weekdays Here are some reasons why.
1. If it's raining and you can't go outside.
2. If you finish your homework.
3. If your favourite shows on.
4. If theres speical shows on.
5. If your doing a project and somethings on about it.

[9M14AR4]

[13]   Dear Editor,
        I am writting to reply to a letter .... Children should be allowed to watch T.V on weekdays not only weekends and holidays. Some of the resons why are:

1. Some programs are educational and would help the children to Learn.
2. It keeps them entertained. Lots of perants...
3. It keeps them out of trouble.
4. Kids can get ideas from T.V...
5. It keeps them informed...
But Childrens T.V time should be limeted...
Thank you for taking time to read this letter,
     A Concerned Perant.
        [11F20AR5 - extracts]

[14]   In my opinion, I think that high school students should be allowed to watch TV on weekdays after school and at weekends and on holidays.
I think that it is not healthy doing your homework...
Another point, is that there may be some documentries...
Another reason, is that each person should have their own freedom...
        [14F8AR4 - extracts]

[15]   Dear Editor,
I have just visited our local library. I noticed,...
My point is, after reading last week's newsletter, I agree with Mr J. Smith that children should be ...
I would like to support my reasons to you. Firstly, with a weekly timetable ... Next, without this interruption, work (homework) would be completed ...
Furthermore, by not viewing television at dinner time, it would allow 'family tabletalk'...   [XF12AR3 - extracts]

By secondary level, students seemed to be able to sustain a more integrated form of text organisation, with less overt support than is perhaps offered by the use of enumeration.

The third form of organisation that will be used to exemplify the developmental changes that occur within text organisation is Problem-solution form. This pattern of organisation may be more cognitively demanding than some of the other forms discussed. Problem-solution form was often organised on a more inductive basis, with the writer's position on the issue likely to occur partway through the text, rather than at the beginning of the text as was the norm with patterns of organisation, such as Logical and Sequential, which were deductively organised. The Problem-solution form of organisation was found most commonly in the adult sample in these data, but it was also used by several primary school level texts. The youngest student employing this form of organisation was a Grade 5 (10-year-old) girl:

[16]   Dear Parents,
        Some of the teachers at school have been descusing that Problem
children are not doing as well as they should   and we all think it's
because they are watching too much T.V. Solution so we thought it would
be a good idea if you limited what they watching. For instence they
could watch T.V. on weekends and holidays. Something like that would
be good   [10F19BR3]

This girl's use of the Problem-solution form of organisation contains
the basic elements, although, unlike more mature writers (e.g., [17],
below], she did not elaborate on the outcomes or benefits that would
accrue to the reader from the application of her proposed solution,
something which this Grade 10 writer did:

[17]   Dear Madam/Sir
In reading the suggestion by a parent in the school newsletter, that high
school student should only be allowed to watch TV at weekends and on
holidays, I have to say that I totally agree with them. Problem If parents
have been complaining about the low marks their children have been
getting, Solution why not take this suggestion up and cut out TV on
weekdays. Outcomes The children will have nothing to do ... they will
remember that home work thats due tomorrow, and that Science test on
Friday...   [14F5AR4 - extracts]

Absence of elaboration of reasons, though, was not unique to a 10-
year-old using a Problem-solution pattern of organisation. As was
shown earlier, absence of elaboration was also a feature of more basic
patterns of organisation such as Logical form, and was not unique to
attempts to use more complex forms of organisation. What is interesting
is that the ability to use the problem-solution form is present in such a
young writer, and without formal teaching. Further, this Grade 5 student
used the form reasonably successfully, as evidenced by the rating (3)
that the text received.

Discussion

The examples of text organisation just given have been drawn from
three of the categories of organisation represented in these data, but the
principles they illustrate could also be demonstrated with texts from the
other categories. In considering the changes that occurred with age, it is
noticeable that even quite young children, who have not received any
formal teaching in writing persuasive text, have rudimentary knowledge

of different ways of organising information in persuasive texts. A related point of interest is the variety of patterns of organisation employed. The texts using these different patterns are not necessarily outstanding examples of their type, but the forms of organisation were, nevertheless, employed with a fair degree of success, judging by the rating scores received, despite the writers having received little or no formal teaching in writing this text type. This observation raises the question of the source of such knowledge. There are several possible influences.

The major influence, especially in the case of the youngest students, is likely to be experience of patterns of text organisation from other communicative contexts, both oral and written. Parents and other caregivers readily attest that young children possess very effective oral persuasion skills, anecdotal evidence that is supported by research (e.g., Weiss & Sachs, 1991) that shows that these skills develop relatively early, so children are likely to draw on a model with which they have been successful in one communicative context (oral language) to assist them in producing a similar type of text in a less familiar context (written language).

Students are also likely to be drawing on knowledge about patterns of text organisation from their experiences with written language through reading. Responses to a question on a participant background information sheet about the type and amount of reading done each week pointed to recreational reading being an important part of the lives of a high proportion of school students in the study.[3] Therefore, it seems reasonable to suggest that reading may be another influence in students' awareness of different ways of organising text.

A further influence on the knowledge of text organisation for children in this study is their involvement in religious activities. The participating schools were all Christian schools, so for many of their students religious activities formed a significant part of their lives outside of school. The purpose of many religious communicative events (e.g., 'devotional talks,' Bible reading) is to persuade hearers/readers to a certain point of view, or a particular way of living. While the underlying organisational patterns of these texts may be varied, such communicative experiences are likely to have served as models on which some school students drew, consciously or unconsciously, for assistance in approaching the unfamiliar task of writing a persuasive text.

One other possible influence on students' knowledge of patterns of text organisation to be mentioned is their general awareness that there are different ways of organising texts for different communicative purposes. Current pedagogic practice in Western Australian schools is for different forms of text organisation (e.g., narrative, procedure, report, exposition) to be explicitly taught from the commencement of formal schooling, although exposition (into which category persuasive texts come) is not introduced until the late primary school years. However, the progressive introduction from the earliest years of formal schooling of different ways of conveying information means that students are cognisant of the fact that different communicative contexts are organised according to different principles. It therefore seems reasonable to suggest that student writing, even of an unfamiliar type of text, is likely to reflect this awareness, and that students will attempt to draw on their existing linguistic resources to assist them in handling an unfamiliar task.

This discussion has suggested possible influences on children's knowledge of forms of text organisation. However, while it is possible to speculate about influences, it is not possible to identify precisely which communicative events may have been drawn on by any given student in writing a persuasive text for this study. To find this out would have necessitated a different methodology, such as interviewing writers immediately after the text had been written. Although not all students would know or be able to articulate what had influenced their writing, this would be a worthwhile avenue of future investigation to help to identify the sources of rudimentary knowledge many young students have about patterns of text organisation.

There is a further issue in relation to influences on students' decisions concerning the patterns of text organisation employed that is relevant to consider here. That is, that while it is relevant to suggest that some or all of the communicative experiences outlined above are probably common to many of the children in the sample, not all students have had exposure to exactly the same communicative events, nor are all students influenced in the same way by a particular event. Hence, differential outcomes can be expected, in this case, in the extent to which children successfully transfer knowledge of a pattern of text organisation from one context to another without explicit teaching. It is likely that many students need formal teaching to be able to organise texts successfully.

The influence of formal teaching on patterns of organisation seems to be evident in the texts of older students in these data, as the texts generally used more complex patterns of organisation and received higher rating scores than did those of younger students, suggesting greater 'success' in meeting audience expectations. Nevertheless, the data also point to young students having at least rudimentary knowledge of a basic generic form of persuasive text (*I think X because Y.*), and in some cases more complex organisational patterns, which is knowledge on which teachers can build in later formal teaching of persuasive writing. The results from this study are not, of course, generalisable beyond this sample but they provide a basis for further investigation of developmental patterns in organisation of persuasive texts using data from a more diverse student group.

Notes

1. Logical form of organisation was the dispreferred pattern in the H-rated group, but this was due to factors such as the failure of writers to state their position clearly or to elaborate on their reasons. Thus, the reasons for Logical form being dispreferred had nothing to do with the particular pattern of organisation *per se*.
2. All texts carry a code number, indicating the age and gender of the writer, plus the rating score the text achieved. For example, 9M13AR1 indicates a text written by a 9-year-old (Grade 4) boy which received a rating score of 1, indicating that it had been selected by one of the six raters as meeting his/her idea of a readable, well-structured, coherent response to the topic. Texts with X as the first digit of the code were written by tertiary students.
3. The question about the type and amount of reading done each week was quite general, and intended simply to provide an overall guide to participants' reading activity. The question was not intended to form the basis of a correlational study of the relationships between types and quantities of books read, and patterns of text organisation employed.

References

Bamberg, B. (1983) What makes a text coherent? *College Composition and Communication* 34:417-429.

Brown, G. & Yule, G. (1983) *Discourse Analysis*. Cambridge: Cambridge University Press.

Cook, G. (1989) *Discourse*. Oxford: Oxford University Press.

Gernsbacher, M. A. (1990) *Language Comprehension as Structure Building*. Hillsdale, NJ: Lawrence Erlbaum.

Gernsbacher, M. (1997) Coherence cues mapping during comprehension. In J. Costermans and M. Fayol (eds.) *Processing Interclausal Relationships*. Mahwah, NJ: Lawrence Erlbaum.

Givon, T. (1992) The grammar of referential coherence as mental processing instructions. *Linguistics* 30/1:5-55.

Givon, T. (1995) Coherence in text vs coherence in mind. In M. Gernsbacher & T. Givon (eds) *Coherence in Spontaneous Text*. Amsterdam/Philadelphia: John Benjamins.

Lawe Davies, R. (1998) *Coherence in Tertiary Students' Writing*. Unpublished PhD thesis, University of Western Australia, Perth, Western Australia.

Perera, K. (1984) *Children's Writing and Reading: Analysing Classroom Language*. Oxford: Basil Blackwell.

Van Dijk, T. (1977) *Text and Context*. London: Longman.

Weiss, D. & Sachs, J. (1991). Persuasive strategies used by preschool children. *Discourse Processes*, 14:55-72.

4 Discourse and synchronous computer-mediated communication: uniting speaking and writing?

JAMES SIMPSON

University of Reading

This paper presents an exploration of the discourse of text-based synchronous computer-mediated communication, henceforth *synchronous CMC*. I argue that when engaging in synchronous CMC, participants are faced with a phenomenon that though written, the discourse is conversation-like. Yet in part due to the technological aspects of CMC system design, and in part due to the novel situation in which the participants find themselves, the discourse has features which are not found in either prototypical spoken or written discourse.

The paper commences with a description of the discourse under discussion. What follows is an examination of the discourse from two broad perspectives. Firstly I discuss the extent to which the discourse is affected by the technology of the substance (the computer system). Secondly I show that the participants themselves strive to increase interactivity within the discourse through the development of novel discourse features which are appropriate to the medium. Within these perspectives, the discourse is investigated here on two levels: the medium-generated effects on turn-taking and exchange structure; and the attempts by participants to increase interactivity through the representation of the prosodics and paralanguage of face-to-face discourse in text, and through the breaking up of conversational turns.

Unity and diversity

The discourse of synchronous CMC bears upon the theme of this collection in a contradictory fashion. Communication in the text-based synchronous mode of CMC straddles a basic parameter of linguistic differentiation: speech and writing. *Prima facie* this would suggest a unity, a melding of the spoken and the written into a hybrid form. Yet though the discourse of CMC has a strong relationship to both prototypical speaking and writing, within the text we can identify the development of features which relate to neither. Thus this discourse exemplifies the diversity of language as it is actually used.

Susan Herring (1996:4) maintains that research into CMC aims to understand: '...to what extent does the computer medium alter human interaction, and to what extent do people simply map their existing patterns of behaviour onto communication in the new medium.' This paper represents an attempt to shed light on this question.

Part one of the paper is a brief description and explanation of synchronous, text-based CMC. Here some terms are explained, and there is a presentation of examples of the data which are used to illustrate the discussion.

The second part is a demonstration that the conversation-like discourse of synchronous CMC is both similar to, and differs from, the spoken conversational mode. We examine the interplay of individual users and the computer system: how the participants' appetites for interaction lead to a tolerance of reduced interactional coherence (Herring, 1999) which is partly a medium effect of the technology. This is exemplified in discussion of two inter-turn synchronous CMC characteristics: multiple threads (or competing collaborative floors) of written conversation, and overlapping turns.

In part three the focus is more firmly on the participants' responses to the medium. Though the discourse bears a strong resemblance to spoken face-to-face communication, the demands of the computer medium enable, or require, participants to adapt their practices. We examine two of the inventive ways in which the participants in synchronous CMC strive to maintain the speech-like qualities of the discourse through the mediation of the computer interface: reduplication of letters and punctuation to represent reciprocity, and the splitting of turns. It is suggested that these practices lead to the creation of novel discourse features, in addition to features which are parallel to those found in spoken face-to-face communication.

Part One: Text-based CMC, Internet chat and instant messaging

Herring (1996:1) defines CMC as: '... communication that takes place between human beings via the instrumentality of computers.' This implies inclusion of video conferencing and the use of computers for telephony within the definition. Some writers (for example Murray, 2000) restrict the definition of CMC to include only text-based modes. This restriction would embrace telephone text-messaging (SMS), but would exclude future applications of text recognition and speech synthesis. As the technological possibilities for audio and video CMC conferencing become ever more feasible, and as CMC modes are frequently used in combination, I feel the limitation of the definition to include only text-based modes to be unnecessarily exclusive. Notwithstanding this, much CMC research to date has concentrated on the text-based mode.

Text-based synchronous CMC is an umbrella term for a family whose members include internet relay chat (IRC) and its cousin, instant messaging, which are the sources of the data in this discussion. The chat text presented here is from a variety of rooms hosted by MSN, and the messenger text is from MSN Messenger. Their common features are that communication is text-based, but takes place in real time, and that participants are separated by distance. Internet chat rooms are public, and each has a theme; most are light-hearted in content (hence 'chat room'). This form of interactive written discourse was developed by Jarkko Oikarinen in Finland in the late eighties as a more immediate substitute for 'talk' on his bulletin board (Hentschel, 1998). It was until recently relatively specialised, confined as it was to UNIX (Eastment, 1999:9). Today, however, it continues to grow in popularity and is available to anyone with access to the internet, as chat software is included on the websites of many internet service providers (ISPs). Instant messaging works on the same principle as IRC; however, participation is between interlocutors who are known to each other.

The ambiguous status of IRC as a discourse type is reflected in its name: though called *chat*, it is text-based. To participate in IRC, a user chooses a nickname by which he or she is known to other users. When using IRC or instant messaging, the computer screen is split: interlocutors type turns into a lower window which, when sent, are immediately viewed by all current participants in a larger window. Turns in IRC and instant messaging cannot be viewed by other participants until they are sent, but the brevity of a typical turn coupled with the speed and number of the exchanges creates the impression of synchronous communication. Kitade summarises the text-based but synchronous interaction of IRC participants thus (2000:152):

> Text-based interactions with computer technology allow interlocutors to scroll back and re-think what has been discussed and re-formulate their own utterances before sending them. Reworking a constructed utterance is possible as in other types of writing, but such reworking is limited because the interaction in IC [internet chat] is synchronous. Although IC facilitates more spontaneous interaction than other written interaction such as email and letters (asynchronous), in IC one can edit what one says (submits) before saying (submitting) it.

Extracts one and two below are examples of IRC and MSN Messenger text. The text is not static as shown here: it scrolls up the screen as the messages are sent. Each extract represents about thirty seconds' worth of communication.

Extract 1: Internet Relay Chat

Guest_Kyslin: And if I found out the same about Bush, I'd want him out, too.
Guest_jenn: Moofing, wold she be ok had she supported Gore?
Guest_hagen: jag...

MSNBC-Debb hands Jayde a dirty gym sock to gag jag
Guest_risa has left the conversation.

Guest_hagen: asarte.. i agree
Guest_EDINVA: jenn ... the state's AG supported Gore and he's still in office
MSNBC-Jayde: I have some dirty diapers
Guest_Bill: The "W" stands for Winner.......
MSNBC-Debb: even better
Guest_raggedyanne: anna so true about the media but maybe just maybe President Bush is not doing a stunt
Guest_Astarte: Debb hahahaha

Extract 2: MSN Messenger

Miss.Shaikha says:
hy mona
mona says:
how u doing
Miss.Shaikha says:
guess where I am?
mona says:
don't say in qatar
Miss.Shaikha says:
yes
mona says:
noooooooooooooooooooooooooooooo

Part two: written conversation and the influence of the medium

Prototypical speech and writing have different functions. As Halliday (1985:41) notes: '... the kinds of meaning that are transmitted in writing tend to be somewhat different from the kinds of meaning transmitted through speech.' And though speaking and writing should not be viewed as dichotomous, one nevertheless tends to think in terms of features typically associated with written communication (messages, information) and with spoken communication (interpersonal involvement). Tannen (1985), uses the term *relative focus of involvement* to characterise this difference: typically spoken communication has a closer focus of involvement than typically written.

The essayist William Hazlitt described the difference between speaking and writing: 'The great leading distinction between writing and speaking is, that more time is allowed for one than the other; and hence different faculties are required for, and different objects attained by, each' (1820/1998:140). Synchronous CMC discourse is not face-to-face spoken communication, however. But it shares a similar temporal relationship to speech. We therefore are obliged to reconsider Hazlitt's assertion. Written communication on-line can seem akin to face-to-face conversation. In the words of Kress (1998:53-4), it is '...this remaking of the social situation which then reshapes language in the direction of speech-like form.' Participants in synchronous CMC can overcome the limitations of the substance of the discourse (the computer system) by utilising the technical potential of the computer and CMC programs to create discourse which for them seems speech-like.

So one way of approaching the interactional discourse of synchronous, text-based CMC is, as its participants do, to conceptualise it as a written conversation. In addition to the obvious fact that it is written, not spoken, synchronous CMC as written conversation nevertheless deviates from the spoken mode in other ways.

Sacks, Schegloff and Jefferson (1974) present 14 general properties of conversation. Of all these criterial features, only two do not apply to synchronous CMC. These are: 'Occurrences of more than one speaker at a time are common, but brief'; and the related: 'Repair mechanisms exist for dealing with turn-taking errors and violations; e.g., if two parties find themselves talking at the same time, one of them will stop prematurely, thus repairing the trouble' (1974:700-701). These exceptions relate to two features of face-to-face or even telephone discourse which CMC participants lack: feedback, in the form of paralinguistic cues and back channels; and the potential for turns from more than one interlocutor to take place simultaneously. Typing a message can be carried out by more than one party at a time. Yet, as noted earlier, in most forms of synchronous CMC the messages themselves do not appear on the screen until they are sent, and therefore participants cannot view utterances as they are being formulated.

Herring (1999) suggests that far from being obstacles to interaction, these features of the system, what she terms a reduced *interactional coherence*, serve to increase interactivity. Says Herring (1999:15-16):

> ... text-only CMC remains loosely coherent in comparison with the interactional norms for face-to-face conversation ... yet clearly, given the popularity of Usenet, IRC and MUDs [*multi-user domain*, a virtual, network-based collaborative space], reduced interactional coherence is not a serious impediment to users' enjoyment of CMC. Not only that, it might be an advantage.

We can view reduced interactional coherence in the patterns of turn-taking and exchange combination in synchronous CMC. What can be seen is the similarity of spoken and written conversation, and at the same time the effects of the medium on turn adjacency. Stenstrom's (1994:34) definition of a turn as being: '... everything A says before B takes over, and vice versa' is workable when describing synchronous CMC. Below we explore two areas where turn-taking and exchange combinations in CMC work in similar, though distinctly different ways to those in spoken conversation.

Multiple threads

In extract three (opposite), a large number of participants are engaged in IRC simultaneously. As previously stressed, the participants may well be typing at once; their turns, however, cannot be viewed until they are received by the system.

At first sight the turns seem unrelated and confused. There are ten different participants, and as the discourse unfolds, it initially seems that they are all taking part in the same conversation. There are, in fact, a number of different conversations continuing simultaneously. If we follow ticcan, LittlePip1 and zen, we can see that the pattern of exchanges is quite clear. In addition to the display of nicknames, interlocutors employ distinctive fonts and colours (which did not survive formatting in this paper); these combine to help the discourse to proceed smoothly by making it easier for interlocutors to follow their particular thread. Ticcan and LittlePip1 are in the midst of a discussion when zen suggests to LittlePip1 that Ticcan is goading the latter into responding.

Extract 3: Multiple threads in typical IRC discourse

```
1     ticcan : how is it not the same pip
2     Conrad523 : hi wife and rob
3     Ådæpt™ : heya tw
4     trophywife0 : GOTEY
5     trophywife0 : tight
6     Serpentula_Chrysalis : ChristianCastration, I want
      that nickname
7     RothkoX : one pleasure giver sage
8     LittlePip1 : because theft has nothing to do with
      bodily assault
9     Conrad523 : she has heaps of work, sage
10    zen™ : dont play along pip,hes thinks hes clever
11    trophywife0 : z
12    ticcan : u are removing the instrument of the crime
      pip
13    RothkoX : you see philosophically speaking the smurf
      village was a metaphor for one enitre human body
14    †wï§mÃƒ£Üþïñÿå : i think smurfet had a disease
      thats why they were all blue
15    zen™ : by acting stupid
16    Robert2323_ : whats up everybody
17    LittlePip1 : it's okay, I'm well aware he's not
      clever
```

If we remove the turns from the other current participants so only the turns from these three remain, a straightforward pattern of initiation and response (following Hoey, 1991; Sinclair and Coulthard, 1975) emerges:

Extract 4: Initiation and response in IRC

1	ticcan : how is it not the same pip	initiation 1
8	LittlePip1 : because theft has nothing to do with bodily assault	response 1
10	zen™ : dont play along pip,hes thinks hes clever	Initiation 2
12	ticcan : u are removing the instrument of the crime pip	Initiation 3
15	zen™ : by acting stupid	(initiation 2 continued)
17	LittlePip1 : it's okay, I'm well aware he's not clever	response 2

In turn 8 LittlePip1 responds to ticcan's initiation of turn 1. Zen (turns 10 and 15) then initiates LittlePip1's response of turn 17. Meanwhile, ticcan makes his or her second initiation of the exchange in turn 12. While it is progressing, nicknames, font type, size and colour all facilitate the discourse. The overall pattern of exchanges in a busy chat room is somewhat reminiscent of that which might take place in a crowded room at a party, where many conversations happen simultaneously.

Negretti (1999) refers to 'multiple strands' in synchronous CMC discourse. Its structure is characterised (1999:81) as exhibiting: 'a parallel architecture, with speakers simultaneously contributing to different strands of the conversation'. Shield *et al* (2000:43) note that users of synchronous CMC become: '... adept at managing multi-threaded exchanges.' A detailed treatment of multiple threads in synchronous CMC is found in Cherny (1999). She states (1999:174):

Given that there is no competition for the channel per se, but rather competition for attention or control of the discourse, notions of shared or collaborative floor seem to be more helpful than the standard turn-taking literature. These notions also appear more useful for theorising multi-threaded topic discourse.

In a 'multiple conversational floor' she distinguishes between instances where a side floor and a main floor exist together, and where two main floors coexist. Cherny's observation brings to attention that it is a result of the technology of the medium that the emphasis in turn-taking is not on gaining attention and deciding who has the next turn. Rather, it is on holding the floor and maintaining position in one or more of the threads of discourse underway.

Overlapping turns

In terms of turn-taking, spoken casual conversation bears a far greater similarity to synchronous CMC than it does to some other forms of interactive spoken discourse such as meetings, debates, and interviews, although synchronous CMC is in written mode. We can nevertheless already see ways in which it differs.

In the previous exchange we witnessed that Zen's initiation was interrupted by ticcan. In the following extract we can see more clearly that the effect of the lag between writing and posting a turn produces a feature we might term the overlap:

Extract 5: Overlapping turns in MSN Messenger

	mona says:
1	could u tell me what 1 mean in Arabic
	cuteOoO says:
2	so ....tell me when u gonna go back
	cuteOoO says:
3	i mean 2 ur hall
	mona says:
4	a bout 3pm
	cuteOoO says:
5	1 ,,,,, nothing ,,,,,,,,, 1 = one ...hehehehe
	mona says:
6	then ill go to asda with hameeda

In turn 1, Mona asks a question which is posted just before the question posed by CuteOoO. The continuation of CuteOoO's question elicits the response in turn 4 from Mona. Only then, in turn 5, does CuteOoO respond to Mona's original initiation. Finally, in turn 6 Mona continues her response to CuteOoO's question from turns 2 and 3.

A general characteristic of spoken conversation, say Sacks *et al* (1974:699), is that: '... there are techniques for the construction of utterances relevant to their turn status, which bear on the coordination of transfer and on the allocation of speakership.' In contrast, the overlap is a general characteristic of synchronous CMC. Herring (1999:9) refers to the violation of sequential coherence as being the rule, rather than the exception, in CMC; a point also made by Negretti (1999:83). It makes the identification of adjacency pairs problematic for participants and analysts. As Herring (1999:9) suggests: 'The greater the temporal and/or spatial distance between related turns, the greater the difficulty for users in identifying which previous message a current message is responding to.'

Herring attributes the interactive possibilities of CMC to the *conversational persistence* of the medium. Sacks *et al* note (1974:697) that: '... the natural home of speech is one in which speech is not always present.' This is not the case with synchronous CMC. At the current stage in its technological development, synchronous CMC is presented in linear fashion, where the text scrolls up the screen as new turns are posted. There is a constant visible record of what has recently been uttered. Thus even though synchronous CMC approaches spoken conversation in its immediacy, it is nonetheless possible for participants to scroll back up the screen to see a record of previously posted turns, and thus keep track of the multiple threads of the discourse. Herring suggests that this persistence aids a participant's cognitive processing (1999:18): '... CMC persists as text on a screen and is subject to conscious reflection in ways that spoken language is not, thereby facilitating a heightened metalinguistic awareness.'

We have considered some of the speech-in-writing characteristics of synchronous CMC, in terms of turn-taking and exchange structure, and have investigated some ways in which it differs from the spoken mode. We now turn to areas of the discourse below the level of the turn which show how interactivity is achieved in a medium which lacks the prosodic and paralinguistic cues of spoken communication.

Part three: Striving for interactivity in synchronous CMC

It is tempting, though erroneous, says Kress, to attribute the changes in language noted in CMC to the technology of the medium. He prefers to make the social prior, stating: 'We could say that the informality of language in general and of speech in particular is a factor of social proximity' (Kress, 1998:54). To an extent I agree. As we have seen, there are some features of the computer medium which serve in part to shape the discourse. They also act as potential, if not actual, constraints on the interaction (see, for example, the overlaps caused by lags). Typing speed has a delaying effect, somewhat counteracted by the use of acronyms and abbreviations, and a disregard for the conventions of spelling, capitalisation and punctuation. But when I am using synchronous CMC, I am in the temporal, if not spatial, co-presence of my interlocutors, and, following Kress, this puts me in a situation somewhat typical to that of the use of speech. The tendency is to increase interactivity, and this tendency results in the emergence of discourse features which I hold are particular to the electronic medium. The term *interactivity* here is more general than that conceived by Rafaeli and his colleagues (see for example, Rafaeli and Sudweeks, 1997), where the level of interactivity of a message, a turn in synchronous CMC, is defined by how it relates to previous messages in a sequence. For the purposes of this paper, interactivity refers to the user's drive to produce turns which require a response. The examples are firstly of the representation of the prosodics of speech in writing, and secondly of the splitting of turns.

Reduplication and reciprocity

The discourse of synchronous CMC can be conceptualised as written conversation. I hold that the emergence of new discourse and linguistic features in synchronous CMC is a result of its participants' efforts to render the discourse speech-like. The key to the understanding of this is that the non-verbal aspects of speech (prosodic and paralinguistic cues), along with other presentational codes of face-to-face communication such as head nods, gestures, and so on, can be partially performed by representational codes in the written text of CMC discourse. It seems that participants do this in part to reciprocate communicative messages.

O'Sullivan *et al* (1983:157) suggest that reciprocation is a common quality in face-to-face interaction: 'It seems that we often seek some kind of balance in communication when speaking with our bodies. The major consideration is that of reciprocation, meaning the answering of another's body questions.' In our case the immediacy of the response, or the real-time nature of the interaction, encourages not only adoption of the strategies for representing non-verbal features of speech, but also reciprocation, which exists clearly enough in the prosodics of synchronous CMC.

In Robert Graves' fantasy novel *Seven Days in New Crete* (1949) a man from the distant future asks a twentieth century Englishman: 'Do I speak with correctitude?' 'With great correctitude,' he is assured, 'but without the modulations of tone we English use to express, or disguise, our feelings.' These modulations of tone are represented through inventive stretching of words and extended strings of punctuation marks in synchronous CMC. This is known as *reduplication* (Hentschel, 1998; Werry, 1996) or *adornment* (Rintel *et al*, 2001). It is not only used by 'we English', as is shown in the following extract, turns 1, 4, 5 and 6, from a French language chat room. The reduplication seems to represent drawn out and expressive intonation:

Extract 6: Reduplication for reciprocity on a French language chat room

```
1    diamont_PF : Me revoilouuuuuuuuuuuuuuuuuuuuuuuuuuuu
2    BattingFouine : coucou diamont
3    pimousse6 : pkoi tu dis ca vesse
4    pimousse6 :
     diamonttttttttttttttttttttttttttttttttttttttttt
5    diamont_PF : slt a tous ce que j'ai
     manquééééééééééééééééééé
6    diamont_PF : Pimmmmmmmmmmmmmm
```

The outstanding feature in this series of turns is that pimousse6 reciprocates the general greeting of diamont_PF. In turn 1 diamont_PF enters the chat with her or his extended reduplication of the vowel 'u'. Pimousse6, engaged in another floor of conversation, drops everything to greet diamont. Interestingly, pimousse6 chooses the 't' to reduplicate, rather than the 'o' or the 'n', which would correspond more closely with the voiced phoneme of its spoken equivalent. Finally, in turn 6 diamont_PF reciprocates pimousse6's reduplicated greeting.

In this second example, two Arabic speakers, a brother and sister from Qatar, greet each other in English, on MSN Messenger. Dodee uses reduplication to achieve the sought-after balance in communication:

Extract 7: Reciprocation using reduplication on MSN Messenger

```
     mona says:
1    Hiiiiiiiiiiiiiiiiiii
     dodee says:
2    Hiiiiiiiiiiiiiiiiiiiiiiiiiiiiiiiiiiiii
     mona says:
3    how u doing
     dodee says:
4    ok
     mona says:
5    how is all
     dodee says:
6    all our right
     mona says:
7    why didin't u call me in morning
     dodee says:
8    I was to busy
```

Rintel *et al* (2001) refer to this reciprocation as 'adornment matching'. They suggest two motives for its use: the establishment of intimacy; and the foundation of turn sequencing. Thus (2001:21): 'Matching can be a powerful demonstration of alignment to the dyad ...'.

Splitting turns: holding the floor and increasing interactivity

In this final set of examples, we can see that the objective is not so much to reproduce the features of face-to-face spoken communication; rather, holding the floor and increasing interactivity seem to be the aim.

In spoken conversation, one way of holding the floor is simply to keep speaking. In most forms of synchronous CMC, if a participant just keeps typing, nothing is seen until the entire message is sent. So what participants do is to split their turns and send them as multiple units, where in spoken mode the utterance would be delivered as one turn. Some (e.g., Hentschel, 1998) see this as simply a technique for floor-holding, for keeping the turn. This is certainly the case when it is deliberately done to prevent others from taking the turn.

In this extract from IRC, IPFreely uses capital letters and swiftly-repeated postings to produce a vertical representation of his over-riding topic of interest:

Extract 8: Split turn on IRC

1	Guest_ILunn : that was a good laugh
2	Guest_IPFreely : jimbo are u a girl
3	Guest_IPFreely : G
4	Guest_IPFreely : I
5	Guest_IPFreely : R
6	Guest_IPFreely : L
7	Guest_IPFreely : S
8	Guest_ILunn : lad2k in dirty flirty

On other occasions, splitting turns increases the interactivity of the discourse by allowing for interjections; a richer, more varied conversation ensues. Note that the turns in this last example break in places which would be considered tone units or information units in spoken discourse.

Extract 9: Split turns and abusive statements on IRC

1	burbilzen3cc : I am but a redwood to your itch weed
2	Guest_null : hahaha, your a total loser
3	AbnormalChick : Hi Pie
4	burbilzen3cc : make me you criminal
5	AbnormalChick : lol
6	burbilzen3cc : you are but null null
7	Guest_AmericanPie : Hi Chick!
8	burbilzen3cc : I am the greatest man in America
9	burbilzen3cc : you jealous twit
10	AbnormalChick : there can be stupid and arrogant ppl
11	burbilzen3cc : I feed people like you to my rodents
12	AbnormalChick : i have got used to that

Burlbizen and null are engaged in an abusive exchange. Turns 3 and 5 from AbnormalChick can be ignored at present; they are from another thread, or floor, of conversation. Turns 1, 4 and 6 can be considered separate turns rather than continuations. However, if we examine turns 8, 9 and 11 from burlbizen, all three utterances are more closely linked. They might be considered part of one 'unit of intention' which has been broken up either as a floor-holding technique, or to allow for interjections. If the latter is true, it is not the case that burlbizen is attempting to recreate a speech-like form (despite the splits occurring at what might be the intonational boundaries of spoken discourse), but rather these split turns increase the interactivity of the discourse.

Conclusion

Halliday has suggested that a significant effect of the invention of printing is that it created the maximum distance between written and spoken text (1996:354). In conclusion, we can say that at the very least synchronous CMC discourse represents a blurring of the barrier between speech and writing. The objectification of writing by print brought about a dichotomy which is now deteriorating. Speech becomes an object, like printed writing, through recording; writing becomes an event, like speech, through synchronous, text-based computer-mediation. More so now than ever, writing cannot be regarded as a solitary activity. In our examples of synchronous CMC we have seen instances of how the patterns of turn-taking resemble, but differ from, those of spoken interaction, of how attempts to recreate speech-like features in CMC text result in the emergence of novel linguistic features, and how increased interactivity, rather than the strict re-creation of features of speech, may be the aim of some participants in synchronous CMC.

I do not believe that the changes in language use exemplified here are wholly the result of the introduction of a new technology. Rather, there is a mutual relationship between the new technology and the broader social contexts within which the technology exists. In the case of synchronous CMC, system constraints have an inevitable effect on the textual structure of the discourse; equally, participants within the social space of synchronous CMC discourse themselves shape it in their quest for interactivity.

References

Cherny, L. (1999) *Conversation and Community: Chat in a Virtual World.* Stanford, CA: CSLI Publications.

Eastment, D. (1999) *The Internet and ELT.* Oxford: Summertown Publishing.

Graves, R. (1949) *Seven Days in New Crete.* London: Cassell.

Halliday, M. A. K. (1985) *Spoken and Written Language.* Oxford: Oxford University Press.

Halliday, M. A. K. (1996) Literacy and linguistics: a functional perspective. In G. Williams and R. Hasan (eds.): *Literacy in Society.* Harlow: Addison Wesley Longman.

Hazlitt, W. (1820/1998) On the difference between writing and speaking. In D. Wu (ed.): *William Hazlitt, the Plain Speaker: The Key Essays.* Oxford: Blackwell.

Hentschel, E. (1998) Communication on IRC. *Linguistik Online* 1. Retrieved March 27 2001 from the www: http://viadrina.euv-frankfurt-o.de/~wjournal/hentschel.htm

Herring, S. (ed.) (1996) *Computer mediated communication: Linguistic, social and cross-cultural perspectives*. Amsterdam: John Benjamins.

Herring, S. (1999) Interactional coherence in CMC. *Journal of Computer-Mediated Communication* 4/4. Retrieved 25 September 2001 from the www: http://www.ascusc.org/jcmc/vol4/issue 4/herring.html

Hoey, M. (1991) Some properties of spoken discourses. In R. Bowers and C. Brumfit (eds.): *Applied Linguistics and English Language Teaching: Review of ELT* 2:1 1992. Oxford: Modern English Publications.

Kitade, K. (2000) L2 learners' discourse and SLA theories in CMC: collaborative interaction in internet chat. *Computer Assisted Language Learning* 13/2, 143-166.

Kress, G. (1998) Visual and verbal modes of representation in electronically mediated communication: the potentials of new forms of text. In I. Snyder (ed.): *Page to Screen: Taking Literacy into the Electronic Era*. London: Routledge.

Murray, D. E. (2000) Changing technologies, changing literacy communities? *Language Learning and Technology* 4/2, 43-58. Retrieved 19 January 2001 from the www: http://llt.msu.edu/vol4num2/murray/default.html

Negretti, R. (1999) Web-based activities and SLA: a conversation analysis research approach.' *Language learning and technology* 3/1, 75-87. Retrieved 28 February 2001 from the www: http://llt.msu.edu/vol3num1/negretti/index.html

O'Sullivan, T., J. Hartley, D. Saunders, M. Montgomery, and J. Fiske. (1994) *Key Concepts in Communication and Cultural Studies*. London: Routledge.

Rafaeli, S. and F. Sudweeks. (1997) Networked interactivity. *Journal of Computer-Mediated Communication* 2/4. Retrieved 24 September 2001 from www:http://www.ascusc.org/jcmc/vol2/issue4/rafaeli.sudweeks.html

Rintel, E. S., J. Mulholland, and J. Pittam. (2001) First things first: Internet Relay Chat openings. *Journal of Computer-Mediated Communication* 6/3. Retrieved 25 September 2001 from the www: http://www.ascusc.org/jcmc/vol6/issue 3/rintel.html

Sacks, H., E. G. Schegloff, and G. Jefferson. (1974) A simplest systematics for the organisation of turn-taking for conversation. *Language* 50/4, 696-735.

Shield, L., L. B. Davies, and M. J. Weininger. (2000) Fostering (pro)active language learning through MOO.. *ReCALL* 12/1, 35-48.

Sinclair, J. McH. and R. M. Coulthard. (1975) *Towards an Analysis of Discourse: The English used by Teachers and Pupils*. Oxford: Oxford University Press.

Stenstrom, A.-B. (1994) *An Introduction to Spoken Interaction*. Harlow: Longman.

Tannen, D. (1985) Relative focus on involvement in oral and written discourse. In D. R. Olson, N. Torrance and A. Hildyard (eds.): *Literacy, Language and Learning*. Cambridge: Cambridge University Press.

Werry, C. (1996) Linguistic and interactional features of Internet Relay Chat. In S. Herring (ed.): *Computer Mediated Communication: Linguistic, Social and Cross-cultural Perspectives*. Amsterdam: John Benjamins.

5   Methodological issues involved in studying children's interactions with ICT

JULIA GILLEN

Open University

Introduction: Language, methodology and technology

Two boys sit together at a PC for over an hour, playing a computer game and talking quietly.

In this paper, a work-in-progress, I explore some of the methodological issues I have encountered as we endeavour to discover and analyse just what was going on as these two boys played their game. (Other outputs from the project will focus upon placing our findings within a framework of questions regarding the relations between ICT, literacy, schooling and popular culture; see Gillen and Hall, 2001). My concern here is to explore some of methodological problems faced in this study: technical, procedural, analytical and theoretical, interwoven as those levels are.

My principal goal is to show that it might be fruitful to problematize the interrelationships of stages of the research process, which may sometimes be taken for granted within the habitual practices of a discipline. For example, the technologies involved in the creation of dissemination products impact 'back', as it were, upon decisions made about the collection and organisation of data. For example, if I am working towards a research output such as this one that will be disseminated in monochrome print, I need to be aware from the beginning that I will need to reduce my data, insofar as I wish to 'quote' or extract from it, into the medium of monochrome print. Although I may have other opportunities to disseminate this work, such as the original conference presentation in which it was possible to use Powerpoint incorporating a video clip, I have also needed to ensure that I have the capability of communicating in a channel restricted to print if I take advantage of the wider dissemination opportunity afforded here.

I will argue that it can be especially useful to pay attention to the stage of 'data organisation' (Bennett-Kastor, 1988): those processes between the collection of data and its analysis according to theoretically derived principles. Often, the assumptions we bring to the organisation of data can be conceived of as belonging to an academic 'habitus' (Bourdieu, 1991): ingrained dispositions towards specific routine practices that rely on disciplinary precedents and can lie unexamined. At various times in the evolution of a discipline, or perhaps more specifically a significant paradigm within a discipline (Kühn, 1970) the scope of the relatively unexamined stage of data organisation may shift as aspects of it are moved into the limelight for interrogation. These shifts are often stimulated in part at least by recognition of opportunities afforded by new technologies. For example the advent of affordable, portable tape recorders, had far-reaching consequences for what was viewed as data worthy of research attention, and ultimately theoretical understandings of language itself. The advent of recording devices brought new attention to transcription processes, revealing these to be highly theory-laden (Sacks, Schegloff and Jefferson, 1974; Ochs, 1977). Everyday conversation, previously thought of as trivial, chaotic and even theoretically unimportant (as in Chomskyan linguistics) was revealed as existing in a "multiplicity of orders" through the new discipline of Conversation Analysis (ten Have, 1999, p.3; see also Scollon, 2001). Only by identifying the assumptions that have come to shape our data organisation practices can we come to question them and sharpen our research endeavour throughout.

I suggest then that just as a newly occurring technology incorporated into data collection procedures caused ripples on the waters of data organisation, analysis and hence theory building, so the present moment might be one in which the impact of new technologies is such that we might start to reflexively re-examine certain features of our academic habitus at different stages of the research process.

New technologies impact upon this project methodology in three aspects:

- the multimedia nature of the computer activity the boys were engaged in and the possibilities for capturing (to some degree) the multimodalities of the boys' interactions;
- data organisation opportunities;
- dissemination media possibilities.

These are considered in turn below.

Nature of the data and means of capture

Immediate observation of the episode under review showed interactions to be occurring in the following channels:

- face-to-face interaction between the peers, utilising verbal and non-verbal means;

- interaction with the PC via the mouse, keyboard and selection of CD-ROM etc. with a great range of effects visible upon the monitor.

Thus, it was immediately clear that the nature of the data is relatively complex in terms of modalities. Two strong trends in current sociocultural work offer tremendous possibilities for approaching the data in a theoretically principled way. One is afforded by the 'New Literacy Studies' and allied work in the 'linguistic ethnography' wave (see e.g. Street, 1993; Gee, 1996; Barton, Hamilton and Ivanic, 2000), in which a broad variety of text genres garnered from multifarious walks of life are studied. These writers point out that functions that are thought of as 'literate' depend, and must always have done so, upon what contemporary cultural mores have held 'literate' to be; this word has no decontextualised, ahistorical meaning. Literacy processes, even if considered at the level of the individual gaining skills, can only be properly analysed in the context of understanding that individual's interactions as a member of her society, in the light of cultural practices. Lemke (1998) argues that in that event there does not seem to be a principled reason for maintaining the classic distinction between reading and writing texts on paper, on the one hand, as clearly 'literacy', and symbolic representations in all other modes. We might nevertheless continue to find in the notion of literacy a useful distinction between written and oral texts for particular purposes. However, the focus of the New Literacy Studies upon processes of meaning-making utilising culturally-derived symbols within social interactions is certainly highly pertinent to this study. An implication for data collection is that the capture of only verbal data, such as might be used to prepare a print transcription, would be inadequate.

A second strand useful in this project is contemporary work conducted by researchers working with notions of activity theory and distributed cognition, for example contributors to the volumes edited by Chaiklin and Lave (1993) and Engeström and Middleton (1996b). These researchers incorporate examination of (inter)actions with artefacts in their analyses of discourse. They offer a useful perspective that emphasises the multimodal character of communicative action. The force of their arguments here is to shift attention away from the traditional cognitive psychology emphasis on communication as the meeting of two brains, in the ether as it were, and rather to emphasise that human communication is embodied and located in particular physical contexts. The collection of research by Engeström and Middleton (1996b) includes diagrams, photographs, stills from videos, and so on. These occupy a more significant space in the book than 'illustrations' (conceived of, for example, as a group of photographs of events detailed in the book, placed all together in one position) but rather constitute elements of the analytic/communicative process to a stronger or at least more explicit degree than usual in the role of graphics. Video, a prominent data collection tool for these researchers, has been used to facilitate the capturing of multiple perspectives of interactions involving people and technologies. In their introduction Engeström and Middleton (1996a) explain that they endeavour to reconceptualise cognition not as existing in the individual's mind (accessible to psychological methods) or as evidenced in societal patterns (accessible to sociological methods) but rather as distributed between individuals and their artifacts.

These two strands of work feature then principled ways in which the nature of data as multimodal is intrinsic to the purpose of research and the methods by which it is undertaken. As humans are engaged in co-operative processes that involve learning from one another, there is a drive towards using technologies that enable some capturing of the physical world: this is characteristic of research 'subjects' and the researchers themselves. This applies to the strands of work discussed above and to the present project.

An important influence on our work was our intention to focus only on spontaneous activity. Engagements with the PC in this home, we already knew, change greatly in character from week to week in terms of the personnel using the PC and what they choose to do. Particular games operate in 'crazes' as it were – just like playground games through the ages. Deciding to look at spontaneous activity entails acceptance of data of an unexpected kind. Another aspect of child spontaneity is lack of supervision. Since we needed to capture data from the different modalities of action, without having a parent/researcher present, video appeared to be the appropriate technology. We had some initial concern as to whether children would feel uncomfortable being filmed and act with less spontaneity; however our experience mirrored those studies of children where it has been observed that the impact of videoing quickly diminishes. (e.g. Corsaro, 1985). The task of filming the children reasonably unobtrusively was accomplished quite easily by using a video camera placed behind the children.

In addition to recording the children's interactions, we needed to record with equal detail the changing images on the computer monitor. This challenge was met by use of a 'mirroring device'. This effectively intercepted the signal between the PC and the monitor and transferred it into a video signal, which was then recorded.

Activities were self-initiated and self-ending, and so we were presented with a small number of episodes in which we had substantial data from each source, from which we chose the current episode, in which two eleven year-olds were "playing Half Life".

Data organisation

The aim of data organisation is to render the data into a form that most effectively facilitates analysis. As I stated in the introduction, this is a research process that can slip into the background as a disciplinary routine, but that may be thrust into the foreground when new technologies come into play and precedents are felt to be either lacking or inadequate. At these moments, reflexivity as to methodology comes to the fore as we endeavour to connect our theoretical frameworks to the technical details of method, some of which are described here insofar as they are new in my research experience.

The first stage of data organisation was to synchronise the two tapes, each covering around 45 minutes of the episode. With a 'mixer' images from the computer screen were overlaid on part of the film images of the children. Thus it was then possible to view both the screen and the children's behaviour on the same monitor.

The objective of the second stage was to produce a transcript that included information about the children's actions and a brief description of changes in the images on the monitor, placed against a textual version of the verbal interaction.

At this point we encountered unexpected difficulties. Certainly, we had expected and indeed looked forward to the challenge posed by 'transcribing' multimedia episodes. But the immediate challenge posed a greater obstacle: I could understand very, very little of what was happening. The very act of listening was made so difficult because of a general lack of that framework of understanding which usually aids one's perception.

Therefore an intermediate stage of data organisation/analysis was developed. My previous repeated careful but frustrating viewings of the tape were supplemented by two viewings with the boy participants. Firstly I viewed the tapes with the boys, endeavouring to improve my understanding of the events. Several hours later my co-investigator Nigel Hall interviewed the boys while all of us watched the tapes. On this occasion the purpose of understanding the details of the interaction was supplemented by the broader purpose of exploring the boys' attitudes to these activities in a more general way. This second interview was tape-recorded.

I then constructed "an outline of the episode" which appears below. From my prior language research experience this feels awkward, putting the cart before the horse. My preference would generally be to introduce some extracts of data, with overtly inductive interpretation. Any succinct description of 'what occurred' should appear in a later position, emerging as it were from the data. Work conducted in Conversation Analysis, for example, shuns in a principled fashion prior assumptions of personal goals that might perhaps be implied by an introductory overview.

Of course, there are other paradigms in which the offering of an overall summary in an initial place in the presentation of findings is completely unremarkable and assumed to be desirable. As already mentioned, the collection of work edited by Engeström and Middleton (1996b) has been helpful to the current study. Those presentations of interactions with technology often precede the presentation of an analysis of a very short episode within a description of the wider event, in particular outlining the goals or at least major responsibility concerns of the participants. In this piece of work the goals took us considerable time to identify (although they appear to have been relatively unproblematic for the boys) and need to be outlined first in order to facilitate understanding of the transcript for the reader.

It is important to stress that the outline could only be put together after many hours' engagement with the data, including considerable time spent gaining and checking the boys' own insights. In this aspect if no other, I felt considerably challenged by working so outside (and so unexpectedly far outside) my usual parameters in research. I also maintain a slight degree of mistrust for the considerable coherence eventually achieved in the outline. The interview often served to contradict earlier interpretations, and it therefore seems likely that layers of misunderstanding remain.

Extract from broad outline of the episode

The boys had originally stated that they were "playing Half Life" a conflict game played out, of course, in a virtual environment. However the activity of "playing Half Life" has actually stretched to quite a different activity, that of personally constructing the environment in which Half Life will be played, for although the game incorporates its own settings for game play, it is possible for players to create their own. The boys are working on Daniel's earlier individual attempt at constructing a specific virtual environment, called a 'level', using software called Worldcraft 2.1. The particular scenario Daniel had tried to construct is a shop in which the conflicts of the game Half Life can at some later stage be played out. The activity of constructing a level involves using the software to manipulate such 'objects' as 'textures' (defining these are beyond the level of detail required here).

The activity in this episode entails running three kinds of software, Half Life itself (in which one can view the 'level' – here a shop); Worldcraft (in more than one version) - the software in which the 'level' is constructed, and 'dev console'. The last is a general computer utility which acts as a commentary on the loading (starting up) of the other software, so that if a programme crashes, the boys can diagnose the problem. In the extract from the episode here, after 'dev console' is run, Half Life is started so that the shop can be loaded and examined. Worldcraft is then used to critically examine the construction of the shop.

The shop can be viewed in two ways. In one view it fills the screen and appears as a virtual environment, i.e. the player can move around the room and look at it from the inside, from different angles. The players toggle between this and the design view. This appears as a grid of four squares. The top left grid shows the room in the 3D effect view (i.e. as it appears in 'Half Life'). The top right square shows the plan of the room and the bottom two squares two elevations. Certain problems with the room as previously constructed are provisionally identified: stacks of food and vending machines are not touching the floor. Textures are wrong. The version of Worldcraft used (version 2.1 rather than 3.3) is identified as problematic.

Towards Decisions On Transcription And Analysis

The driving force behind transcription decisions was the wish to represent all the following modalities: each boy's speech, each boy's actions and the activity on the screen. How actions across these modalities relate to each other in time must be issues of significance. For example, interpretation of a boy's action might be facilitated through understanding the utterance that has been produced immediately before, interpreted as indicative of intention perhaps. However another impulse driving the formatting of a transcript, potentially clashing with the wish to make it as chronologically accurate as possible, is to make it as readable as possible. Such dilemmas are at the heart of the transcription process, viewed as a process of making decisions that are compromises (Heritage and Atkinson, 1984).

Decisions about the formatting of the transcript were particularly guided in linguistic matters by ten Have (1999, pp. 75-90). This is not to say my practice has necessarily followed his recommendations, but I am indebted to his suggestions as to what it is important to think about. Following is a list of matters considered, although space in this paper precludes detailed discussion of the options considered and compromises reached:

Factors taken into consideration in transcription decisions

Time, date and place of recording
Identification of participants
Actions of participants
Image on the computer screen
Orthography
Phonological/paralinguistic features
Inaudible or incomprehensible sounds or words
Spaces/silences
Overlapped speech
Timings
Layout

Figure 1 (next page) Short extract from transcript June 2001 Daniel and Lincoln at Daniel's home part A

Lincoln = [L] (green in original version)
Daniel = [D] (blue in original version)
t.r. = top right; t.l. = top left

Notes on transcription conventions:
* =	low volume
(then) =	uncertain transcription
(^^) =	untranscribable
[1]	pause of about one second
,	slight pause
.	falling intonation at end of phrase
?	rising, questioning intonation
|	denotes overlapping speech – beginning from stroke until carriage return
:::	elongated

Speech	Actions	Screen	Timing
[L]I think you got the textures a bit wrong here ha'nt you	[L]uses mouse [D]looking around	dev console runs, Half Life starts virtual environment is scrolled around – walls and floors etc	5.04
[D]yeh [1] oh haha ha I made the wall the floor	[D]looks at monitor		5.08
[L]you could have made [1] a proper like freaky level you know so it's like [1]		zooms in towards objects (vending machines)	5.10
[L]I did that once and made	[L]waves both hands		5.15
[D]yeh	[D]nods		5.16
[L]you know it were all on the wrong side	[L]returns hand to mouse		5.17
[D]that's wrong I think as well i'n't it		zooms in further on vending machines	5.21
[L]well you're using um [2] what version were you using	[L]points at screen	dev console runs	5.23
[D]two point one			5.28
[L]oh right 'cos there an easier way	[L]returns hand to mouse	Worldcraft 2.1 is loaded; front window removed; grid of 4 rectangles is maximised;	5.30
[L]that I just found out yesterday of um			
[D]three point three		cursor darts around t.r, briefly to t.l, then t.r.	5.35
[L]yeh how to get textures you know so they fit the right size		cursor clicks on shape in t.r, slight	5.36
[D]um		changes to lines and shapes there and in bottom rectangles	5.40
[L]so you don't have to you know going adjusting it and stuff			5.42
[D]um			
[L]what's this here		cursor rests on shape	5.43
[D](paks^)			
[L] (^^) interlock			5.47

Conclusions: new dissemination media possibilities

Dissemination has to have the closest possible relation in terms of technology with the kind of object being studied. A traditional linguistics paper is delivered orally at a conference (often with the aid of a handout following particular stylistic conventions that differ markedly, for example, from practices at education conferences). The discussion and data extracts are given orally or through the medium of print – either on the handout or an overhead transparency. (Presentation software is beginning to be used but rarely for more than delivery of printed text, albeit with the accompaniment of more graphics). The most significant and successful papers are (then) produced in the form of a published, printed text. Taking one recent relevant publication dealing with multimodal research, the paper by Jewitt et al (2001) was published as a monochrome text with a few monochrome images, which were reproductions of monochrome photocopies. This is totally understandable given issues of accountability, access and prestige. The journal publishing this paper is accessible on-line, but the only advantage the Internet brings to bear in this case (which is the norm) is improved ease of access, rather than expansion of multimodalities. However, it surely desirable to develop a dissemination format that takes advantage of the multimodal potentialities of the Internet, while retaining the peer-refereeing, gatekeeping advantages of the scholarly academy in the near future.

Finally, the most challenging methodological issue for me in this project remains consideration of the interwoven nature of what might have otherwise been formulated as the 'stages' of the research process. If one abandons the well-worn habitus of distinction between collecting data, organising data, analysing data, and dissemination: all laying neatly on a timeline because one suddenly, in advance, questions the form and nature of dissemination (for example), then one allows the opening of new possibilities even 'back' at the data collection 'stage'. Walker and Lewis (1998: 162) express this challenge very skilfully:

> Until recently the conventions of publishing have caused us to treat photographic and video images separately from written words. The convergence of media precipitated by the digitization of practically everything make for a seamlessness which undermines these conventions and makes new forms possible: text becomes image just as image becomes text. Among the new possibilities this creates for research practice are a collapse of the conventional distinctions between 'writing down' and 'writing up' as 'fieldwork' ceases to be a discrete set of activities and writing is

no longer bounded by the act of putting words on paper.

I simultaneously agree and disagree with Walker and Lewis here. They are, to my mind, absolutely right in reflecting so lucidly the interwoven nature of the challenges to the research process I am meeting in this project and reflecting upon in this paper. New possibilities of form in which we might disseminate our research on multimodality should in turn impact upon our procedures in data collection. A multimodal approach to data collection enables a "focus on a rich range of resources, including talk, speech, image and action" (Jewitt et al, 2001, p. 17). In this project we are endeavouring, as do Jewitt et al., to take consideration of these diverse modes of communication and the interplay between them. By extension surely this focus presents a challenge to one's own technologies used in research investigations. The instruments the Jewitt et al (2001) group used were observation, interviews and documentary analysis. It may perhaps be beneficial to take advantage of a variety of technologies that are in themselves multimodal, such as video and the mirroring device of the current study.

Yet, at the same time, I partially disagree with Walker and Lewis in that an implication of their words appears to be that it is the advent of a new multimodality in dissemination that creates the need for attention to the interrelationship of research processes. Reflexivity should perhaps *always* lead us to question our methodologies. Should not "writing down" and "writing up" always be linked as research processes? The opportunities and problems thrown up by one can usefully inform the practices employed in the other.

In the current project, there is undoubtedly further to go in terms of developing a methodology appropriate to a multimedia focus. I particularly aim to improve my abilities to work with new media, e.g. digital editing, electronic software that incorporates video and graphics, etc. Such tools may make possible the development of new analytic instruments. However, we seek a way of working with multimedia as a focus of attention and as research process that is more than being simply technology *driven* but rather theoretically derived. Clearly, this impetus must be extended into analysis, beyond the scope of this paper, which similarly must entail reflections upon the theoretical underpinnings and how these might be drawn upon. Analysis should, among other imperatives, follow Heath's (1997: 198) exhortation, "to abandon some of the traditional distinctions which have informed our understanding of 'non-verbal behaviour' and consider the ways in which visual and vocal conduct feature in the *in situ* accomplishment of particular social actions and activities." We must too consider how dissemination behaviour is accomplished in our own research circles. Gee (1996:46) writes: "the study of literacy ultimately requires us to study the social groups and institutions within which one is socialized to interpret types of words and certain sorts of worlds in certain ways." Certainly then the changes in 'literacies' as technologies advance may encourage us to re-examine our own practices as we investigate those changes and share that research experience with other investigators.

References

Barton, D., Hamilton, M. and Ivanic, R. (eds) (2000) *Situated Literacies: reading and writing in context*. London: Routledge.

Bennett-Kastor, T. (1988) *Analysing Children's Language: Methods and Theories*. Oxford: Blackwell.

Bourdieu, P. (1991) *Language and Symbolic Power* trans. G. Raymond & M. Adamson ed. J.B. Thompson. Cambridge: Polity Press and B. Blackwell.

Chaiklin, S. and Lave, J. (eds.) (1993) *Understanding practice :perspectives on activity and context*. Cambridge: Cambridge University Press.

Corsaro, W.A. (1985) *Friendship and peer culture in the early years*. Norwood, N.J: Ablex.

Engeström, Y. and Middleton, D. (1996a) Introduction: studying work as mindful practice. In Y. Engeström and Middleton, D. (eds.): *Cognition and Communication at Work*. Cambridge: Cambridge University Press.

Engeström, Y. and Middleton, D. (eds.) (1996b) *Cognition and Communication at Work*. Cambridge: Cambridge University Press.

Gee, J. P. (1996) *Social Linguistics and Literacies: ideology in discourses*. 2nd ed. London: Taylor and Francis.

Gillen, J. and Hall, N. (2001) "The application of an instrument" - an exploration of an episode of computer activity by two eleven-year-old boys. Paper presented as part of the symposium in Literacy and Popular Culture at BERA, University of Leeds, 13th-15th September.

Have, P. ten (1999) *Doing Conversational Analysis: a practical guide*. London: Sage.

Heath, C. (1997) The Analysis of Activities in Face to Face Interaction Using Video. In D. Silverman (ed) *Qualitative Research: theory, method and practice*. London: Sage.

Heritage, J. and Atkinson, J.M. (1984) Introduction. In J. M. Atkinson and J. Heritage (eds.): *Structures of Social Action: studies in conversational analysis,* Cambridge: Cambridge University Press. 1-15.

Jewitt, C., Kress, G., Ogborn, J and Tsatarelis, C. (2001) Exploring learning through visual, actional and linguistic communication: the multimodal environment of a science classroom *Educational Review* 53/1 5-18.

Kühn, T. (1970) *The Structure of Scientific Revolutions*. 2nd ed. Chicago: University of Chicago Press.

Lemke, J.L. (1998) Multimedia literacy demands of the scientific curriculum *Linguistics and Education* 10/3 247-271.

Ochs, E. (1979) Transcription as Theory. In E. Ochs and B. B. Schieffelin (eds.): *Developmental Pragmatics.* New York: Academic Press.

Sacks, H., Schegloff, E. and Jefferson, G. (1974) 'A simplistic systematics for the organisation of turn taking' *Language* 50/4: 696-735.

Scollon, R. (2001) *Mediated discourse: the nexus of practice.* London: Routledge.

Street, B. (ed) (1993) *Cross-cultural approaches to literacy.* Cambridge: Cambridge University Press.

Walker, R. and Lewis, R. (1998) Media Convergence and Social Research: The Hathaway Project. In J. Prosser, (ed.): *Image-based Research.* London: Falmer.

6 Students' interpretations of teachers' gestures in the language classroom – what do teachers mean and what do students see?

DANIELA SIME

University of Stirling

Introduction

When evaluating recent research in applied linguistics, it is relevant to assess critically the study of individuals' non-verbal communication as an intrinsic component of human interaction process. For too long, linguistic tradition blinded the investigators of human interaction so that "what we hear" became the substitute for what is actually going on in terms of communication between individuals. In FL classroom research, the interest in teacher-student / student-student(s) interaction fell into the same trap of extrapolating and considering linguistic variation as the sole dimension of any research investigation. More recent work in the field of SLA has documented the importance and possible dimensions of participants' own beliefs and expectations of the interactional process (Breen, 2001), the influence of contextual variation in interaction (Breen, 1985; Candlin and Mercer, 2001; Kramsch, 1993; Lantolf,1994; Lantolf and Appel, 1994) and the broader implications of current psychological rationales of strategic language acquisition (Breen and Littlejohn, 2000; Lantolf, 2001). If we attempt to reveal what learners actually do while learning through interaction or how they actually make sense of various aspects of communication in the classroom, we might obtain a more complete picture of the process of FL learning, if we do not rely exclusively on a verbatim transcription and analysis of talk in interaction alone.

Communicative bodies

The purpose of this paper is to restate the role that language and gesture play jointly in the specific interactive context of the language class. My research frame is intersemiotic and communicative. Rather than favouring the popular linguistic descriptions of meaning, I favour the "corporeal turn" (Ruthrof: 2000) as a rediscovery and reintegration of the body into the study of human interaction. The argument that follows offers a re-assessment the visual aspects of classroom interaction, particularly of gestures, by investigating the linkage through which language and gesture construct meaning.

The arbitrary association between a given word and a certain aspect of reality does not reflect a subjective process of attribution of meanings. This is rather a culturally embedded regulatory process which individuals learn since childhood. "Why do we choose the words we do for our description? Because we have been trained to expect a certain fit between specific expressions and the world, which means we have already learnt how to fill linguistic schemata with quasi-perceptual signs" (Ruthrof 2000: 46). This view of language as gaining meaning through a socially regulated process of associating certain words for particular aspects of reality could be illustrated by the common example of a child learning to speak. Until fully competent in speaking a language, the child will be trained by the adults around them on how to associate a word like "chair" with any object which is adequate in shape and design for sustaining a person while sitting.

The development of the conceptual schemata (Lakoff and Johnson, 1981) for objects in the immediate reality is mostly based on direct perception. The role of imagination in our understanding and interpretation of the world is more obvious in the processing of abstract concepts. Words like *faith, solitude, interest* constitute concepts with a different surplus of meaning for each individual, depending on previous experience and personal use of mental processes. An infinite diversity of interpretations is theoretically possible in any given social construct: "there is no fully shared stock of concepts (...) As a result, meaning identity is a highly unlikely event" (Lakoff and Johnson, 1981).The social move, as a unit of research analysis, needs a holistic approach when investigated, as does the individuals' perception and interpretation of the world. The linguistic tradition unbalanced the investigation of human interaction by a tendency to resolve all questions about communication in terms of linguistic relations. Individuals communicate not only through their words, but also with their bodies. The intertwined verbal and non-verbal codes are used simultaneously by speakers in order to convey meanings. Just by using these apparent antonyms – verbal and non-verbal – we infer the salience of distinguishing between the two codes. However, if dissecting a communication act for investigatory purposes, we must not ignore the more integrated and complex context in which these acts take place. My present focus is on gestures as interactive phenomena, which convey meanings in different ways from language.

Vygotsky's theory of semiotic mediation is initially explored in this paper as a framework for the interpretation and analysis of gestures as meaning constructs in language learning. The activity of FL learning in the classroom context is then investigated as a continuous process of simultaneous construction of meaning through language and gestures. Gestures mediate the learning of verbal constructs and the latter support the attribution of meanings to gestures. This is a two-way process which involves mental representations of both gesture and word in a symbiotic process of meaning construction. The data presented in this paper focuses specifically on students' interpretations of teachers' gestures in a language class as meaningful signs which mediate the learning of a FL. Finally, the paper argues for a perspective on the communicative process as more than linguistic, being corporeal and intersemiotic.

Gestures are ephemeral bodily actions, mainly of the hands, which occur in human interaction and attract meaning in the particular context in which they occur. In this paper, I refer to gesture in the restricted sense of spontaneous gesture which synchronises with speech temporally and accompanies it in meaning (McNeill, 1992). As in the case of utterances, gestures seem to be adjusted for the receiver, in the manner that words are (Bavelas 1994). Gestures are designed for spontaneous face-to-face interaction, and it is in this context that they need to be analysed and interpreted. The context gives gestures a certain shape, a function and a particular meaning. Any investigation concerning gestures needs thus to consider them as interactive phenomena and occurring in specific contexts.

Gestures as signs – mediators or mediated?

Vygotsky (1978) bases his theory of mental activity on the analogy with the mediational action individuals perform when interacting with the objects of the real world. Individuals need symbolic tools to perform a certain mental function in the similar way they use material tools in performing an action in the external environment.

From the perspective of a sociocultural framework, mental processes and the use of communicational signs develop in context. The learning of the language is seen as emerging from the social and cultural activity; children develop first as participants in non-verbal interaction and through their actions, they develop as speakers of a certain language. So at the beginning it is not the word but the action which functions as a pre-conditional stage of language development. In the case of FL learning, people develop meanings long before becoming fully competent speakers of the target language. This suggests that meaning is an extralinguistic construct.

In this process, gestures as visual signs become potential stimuli, which are created by the individuals and oriented towards a potential receiver. Vygotsky (1978:56) gives the example of a child's pointing to a particular object they want to reach. The initial pointing with the finger in the air is initially just a meaningless gesture; when the mother explicitly attends the gesture, "pointing becomes a gesture for the others". Only when the child begins to understand the meaning of their gesture when understood by the others accordingly, the internalisation of the external activity takes place and the sign functions as a developmental factor. One could identify a similarity between the child in this example and the FL learner. A gesture produced in a FL learning situation can transform from a purely external movement into an internalised meaningful sign as a result of attendance to the gesture and its association to a particular meaning.

In the learning of a FL, the role of gestures as compensatory devices might seem the most obvious one. One would be tempted to accept that, at least in the beginning stages of the FL learning process, learners will use more gestures to compensate for their lack of verbal skills in the FL language. What I am suggesting is that gestures continue to be an important component of the communication system at all stages of FL learning. The preponderance of attention a subject may give to gestures or utterances at any given moment varies considerably, depending on factors like linguistic competence in FL, domination of one set of signs over the others, own definition of context, individual expectations of interaction, etc.

What is salient for one learner might be overlooked by another. Any two learners may value differently the signs received at any given moment. A gesture suggesting a shape in the air might help a learner to understand the meaning of a word or sentence. In this case, the gesture functions as a mediator for the understanding of the language. The same gesture might have a different relevance for a student who already knows the word the teacher tries to suggest. This student might use the word as a mediator to understand the visual representation. While s/he knows the word in the target language, the learner may add new elements to the old semiotic frame. The role a gesture fulfils depends thus on the whole dynamics of the communication process. Depending on previous experience, content, individual psychological processes, linguistic ability in FL etc., individuals may use the same signs in different ways to construct meanings. The data below will show how individuals process signs differently in FL learning.

The study

The focus of this research is on students' attribution of meanings to teachers' gestures in the FL class. It was thought that, apart from the analysis of the observable classroom exchanges of verbal and non-verbal signs, an introspective paradigm would reveal more about the individual interpretations of gestures.

Three classes of English as a FL were videotaped. Two female British teachers were involved in the teaching and the classes lasted approximately 90 minutes each. Samples of 2-3 minutes video extracts were selected by the author from each of the videotaped classes. The criteria for selecting the samples were: (i) a fair density of teacher's gestural behaviour; (ii) the segment to be representative for a 'typical' language classroom interaction (explaining vocabulary, clarifying task etc.) (ii) the sample to have a clear cut beginning and ending. The students were all adult learners of EFL, of different nationalities (Japanese, Spanish, Italian), of mixed genders and ages between 20 and 25 years old. Fourteen accounts were generated through individual interviews organised on the same or the second day after the class took place. The subjects were asked to watch the video samples and to interpret any of the teachers' gestures they notice in the video sample. They were also encouraged to mark the gestural elements identified as relevant by stopping the video whenever a comment was to be made. A stimulated recall methodology (Gass and Mackey, 2000) was used to prompt participants to recall their perception and interpretation of gestures during the class. The purpose was to get as close as possible to the students' mental representations of teachers' gestures and to identify the functional roles they gave to gestures in the FL classroom context.

Teachers' use of gestures in the FL class

To begin with, I will offer examples to illustrate the way in which teachers used gestures in the classes videotaped. Gestures occurred mainly in the presence of speech, although teachers performed gestures without speech as well. McNeill (1992:23) argues that gestures that occur during speech "present the same or closely related meanings semantically and perform the same functions pragmatically".

The following excerpt from one of the sessions is an example of a teacher's simultaneous use of gesture and speech in providing meaning. The description of the gesture is provided in brackets, the first bracket indicating the moment when the gesture started in relationship with the verbal input. For example, the gesture described in line (3) coincides temporally with the words "which people sometimes confuse".

Excerpt 1
Teacher (1) There are two expressions (.) the cost of living
                              [left hand in a cup shape,
                                  points to desk]
            (2) and the standard of living
            [right hand raised in the air,
            fingers in a cup shape]
            (3) which people sometimes confuse (.) 'cause they are not
            the same
            [both hands in a cup shape,
            moving up and down in a
            counterbalanced oscillation]

Each of the gestures in lines (1) and (2) synchronises with an instance of the utterance. The dichotomy expressed verbally is emphasised by the visual display of the hands. They are opposing each other horizontally (left-right) and vertically (up-down), each hand signifying a different concept. In line (3), the teacher balances both hands, still in a cup-shape form (to emphasise the difference between concepts?) Then, after the gesture is finished, the teacher says " 'cause they (the concepts) are not the same". The relationship between speech and gesture is different in line (3) as opposed in lines (1) and (2). The first two gestures are synchronous with the speech, while the third gesture anticipates the speech. The same intended meaning is conveyed in line (3) twice, but at different intervals and through different semiotic codes.

In the following example, the meaning conveyed through gesture seems to contrast with the meaning conveyed verbally. The figures between brackets indicate the time in seconds.

Excerpt 2
Teacher (4)   your good ear enables you to   (0.5)
                [right hand fingers   [both hands to mouth,
                rotate around mouth twice]   then   palms   open
                                                   towards class, twice]
Student (5)   pronunciation?

Teacher (6) ye:::s   (0.1)   to pronounce
    [nods, points to S]   *[repeats second gesture above]*

The first gesture in line (4) seems to not to refer to what is said. The teacher says "good ear" while pointing to her mouth. In fact, the teacher anticipates by gesture the desired answer. She is eliciting the word "speaking" or "pronunciation" and the second gesture in line (4) is performed in the complete absence of speech for five seconds. The student seems to attend to the gesture as s/he gives the expected answer and the teacher then repeats the same gesture in line (6) to emphasise the word "pronunciation/to pronounce". In this extract, one can see how the same gesture is used within a short interval with two different roles - in line (4) the second gesture substitutes the speech and it is used as an elicitation technique, while in line (6) the same gesture is used to emphasise the verbal message. Once again, this shows how the gestural expression and the verbal expressions can be used in different combinations to convey meaning.

Finally, the third excerpt illustrates a typical classroom situation of turn-giving, in which the teacher indicates the student whom she wants to get involved in the conversation by simply using a pointing gesture. The teacher points to the student after asking a question and the student picks up the conversation line.

Excerpt 3
 Teacher: (7) so good standard of living in Spain
(8) what about Italy? (0.2)
           *[looks at S2 and points with left hand open in
           his direction]*
Student 2: (9) the same (as) Spain

This co-construction of interaction by the participants relies not only on the interpretations of words. There is also a prevalent understanding of the classroom as a social stage with certain unwritten rules for all participants (Breen, 1998) . Here there is no clue in the teacher's verbal sentence which to indicate to whom is she addressing the question. We might expect by the reading of the question in line (8) that any of the students in the class could answer it. But there are the non-verbal cues that identify the addressee and the rule which empowers the teacher as the interaction conductor; the teacher asks the question in line (8), then establishes eye-contact with S2 and points at him with the left palm open. The student interprets these cues accordingly and so do the other participants in the class - no other student attempts to answer the question.

The examples illustrate that there are several ways in which gestures are used by the teachers in class. The differentiation in the functional involvement of gestures indicate the flexibility of gesture-speech combinations for the purpose of conveying meaning. In general, gestures appear as a complement of speech, by supporting, emphasising, complementing or even substituting the verbal. The examples above indicate instances of clear attendance to the teacher's gestures and evidence to claim that gestures are not a by-pass product of interaction. It seems thus reasonable to investigate the students' interpretations of teachers' gestures.

Students' interpretations of teachers' gestures

Farr (1991) suggests that the symmetry of any dialogical interaction when both speaker and listener hear the same thing is matched by an asymmetry in the visual plan. A speaker's perception of his own gestures is different from a listener's perception of the same gestures. The listener has the advantage of the observer, being conscious of what s/he sees, while the sender is rarely self-conscious. Thus, gestures as symbols are different to speech when considering symmetry of roles and viewpoint. We would expect the learners of a FL to be conscious of teachers' gestures, especially in the given context of the high asymmetries of knowledge, linguistic skills and status between them and the teacher.

As students were shown the videotaped extracts, they were asked to comment on teachers' gestures from their perspective as language learners. The purpose was to get as close as possible through the students' interpretations of particular classroom extracts to their interpretation of gestures as visual signs during the language learning process. In a Vygotskian perspective, asking students to reflect on their semiotic interpretations provides some insight to their mental processing of meanings.

One constraint in interviewing the learners was their ability to talk about gestures, the difficulty in describing a hand move being increased by the need to express this is a foreign language. I am aware that this must have influenced not only the length of the responses, but also the amount of gestures selected for comment by each individual. However, in many instances, subjects often seemed to choose to reproduce the gesture themselves instead of providing a minute verbal description. They usually combined the reproduction of the gesture with a verbal explanation of the function the gesture played in the context. In commenting on teacher's gesture in *Excerpt 1* (above), a student reproduces the gesture himself, by counter-balancing the hands while saying:

> each hand is one thing, now it's talking about two things, one is standard of living and the other is cost of living, so each hand is one thing, one concept ... if there are confusions

This student does not perceive the hands as hands anymore; they become symbols which embody the conceptual dichotomy. While perceiving the linguistic differentiation, the student also perceives the same relationship visually, the meaning conveyed verbally being reinforced gesturally. In his comment, the gesture gets a shape (actually reproduced by the student), a context (linguistic and extra-linguistic) and a function (to dispel any confusion). The same gesture is commented on similarly by other students:

> she (the teacher) wants to make the difference between one word and another word

> there are two similar things and a relationship between them, a similarity

> she is talking about two things and (...) then with her arms she is doing like this [repeats gesture] to explain there are two things because there are two arms and she is moving like this to explain that the two things are similar, but not quite

These interpretations suggest how the same gesture has a slightly varying value for different individuals. Some identify the difference between the two concepts discussed ("cost of living"-"standard of living"), some identify the connection between the two concepts (there is a "relationship"), while others suggest the lexical variation as being illustrated by the teacher's gesture.

In the following instance, the teacher discusses the relationship between prices and standard of living:

Excerpt 4
Teacher: (10) if the prices are increasing
                    [left hand, fingers together, makes an
                    ascendant move from left hip to the chin level]
            (11) the standard of living is usually decreasing
                    [hand descends back to the hip
                    level on the right side]

Students interpretations for these gestures varied as follows:

with the hand, up the hand [reproduces gesture], and you know means increasing, means up, price goes up

the gesture is suggesting something which goes up, like money or cost, then she makes the opposite of going down, to suggest the decrease

this means an increase of price, but for me this is not a relevant gesture; I know the word increase, so I don't need the gesture; some gestures may help you understand what the teacher is talking about; when you don't know the word or it is an abstract noun, then it's quite difficult to understand only with the gesture

In this last case, the student not only gives the verbal equivalent for the gesture, but he also makes a general judgement about the relevance of gesture in language learning. In his view, gestures are aids to verbal communication which can not provide the meaning in themselves but can clarify a context or help clarification. The three different reports on the same gesture give indications of students' attributions of meaning to gesture. While the first student uses the gesture to identify the word ("you know it means increasing"), the second student seems to use both gestures (increase-decrease) to understand the two phrases, while the third student seems to use the words in order to interpret the gesture. This last student's construction "for me this is not a relevant gesture" raises the issue of gestures' significance for different students while learning the FL. What do students consider as "relevant gestures" and more generally what roles do students attribute to gestures in the class? Here are some of the learner responses which might answer these questions:

if the teacher makes gestures , we can understand more

you see the gesture and then you remember the word, if you know it, but if you did not know the word before, it's hard to guess only by seeing the gesture

you can sometimes associate the word with the gesture, or the idea with the gesture

when you talk about feelings , its easy to show it in gestures; when you talk about concepts or technical things, it is more difficult

gestures are like pictures for words, if you see them clearly, it makes you understand easier

These interpretations indicate not only the differences in individual beliefs of teacher's gestures as meaningful signs, but also the individual identification of certain functions the gestures play in the context. The students identify the gestures as clarifying meaning, substituting a verbal command, conveying information or emotions. Also relevant is the students' choice of verbs when reporting during the interviews. Words like "understand", "associate", "represent", "know", "remember", "memorise" -frequently used in the interviews- are indicators of students' expressions of the ongoing learning processes.

Significant attention was given by the students to the role that gestures played in teacher's interaction management. Gestures made by the teacher to give students the turn to speak were interpreted as meaningful signs and analysed in the context. For example, the teacher's gesture of pointing to a particular student after asking "what about Italy?" (see *Excerpt 3*,above) is interpreted as follows:

this is to design someone to speak, it's like an invitation to say to someone now it's your moment to speak

she was waiting for the answer and she keeps the hand on the direction of this student until he speaks

this is to design Mariano to speak, it's like an invitation to tell him now it's your moment to speak, tell me about your country; when she points with the hand is lovely, pointing with the finger is threatening, but with the palm is warmer

The role that the pointing gesture is seen to play indicates the student's sensitivity to gestures as signs which influence the others behaviour. Here the pointing is interpreted not only as a behaviour generator, but also as an indicator of feelings. In general, the subjects interviewed offered several interpretations of gestures as emotional signifiers, especially when connecting the meaning conveyed simultaneously through different channels:

if the teacher looks at you, smiles and nods, you know that he wants you to continue talking; when the teacher avoids looking at you or shows you a finger or a palm, it means he wants you to stop talking

if you don't understand, you look at the teacher directly or raise your eyebrows; that means you need clarification; sometimes you can raise your hand to ask a question

These two extracts from students' comments indicate the simultaneous analysis which students perform on information coming through multiple channels. The classroom context gives meanings to complexes of signs and during the interaction, students learn how to manipulate these signs and use them in the process of meaning making.

This double perspective, teacher-student perception of signs, was flexibly adopted by most of the students during the interviews. Students shifted their observing perspectives, from that of mere observers of the interaction to that of the involved learner. The same visual sign was interpreted by different perspectives when the subjects had different roles in the interaction; a direct participation involved usually a first or second person narrative:

> she (the teacher) is pointing with the arm in my direction and I know that I have to speak

> you see this move and you know that it means increase

> I did not know the word, and when I saw this gesture, I guessed it might be about prices which become higher

Otherwise, the observer's perspective was reflected by a more analytical stance and use of third person singular:

> she is talking about catching the word metaphorically, so she makes this move like catching something in the air

> she is pointing to herself to suggest that this is a personal example

> she thinks it is not exactly the right answer, so she moves her hand to say like 'so and so', she wants a better answer

The examples analysed, although limited in number here due to space, may be seen as sufficient to show that learners are able to build intersemiotic constructs, where the linguistic and the visual signs are jointly used to construct meanings. Students use their previous knowledge, the linguistic context and the interaction context to understand the situation. The accounts summarised here indicate certain uses of gestures as semiotic devices by the learners in a FL learning context.

Conclusions

Gesture, as a sign, accompanies speech and individuals who learn a FL seem to treat gestures as semiotic devices with certain meanings and functions in the particular context in which they occur. We still need to investigate the more complex role that gestures play in acquiring a foreign language and culture. But at the moment, the following conclusions emerge from the data analysed:

Teachers often use specific gestures when teaching a foreign language and students in the class perceive and interpret these gestures in particular and various ways as meaningful signs in certain contexts. While the teachers might not be fully aware of their gestures while teaching, the learners have the advantage of being observers and the motivation to make sense of any instance of classroom interaction. Under these circumstances, gestures become valuable meaning carriers, especially when learners are not fully competent in the target language.

Learners are more likely to perceive the intersemiotic construction of a communicational instance and to use signs from different semiotic codes as mediators of understanding and learning at different moments in their FL acquisition process. It is not only the linguistic signs that act as mediators, gestures also mediate learning, and this fact is worthy of closer consideration when conducting language learning research.

Acknowledgements

I thank both my supervisors, Prof. Michael Breen and Dr. Richard Badger, for illuminating discussions and constant support and express my gratitude to all teachers and students involved in the project in CELT, at the University of Stirling.

References

Bavelas, J. (1994) Gestures as part of speech: Methodological implications *Research on Language and Social Interaction* 27/3: 201-221

Breen, M. (1985) The social context of language learning: a neglected situation? *Studies in Second Language Acquisition* 7:.135-158

Breen. M. (Ed). (2001) *Learner Contributions to Language Learning: New Directions in Research*. London: Longman

Breen, M.P. & Littlejohn, A. (Eds.) (2000) *Classroom Decision-Making: Negotiation and Process Syllabuses in Practice*. Cambridge University Press.

Candlin, C.N. and Mercer, N. (Eds) (2001) *English Language Teaching in Its Social Context*. London: Routledge

Gass, S. and Mackey, A. (2000) *Stimulated Recall Methodology in Second Language Research*. New Jersey: Lawrence Erlbaum Associates

Faar, R. (1991) *Bodies and Voices in Dialogue*. In Markova,I. and Foppa, K. (Eds) *The Dynamics of Dialogue*. New York: Springer-Verlag, pages 241-258

Kramsch, C. (1993) *Context and Culture in Language Teaching*. Oxford: Oxford University Press

Lakoff, G. and Johnson, M. (1981) *Metaphors We Live By*. Chicago: University of Chicago Press.

Lantolf, J.P. (1994) Sociocultural theory and second language learning: Introduction to the Special Issue. *The Modern Language Journal* 78:418

Lantolf, J.P. (Ed) (2001) *Sociocultural Theory and Second Language Learning.*
Oxford: Oxford University Press
Lantolf, J.P. and Appel, G. (Eds) (1994) *Vygotskian Approaches to Second
Language Research.* Norwood, NJ: Ablex
McNeill, D. (1992) *Hand and Mind: What Gestures Reveal about Thought.*
Chicago: University of Chicago Press.
Ruthrof, H. (1997) *Semantics and The Body: Meaning from Frege to the
Postmodern.* Toronto: University of Toronto Press.
Ruthrof, H. (2000) *The Body in Language.* London: Cassell.
Vygotsky, L.(1978) *Mind in Society: The Development of High Psychological
Processes.* London: Harvard University Press.

7 Mapping and assessing medical students' interactional involvement styles with patients[1]

CELIA ROBERTS

King's College London

SRIKANT SARANGI

Cardiff University

Introduction

In many contemporary societies, interactional performance, alongside relevant bodies of constitutive knowledge and transferable skills, is regarded as crucial for achieving success in employment and professional education. The training of medical students in the UK, which is the focus of our discussion here, now includes an assessment of communication skills in most medical schools through some form of real or simulated consultations under examination conditions. Both the training and the assessment tend to be based on the literature on communication skills, which has its origins in psychology, and in the practice of healthcare professionals (e.g., Buller and Buller 1987, Cohen-Cole 1991, Silverman et al 1998). Students are expected to demonstrate skills such as 'active listening', 'open questioning' and 'rapport building' while at the same time they are also assessed on their ability to follow a medical agenda. However, when the analytic gaze shifts from this agenda and from the general psychological notions underpinning communication skills to an understanding of how these consultations are interactionally achieved, the fine-grained detail of what makes for (un)successful medical interviews comes into focus.

Within the applied linguistics community (broadly defined here to include interactional sociolinguistics and discourse analysis), many researchers have provided descriptions of what constitutes interactional/communicative competence in context-specific ways. The challenge however remains: can our descriptive models adequately account for the professional ethos in which these competencies are assessed? And also, to what extent can a sociolinguistic/discoursal description of the interaction process become a useful measurement tool for the professional tutors and examiners in their attempt to discriminate between good and bad performance styles?

Background to the present study

Our discussion here is based on a recently concluded study of final year medical students at the Guys, King's and Thomas's (GKT) Medical School in London (Roberts et al 2000). As part of their final exam, students are subjected to 25 simulated consultations – each lasting seven minutes – with trained actor-patients. The data discussed here are taken from 309 video-recorded consultations involving 179 students. All the videos were viewed and together with field notes from observation of the exam, formed the basis for selecting 28 encounters which were transcribed in some detail.

The aim of the study was to look closely at the candidates' interactional performance in order to shed some light on their styles of consultation. Despite the increased attention to communication in the undergraduate curriculum, some 10% of candidates regularly fail the simulated consultation exam and large numbers reach a bare pass level.

We will concentrate here on two main issues – one analytic and one methodological – which arose from the study but firstly we will discuss the context within which we were working and which framed these two issues. This study was carried out with and for medical colleagues who had no background in discourse analysis but have had years of experience of designing and implementing communication exams for medical students. They were also representative of the mainstream of medical education in that they had no experience of and were rather sceptical of qualitative research paradigms. Our challenge, therefore, was to work jointly and convincingly with colleagues from a different disciplinary background and with different traditions of research (Roberts and Sarangi 1999, Sarangi, in press; Roberts and Sarangi, forthcoming). As well as presenting our analysis to them in ways which were persuasive and relevant, we also needed to represent it in practically relevant ways which could feed directly into curricular outcomes.

Involvement Styles: From psychological to interactional models

Medical schools such as GKT tend to work with biomedical models of diagnosis, explanation and treatment and with psychological models of relationship building, rapport, empathy and so on. These two sets of models are realised in the assessment procedure by having an experienced doctor as examiner and actors role-playing patients. The examiners rate the candidates on whether they have covered the necessary medical ground in appropriate ways and the actor-patients rate them on their capacity to build a relationship with patients. The actor gives a global rating and often makes off-the-record comments about the candidates to the examiner after they had left the room. For example, 'When they are good they almost make you cry'. By contrast, the examiner has a checklist covering essential medical ground and sometimes communication skills such as 'listening', 'ask open questions' and so on. Despite the increasing emphasis on 'patient-centred' consultations, how precisely notions such as empathy or rapport are interactionally accomplished is not made explicit to either examiner or actor-patient.

From a traditional linguistic perspective, empathy has been defined as 'the speaker's identification, which may vary in degree, with a person/thing that participates in the event or state that he [sic] describes in a sentence' (Kuno 1987:206). A notion of placement in relation to the events and people and the grammatical realisations can be seen in the use of active agent, modalisation, pronoun use etc. So, empathy can be grammaticalised, but it can also be lexicalised as in 'I know how you feel', 'I can understand your concerns', but such formulations, including repetitions, often run the risk of being produced and perceived as 'trained empathy' (see below).

The notion of 'involvement' with its counterpart 'detachment' which has developed out of the sociolinguistic literature provides a useful interactional handle.[2] Based on Goffman (1961), Gumperz and Cook-Gumperz (1982:15) suggest that 'conversational involvement' or what they refer to as 'communicative flexibility' 'enables us to tell, by looking only at actual performance features and without knowing the content, whether two speakers are actively communicating'. Participants have to be conversationally engaged for talk to happen, but involvement is also the result of speakers and listeners making inferences together. And since listening and speaking are interconnected (Erickson 1986), maintaining involvement is the responsibility of both speaker and listener all the time. So, for example, in a medical interview, the doctor's standard history-taking which often consists of apparently disconnected questions may not be properly involving since the patient may not be able to infer any coherent line from the doctor. In this respect, the latter may have failed to take responsibility for the patient's involvement.

Tannen (1984, 1989), drawing on the work of Chafe (1982) and Becker (1982), argues that there is an emotional dimension to involvement, giving the term a positive gloss which connects it to rapport and the positive face work used to build up solidarity in talk. For example, she quotes Lakoff (1979) in defining one of the involvement strategies as indirectness or ellipsis and the rapport which comes from being understood without having to make meaning explicit. Tannen distinguishes between two types of involvement strategies: sound and sense. In the first category come rhythm and other paralinguistic features, patterns of repetitive sound and collocations. Sense-making involvement strategies include indirectness and ellipsis, tropes and imagery and narrative. One recurring example in our data which stems from the anthropomorphizing tropes of the human body is when candidates talk of an organ of the body as 'being challenged' or 'unhappy' or 'not liking' what the patient is inflicting on it. Such image-making seems to enhance the positive side of conversational involvement as long as the understanding aspect of it is present. But where patients cannot make the necessary inferences, then it can be counter-productive and lead to detachment.

Alignment in the Conversation Analytic (CA) tradition

Underlying the idea of involvement/detachment is the assertion that interaction is jointly produced. This is not just a case of actively participating in the interaction but in working to produce what the conversation analysts call 'alignment'. The now relatively long tradition of CA in medical encounters (Drew and Heritage 1992, Frankel 1987, Heritage and Maynard, forthcoming) has shown how the two key notions of turn design and sequential organisation account for interactional outcomes in the consultation. As Heath (1992) and Maynard (1992) demonstrate, the finely tuned design of a turn manages the tension between on the one hand, maintaining the authority of the medical voice and its attempts to be persuasive, and on the other, issues of face and solidarity. These studies show the context sensitive ways in which turn design aligns the patient to the doctor's diagnosis and explanation (Sarangi and Roberts 2002).

As these studies of experienced doctors show, turn design creates alignment without, usually, the explicit voicing of solidarity features such as 'I understand how you feel'. In fact, formulaic tokens by the novice doctors in our data were nearly always received badly by the actor-patient. High rated candidates tended to align themselves with patients in more indirect ways by being more attentive to patient responses and building on them.

But it is not just a question of turn design. It is also a matter of sequencing. A turn which is apparently aligning in its particular location in the sequence is just the opposite in another location. For instance, asking how the patient feels about bad news immediately after it has been broken to them, or running a pre-sequence to display the patient's orientation when the patient is keen to get on with the business of hearing the diagnosis may seem out of place, and hence a marker of detachment.

CA has tended to look at phases within the consultation (as have even the best textbooks on communication skills) rather than the sequencing or staging of the entire consultation. In these medical exams the assessment is based on the entire seven minute encounter, and it was therefore important to look at the effect of sequencing on the whole consultation. It is important to look at how the content of the medical work – for example, history-taking, diagnostic reasoning – is *staged* overall to be relatively patient centred or not. Alignment is created through turn design but is also achieved indirectly throughout the whole sequence.

Analysing empathetic and retractive involvement styles

As indicated earlier, our discourse analysis had to speak to our colleagues and to medical students in practically relevant ways. This meant finding common ground between the more psychologically orientated discourses of our medical colleagues and our own sociolinguistic and CA discourses. Given that the notion of empathy used in the exams and in text books generally has its interactional counterpart in Tannen's positive face involvement strategies, we chose to keep the label of empathy. Detachment, however, was inappropriate since we were looking for a label which would suggest an active emotional distancing or drawing away from the patient. So we coined the term 'retractive' since the technical opposite of empathy – 'apathy' – has very different connotations. In order to display how these two notions accounted for relative success or lack of it in candidates' performance, we chose those encounters which were highly rated by actor-patients and contrasted them with the encounters where candidates had been given the lowest grades.

Discourse analytic findings based on holistic comparative analyses are, we consider, more likely to appeal to professionals for purposes of uptake and change in practice. Both CA and most current discourse analysis take turns, formats or utterances as the units of analysis. But our remit of analysis, as far as our professional colleagues were concerned, was the whole encounter. We, therefore, focused both on turn design and the sequential organisation of the whole consultation.

The empathetic and retractive styles were analysed in four different exam scenarios:

Cancer: an older white woman is advised to have a bronchoscopy because of possible tumour recurrence, although she denies the possibility that the cancer may have returned.

Sexually transmitted disease: a young Muslim woman has had unprotected sex and is concerned that she might have caught something. She also feels very upset about what has happened.

Alcohol: a Chinese businessman has come for the results of liver function tests. The results indicate he may be drinking too much.

Drugs: a young Afro-Caribbean man is seeking a methadone prescription because he says he has lost the one recently given to him at the drug rehabilitation centre.

Our overall interpretations suggest that candidates with high ratings tended to be empathetic, organically building solidarity and a joint problem-solving framework with the actor-patients. The failing candidates produced a retractive interactional climate, using questioning formats and responses which distanced them from the patient. The empathetic and retractive interactional styles are each grouped under three main headings. These coincide with several of the involvement strategies described by Tannen (1989) and the CA studies of alignment in medical interviews. However, as we shall see, the involvement strategies differ in their realisation in some respects from the Tannen list. This is because, as Silverman (1987) suggests, more social and patient-centred consultations are not necessarily like ordinary conversations. Some of the rapport work of ordinary conversations is done more explicitly in medical encounters, given their institutionally framed character.

Empathetic interactional styles

The first of these styles is 'attentive responding'. This involves the candidate picking up themes and making inferences from the actor-patient; making coherent a relatively loose patient narrative and giving positive evaluations and commentary to patient narrative.[3]

Empathetic Style/1

> **act**: what what you're not aware of i- probably is that m- my husband died of lung cancer about two years ago (..) and he had to have a bronchoscopy and he found the whole thing very (.)
> **can**: very unpleasant = ((nods)) (mm) =
> **act**: = very traumatic yes = he did
> **can**: ok well
> **act**: so you = must forgive me =
> **can**: = if = ((nods)) I I completely understand
> **act**: thank you

By this stage in the consultation, the doctor and patient have developed a climate of involvement so that the patient's hesitation after 'very' is picked up by the doctor with 'very unpleasant' and then acknowledged by the patient as she rewords it as 'very traumatic'. This type of overlapping and finishing off of each other's sentences (Lerner 1991) is perhaps common particularly in conversation among women (see Coates 1996). It turns the patient's monologue into a dialogue, supporting rather than disrupting the flow. This is another way of 'connecting' (Neighbour 1987) or showing empathy with the patient. Buller and Buller (1987) call this an affiliative style and suggest that it correlates with patient satisfaction.

The second empathetic style describes strategies used for joint problem-solving in the consultation. This includes ways of including the patient in the decision making, for example, 'we'll see if we can work something out together', eliciting patient awareness and thinking – what Maynard (1992) calls 'perspective display sequences' – and checking own and patient understanding and commitment. One of these involvement strategies is, as we have mentioned above, the use of tropes in which the assumption is that interactants share an understanding of the metaphorical work that is going on:

Empathetic Style/2

> **can**: what's happening is that you're drinking more than you should (..) and your stomach doesn't like it
> **act**: ah = =
> **can**: = = and your liver doesn't like it either
> **act**: mm (.) mm = =

The third empathetic style is contextualising and face work. We have mentioned earlier that conversational involvement entails the participants knowing where they are going together. As Gumperz (1982) suggests, this means understanding how to interpret contextualisation cues. But, in medical interviews, this contextualisation work is routinely done more explicitly than in casual conversation. It also functions to save face in potentially embarrassing question and answer sequences. So, in the next example, taken from the HIV encounter, the candidate shifts topic from the medical agenda to a narrative account of what actually happened at the party:

Empathetic Style/3

> **can**: ok (.) I'm going to ask you about a bit more about what (.) went on ok erm (.) what actually happened that that day when it all happened
> **act**: er it was like a party
> **can**: right

She sets the context, 'Im going to ask you...' and then is careful to refer back to the incident in a general way which will not cause embarrassment or loss of face to the patient. This contextualising helps the patient to distance herself from the here and now emotional trauma. The event is now seen as belonging to the past which makes it easier to narrate. The actor-patient can talk more openly to the candidate which, in turn, helps to bring them interactionally closer together. Her narration is both discursively and interactionally involving.

Retractive Interactional Styles

The three types of retractive styles contrast with the three empathetic ones. The first is inappropriate or inattentive responding. Here the candidates' responses are minimal and often formulaic or mechanistic – what we call 'trained empathy'. Utterances such as 'How do you feel about that?' immediately after bad news is given or 'I understand how you feel' when the patient expresses disgust or anger, for example, can be quite counter-productive given its particular location in the interaction. In the next example, the candidate responds inadequately to the actor-patient's feelings about having sex:

Retractive Style/1

> **act**: erm (..) I just (..) ((breath out)) (..) just (.) feel really terrible about it
> **can**: ok (.) erm (2.0) did you use protection at all

Here the candidate's 'OK' does not acknowledge the patient's feeling at all. He simply gives a minimal response token and then moves on to a new topic after quite a long pause. This 'OK' can be contrasted with other 'OKs' in the data where they are confirming the patient's response. Here, however, the patient makes an evaluative comment about her emotional state. An 'OK' after such an expression of affect shows no recognition of the patient's emotional state.

The candidate's rapid topic shift is also an example of the second type of retractive style. This we have termed schema-driven progression and patient labelling. Just as its empathetic opposite is concerned with patient perspectives and inclusiveness, here the weak candidates display styles which are distancing and excluding. These include early categorising of patients, driving through medical agendas, interrogations with little coherence to the patient and rapid topic shifts. Patients are implicitly labelled as worriers, or problems or difficult, when candidates make high inferences from patients' utterances. In this next example, the candidate fails to involve the actor-patient in his line of questioning and uses an interrogatory interactional style which reduces her to minimal responses in long linear phases:

Retractive Style/2

can: any rashes or
act: no don't think so
can: discharge (.) have you yourself had any discharges at all
act: no
can: any erm (.) irritation down there
act: no
can: any pain when you're passing water
act: no
can: erm (..) any blood in your urine
act: no

The last retractive style contrasts with the successful contextualisation work illustrated above. Whereas contextualisation is central to creating conditions for shared understanding (Gumperz 1982), problems of understanding on either side are retractive. So, misunderstandings, storage failure, issues of clarity and blunders can distance the patient from the doctor. In this next example, the candidate shows his insensitivity to the patient's level of understanding of scientific discourse:

Retractive Style/3

> can: right ok (1.0) erm (6.0) did (.) this patient have any er overt
> signs of any sexual disease did he have any rashes at all or
> act: sorry
> can: did the (.) did the partner that you had sex = with did he have =
> act: = yeah =
> can: any (.) sort of signs of (.) sexually transmitted diseases

The candidate's initial question confuses the patient in a number of
ways, including the slip of the tongue, in which he talks about 'patient'
instead of 'partner'. But the problems of understanding are due largely
to the medical register in which the question is expressed and to the
assumption that she would know what the symptoms of sexually
transmitted disease would be like. In addition, in his attempt to repair
the error in assuming too much medical knowledge, he shifts down to
give a specific example, 'any rashes' without showing through words or
intonation that he is doing so. Instead of bracketing the reformulation
within a falling intonational contour, he uses the same questioning
intonation as he does with the opening question. His attempt at
clarification, when the patient fails to understand, is no more helpful
since he is still using the same medical jargon, assuming that she will
know the portmanteau term 'sexually transmitted disease'.

Interactional hybridity

It is worth stressing that no one question or response is necessarily
empathetic or retractive. An empathetic move such as 'responsive
listening', which often depends on making inferences from the patient's
remarks, may in another context be treated as high inferencing and
produce the negative labelling of a patient. For example, a question
such as 'you're not worried about ...' may be an attentive response to a
patient's narrative or may make the patient feel they are being labelled
as 'a worrier' in which case it may not be perceived as empathetic at
all. Similarly, one candidate's reassuring moves, which contribute to an
overall high grade, appear as set responses, or what we call 'trained
empathy', for another candidate. The success, or not, of a particular
remark or question by the candidate depends on its location in the whole
interaction and the kind of climate which their communicative style has
already established.

The idea of involvement from the sociolinguistic literature and of
alignment from CA studies conjure up analytic frameworks which shed
light on that side of the consultation not concerned narrowly with

medicine. The social, the relational, the rapport aspects of the interview have been distinguished from the medical through the notion of the voices of medicine (Mishler 1986, Silverman 1987, Atkinson 1995). The contrast here is at the ideational and textual level of discourse. In other words, the expert scientific authority of medicine as it is constructed through the grammar and lexis of scientific discourse produces the voice of medicine. The lifeworld, by contrast, draws on the grammar and vocabulary and ways of knowing of ordinary, everyday life. Although the distinction between these two voices is a useful one, it does not account for the interpersonal level of discourse which is our focus here. Although the voice of medicine would seem to fit with the detached style and the social with the involved, data from doctor-patient interviews suggests that the mix of voices and interactional style is more complex and hybrid than this. In addition, as CA studies have indicated, it is the particular design of an utterance (or some other interactional feature such as pausing) in that particular location which produces an involved or detached effect.

For example, in our data, the actor-patient presented with feelings of guilt and disgust after having had unprotected sex. Candidates were expected to deal with both medical and social agendas. But in shifting to the social to find out why she felt so upset and guilty, candidates had to choose between an interactional style which was relatively detached – a series of probing questions – or one that was relatively involved. In the latter case, successful candidates managed to integrate aspects of Tannen's involement strategies with the more detached interactional style of medical history-taking. For example, some candidates were able to participate in the young woman's narrative of the party (which led up to the incident) by making evaluative comments which emphasised positive face or by finishing off the actor-patient's own comments when she paused. In other words they used some of the strategies of social conversation.

As well as the hybridity of voices and interactional styles, the exams require the candidates to manage the hybrid nature of all professional gatekeeping encounters (Roberts and Sarangi 1999, Roberts 2000, Sarangi 2001). In addition to the professional discourses (primarily the voice of medicine) and the interpersonal, interactional aspects largely assessed by the actor-patient, there is the institutional frame of the whole event. The consultations are assessed within a strict seven minute time constraint, the 'patients' are themselves assessors and the candidate is performing to an examiner's checklist. The candidate is not a qualified doctor but remains a novice still only partially socialised into the doctoring role (Becker et al 1961, Erickson 1999, Merton et al 1957).

The intricate but seamless architecture of the experienced doctor's consultation contrasts with the rough edges that novice doctors and actor-patients may give each other. One reason for this is the complex orientation of the actor-patient to the candidate. The actor-patients often voice feelings and attitudes which are kept hidden or managed in more face-saving ways in naturally occurring consultations. These more explicit voicings in gatekeeping settings may be due to the shift in power relations in which the asymmetry of the doctor-patient relationship is inverted and the actor-patient becomes the assessor. (The actor-patient may also help the candidate by nudging them towards a preferred response.) These vocal actor-patients tend to trigger more formulaic responses from, particularly, the weaker students who have been trained in 'rapport *words*' rather than 'rapport *work*'. So, for example, where the actor-patients voice their refusal to comply rather than remain silent or spell out their feelings, the weaker candidates resort to responses (often repeated many times) such as 'I understand', 'I'm sorry you feel like that'. These so-called empathetic words have little or no solidarity function unless they are part of the candidate's involvement style (Savage and Armstrong 1990).

Thematic staging

The global impression of candidates and the quality of their communicative style does not depend only upon the empathetic or retractive design of questions and responses in their particular location. The issue of how questions and responses are positioned or sequenced in the consultation to cover particular themes is also significant when the whole interaction is examined. In other words, how the different *themes* of the consultation are *staged* affects its overall emotional climate and helps to define the candidate's communicative style.

Each encounter has a key moment or *crux* (or in most cases a number of *cruces*) around which much of the interaction is organised e.g., the moment when the Chinese businessman asks 'Am I an alcoholic?'; the drug addict asks for a repeat methadone prescription; the young Muslim woman conveys her feelings of self-disgust or the bad news is broken to the cancer patient. How candidates build up to, realise and follow up these crucial moments affects the whole climate of the interaction and its successful outcome or not. This thematic element contributes to the relatively empathetic or retractive style of the whole encounter as well as progressing the medical agenda.

The contrast between good and poor candidates in thematic staging is well illustrated in the cancer scenario in which an older white woman resists the advice to have a bronchoscopy to assess whether her cancer has returned. Again we will take two examples, one rated high and one low, to illustrate the point (see appendix A for the full transcript). The good candidate gradually and sensitively takes the patient through the consequences of not having a bronchoscopy. She stages her case for this further investigation so that each time the patient rejects her advice she still has some persuasive resources to bring to the consultation.

Good thematic staging

The sequencing of her case for having a bronchoscopy by the strong candidate:

We need to exclude the worst
We need to investigate in more detail
We would like to do a bronchoscopy
We want to exclude the possibility of a tumour
You had a tumour before
There is the possibility of a recurrence of the tumour

By contrast the weak candidate stages the argument differently. He introduces the fact that she had cancer of the kidney much earlier on in the consultation and then has no strong reasons left to persuade the patient as the consultation continues.

Poor thematic staging

The sequencing of his case for having a bronchoscopy by the weak candidate:

We need to do more investigations
The possible recurrence of the tumour
The possible recurrence of the tumour (repetition of theme two)
It would be better to have the bronchoscopy
Do you have any other worries

Whereas the strong candidate builds up to the most persuasive argument, the weak candidate brings in the worst case scenario early on (some 60 lines before the strong candidate). This produces a confrontational response from the patient. The consultation then tails off, as he runs out of persuasive resources, with some general exhortations that 'it would be better', and an elicitation about any other worries (as if the possibility of a return of the cancer was not bad enough!). These contrastive examples show that candidates not only need to design their questions and responses sensitively but need to be aware of the overall staging of an encounter particularly where persuasion, negotiation or reassurance are the focus of the consultation. This awareness may be brought to the encounter but the candidate with a top-rated communicative style stages the themes in a highly responsive way, designing the progress of the consultation to fit the particular local interactional context produced by the patient.

Representational and Methodological Issues

As we have discussed earlier on, the context within which we were working required us to be persuasive to colleagues who were not familiar with discourse analysis. We, therefore, had to think about issues of presentation early on when we were discussing our methods. We needed to find a means of presenting our analysis which would function in three different but inter-connecting ways. The analysis needed to have an impact on our medical colleagues. The scope of our analysis also had to acknowledge our accountability to the whole data set and not just to one or two selected transcripts. Finally, it needed to integrate local sociolinguistic and sequential inferences with an analysis of the whole encounter.

We, therefore, borrowed from Green and Wallat (1981) the notion of mapping conversations. Their micro-ethnography of classrooms maps the ways in which instruction units of the class are tied together thematically. It is worth noting that such mapping techniques have also been undertaken in narrative research (Labov and Waletzky 1967, Gee 1997), but in focusing on the structure, these maps do not engage with the question of what makes communication effective. Our interactional maps show the relationship between turn by turn empathetic and retractive moves and the overall thematic staging of the consultation (see Appendix B).

As with the approach to analysis described above, the mapping process is contrastive. By contrasting a map of a high rated candidate with one who has failed, it is possible to see a clear visual comparison in the design of questions and responses, in thematic staging and in the ways these two sets of phenomena interact. For example, the prominent features of these maps, around the cruces, tend to show a thick clustering of empathetic or retractive interactional styles.

Since we were concerned from the outset with making our analysis persuasive to medical colleagues, issues of how to represent the data and our method of analysis were inevitably inter-related. By using the metaphor of mapping to summarise the data analysis we were trying to achieve a number of goals. Firstly, visual representations allowed us and our medical colleagues to 'see' the differences in the contrastive maps. They could be quite dramatically compared by putting a good interaction along side a bad one. Secondly by tuning into the 'maps and diagrams' semiotics of medicine, we were able to avoid the criticisms of 'soft' discursive qualitative descriptions! Thirdly, we were able to use this map as a way into actual examples since the mapping refers to a typology which is always supported by examples from transcripts. Finally, the map goes some way towards providing an assessment framework for thinking about interaction as the candidate is assessed. Examiners can fill out their checklists by making mental notes of the kind of empathetic and retractive styles the candidates are using. Of course, it is easy to claim too much for such an attempt. There is the danger of slipping into a coding mode, rather than constantly referring back to the data in an interpretive way. And a map is always and only an interpretation of the much more interesting terrain which it represents.

Conclusion

We are particularly struck by the way in which strong candidates stage the consultations, and design their turns in context-sensitive ways, tuning in to the particular moment. Overall, in our data, high grades were given where candidates achieved 'tunefulness' and managed to integrate authority and solidarity. In other words, diagnosis, suggested treatment, issues of medication etc. were covered in a persuasive way while at the same time candidates were rated as empathetic: 'she was lovely', 'a nice way about him'. Low grades were awarded where these two aspects were not integrated and/or when, as one examiner put it, candidates 'did not take the patient with them'. Such 'tunefulness' is hard to teach and, certainly, trying to improve communication skills with recipe style phrases and 'trained empathy' appears, from the evidence of our data, likely to be counter-productive.

We are also aware that several of the aspects of empathetic and retractive styles which we have illustrated are widely recognised in the communication skills literature (e.g., Platt et al 1994). Where our analysis differs is in our attempt to look at good and poor communicators in the local context of specific interactions, to link specific styles of questions and responses to the overall staging of the consultation and to the ideological underpinnings of individuals' styles.

To conclude, the acts of interpretation that we were engaged in also had to be acts of persuasion for an audience that did not take our disciplinary moorings for granted. So issues of presentation and representation were important as part of the analytic process rather than something to be tacked on to the end. We also wanted to find ways to account for large data sets but remain orientated to local interpretive processes and we had to think of ways of contributing to sociolinguistic thinking and yet speak in relevant ways to clinical colleagues and medical students. This motivated us to compare highly rated candidates with those who failed and the insights from this comparative analysis have now been used to develop appropriate learning materials for the undergraduate medical curriculum. It is still early days but there is the possibility that the Medical Defence Union will disseminate the video and training materials developed from the research. These materials will be used by the communication skills tutors with second year and final year students. It remains to be seen, however, if the interactional mapping we suggest here can be used by examiners as a tool for assessing candidates' clinical competence (Wass et al 2001). So far, the assessment checklists and the examiners themselves have not been involved in any changes or modifications. We are aware of the limitations of the learning materials based on our analysis of the hybrid medical consultations under exam conditions. These are not real professional encounters but institutionally based synthetic ones. So the data-based materials cannot directly improve young doctors' consultation styles in real medical practices.[4] However, although the focus is on their performance in the exams, the analytic language which they are introduced to is designed to provide them with tools for self-analysis in real patient-health care professional communication.

Notes

1   We would like to acknowledge the support of Val Wass and Roger Jones who collaborated on the project. We are grateful to the medical students and the actor-patients who consented to be part of the study and our special thanks to Annie Gillett for her help with the transcription and mapping of the data examples.

2   See Chafe's [1982] characterisation of detachment as typically realised in passive voice and in nominalisation. Here we adopt an interactional approach to involvement and detachment, or what we call 'empathetic' and 'retractive' styles respectively.

3   We use the following simplified transcription conventions: 'can' for 'candidate'; 'act' for 'actor-patient'; (.) denotes short pause; (2 etc) denotes length of pause; ((nods etc.)) signal non-verbal communication; and the equal sign (=) marks overlapping speech.

4   There are plans for a joint research project with the Department of Primary General Practice and Primary Care, using the analytic framework with naturally occurring recordings of general practice.

References

Atkinson, P. (1995) *Medical Talk and Medical Work*. London: Sage.

Becker, A. (1982) Beyond translation: Aesthetics and language description. In H. Byrnes ed., *Contemporary Perceptions of Language: Interdisciplinary Dimensions*. Washington DC: Georgetown University Press, 124-138.

Becker, H., Geer, B., Hughes, E. C. and Strauss, A. L. (1961) *Boys in White: Student Culture in Medical School*. Chicago: Chicago University Press.

Buller, M. and Buller, D. (1987) Physicians' communication style and patient satisfaction. *Journal of Health and Social Behaviour* 28, 375-388.

Chafe, W. (1982) Integration and involvement in speaking, writing and oral literature. In D. Tannen ed., *Spoken and Written Language: Exploring Orality and Literacy*. Norwood NJ: Ablex, 35-53.

Coates, J. (1996) *Women Talk: Conversation between Women Friends*. Oxford: Blackwell.

Cohen-Cole, S. A. (1991) *The Medical Interview: The Three Function Approach*. St Louis: Mosby Year Book.

Drew, P. and Heritage, J. eds (1992) *Talk at Work: Interaction in Institutional Settings*. Cambridge: Cambridge University Press.

Erickson, F. (1986) Listening and speaking. In D. Tannen and J. Alatis eds., *Languages and Linguistics: The Interdependence of Theory, Data and Application*. Washington DC: Georgetown University Press, 294-319.

Erickson, F. (1999) Appropriation of voice and presentation of self as a fellow physician: Aspects of a discourse of apprenticeship in medicine. In S. Sarangi and C. Roberts eds., 109-143.

Frankel, R. (1987) From sentence to sequence: understanding the medical encounter through microinteractional analysis. *Discourse Processes* 7, 135-170.

Gee, J. P. (1997) Thematized echoes. Journal of Narrative and Life History 7, 1-4, 189-196.

Goffman, E. (1961) *Encounters: Two Studies in the Sociology of Interaction*. Indianapolis, IN: Bobbs-Merrill.

Green, J. and Wallat, C. (1981) Mapping interactional conversations – a sociolinguistic ethnography. In J. Green and C. Wallat eds., *Ethnography and Language in Educational Settings*. Norwood, NJ: Ablex, 161-195.

Gumperz, J. and Cook-Gumperz, J. (1982) Introduction: language and the communication of social identity. In J. Gumperz ed., *Language and Social Identity*. Cambridge: Cambridge University Press, 1-21.

Gumperz, J. (1982) *Discourse Strategies*. Cambridge: Cambridge University Press.

Heath, C. (1992) The delivery and reception of diagnosis in the general practice consultation. In P. Drew and J. Heritage eds., 235-267.

Heritage, J. and Maynard, D. eds. (forthcoming) *Practicing Medicine: Structure and Process in Primary Care Encounters.* Cambridge: Cambridge University Press.

Kuno, S. (1987) *Functional Syntax: Anaphora, Discourse and Empathy.* Chicago: The University of Chicago Press.

Labov, W. and Waletzky, J. (1967) Narrative analysis: oral versions of personal experience. In J. Helm ed., *Essays on the Verbal and Visual Arts.* Seattle: University of Washington Press, 12-44.

Lakoff, R. (1979) Stylistic strategies within a grammar of style. In J. Oransanu, M. Slater and L. Adler eds., Language, *Sex and Gender.* Annals of the New York Academy of Sciences.

Lerner, G. (1991) On the syntax of sentences-in-progress. *Language in Society* 20, 441-458

Maynard, D. (1992) On clinicians co-implicating recipients' perspective in the delivery of diagnostic news. In P. Drew and J. Heritage eds., 331-358.

Merton, R. K., Reader, G. G. and Kendall, P. L. eds (1957) *The Student Physician: Introductory Studies in the Sociology of Medical Education.* Cambridge, Mass: Harvard University Press.

Mishler, E. G. (1986) *The Discourse of Medicine: Dialectics of Medical Interviews.* Norwood, N.J.: Ablex.

Neighbour, R. (1987) *The Inner Consultation: How to Develop an Effective and Consulting Style.* Lancaster: MIT Press.

Platt, F. W. and Keller V. F (1994) Empathic communication: a teachable and learnable skill. *Journal of General Internal Medicine* 9, 222-226.

Roberts, C. (2000) Professional gatekeeping in intercultural encounters. In S. Sarangi and M. Coulthard eds., *Discourse and Social Life.* London: Pearson, 102-120.

Roberts, C. and Sarangi, S. (1999) Hybridity in gatekeeping discourse: issues of practical relevance for the researcher. In S. Sarangi and C. Roberts eds., 473-503.

Roberts, C. and Sarangi, S. (forthcoming) Uptake of discourse research in interprofessional settings: Reporting from medical consultancy. Special issue of *Applied Linguistics.*

Roberts, C., Wass, V., Jones, R. and Sarangi, S. (2000) *Ethnicity and Intercultural Communication between Patients and Doctors: Implications for Undergraduate Education in London.* London: The King's Fund.

Sarangi, S. (2001) Interactional hybridity in gatekeeping discourse. In S. Cigada, S. Gilardoni and M. Matthey eds., *Communicare in ambiente professionale plurilingue.* Lugano: Universita della Svizzera Italiana, 47-71.

Sarangi, S. (in press) Discourse practitioners as a community of interprofessional practice: some insights from health communication research. In C. N. Candlin ed., *Research and Practice in Professional Discourse.* Hong Kong: City University Press.

Sarangi, S. and Roberts, C. eds (1999) *Talk, Work and Institutional Order: Discourse in Medical, Mediation and Management Settings.* Berlin: Mouton de Gruyter.

Sarangi, S. and Roberts, C. (2002) Discoursal (mis)alignments in professional gatekeeping encounters. In C. Kramsch ed., *Language Acquisition and Language Socialisation: Ecological Perspectives*. London: Continuum.

Savage and Armstrong, D. (1990) Effect of GP's consulting style on patient's satisfaction: a controlled study. *British Medical Journal* 301: 968 - 970

Silverman, D. (1987) *Communication and Medical Practice: Social Relations in the Clinic*. London: Sage.

Silverman, J., Kurtz, S. and Draper, J. (1998) *Skills for Communicating with Patients*. Abingdon: Radcliffe Medical Press.

Tannen, D. (1984) *Conversational Style*. Norwood: Ablex.

Tannen, D. (1989) *Talking Voices: Repetition, Dialogue and Imagery in Conversational Discourse*. Cambridge: Cambridge University Press.

Wass, V., Van der Vleuten, C., Shatzer, J. and Jones, R. (2001) Assessment of clinical competence. *Lancet* 357, 945-949.

Appendix A

Data Extracts from the Cancer Station

Data Example 1 (high rated candidate: c18S1am7)

```
can:  hello there
act:  hello
can:  my name [is tasha] I'm one of the doctors here
act:  right (.) = and I'm missus = ring
can:  = [what can    ] = missus ring
act:  yes
can:  [ok] I don't think we've met before have we = =
act:  = = no no (.) we = haven't =
can:  = right =
act:  = no =
can:  = erm = (..) can you just tell me a bit about how
      you've been feeling recently
act:  well I I've basically be- been feeling very fi- very
      well (.) but I've got a a (.) tickly cough
can:  right = =
act:  = = erm (.) I've lost a little bit of weight
can:  = ok =
act:  = which = (.) maybe I mean that doesn't (.) do me any
      harm (.) [    ] being over weight = =
can:  = = you're not worried about that at all
act:  no not = worried =
can:  = no =
act:  about it no no erm (.) so I went to my gp to have erm
      (.) some antibiotics or = something =
can:  = mm hm =
act:  you know just to clear = this up =
can:  = mm ok =
act:  but he sent me for a chest x-ray = but =
can:  = right = ok
act:  erm (..) so really I suppose I've come in for the (.)
      result of that and
can:  right
act:  expect you'll give me some antibiotics and that'll be
      it
      [01:19:00]
can:  ok erm (..) we've got the re- we've got the results
      of the chest x-ray now we've actually got the results
      and I'd like to discuss those with you = if that's =
act:  = mm =
can:  ok
act:  mm
```

can: erm the chest x-ray [did] actually show that (.) erm
there's a shadow on one of your lung [   ]s (..)
erm (..) and (.) it may be the cause of some of your
symptoms erm (..) I- I- y- you mentioned you've been
having to take antibiotics it hasn't helped much (.)
so erm this is probably likely to be what is causing
your symptoms the cough and = maybe =

act: = mm =

can: the weight loss (..) erm it's very difficult for us
to say just from the x-ray (.) you know what it could
be = [or] =

act: = mm =

can: exactly (..) erm it could be a number of things (.)
erm (..) we'd we'd obviously just like to exclude the
worst

act: mm = =

can: = = do you do you have any ideas as to what it may be
[or you haven't thought]

act: well no I- I'm not (.) I'm not worried about it = I I
just think =

can: = no mm =

act: I've got a (..) just a bit of a cough there

can: mm ok = =

act: = = erm = =

can: = = well I you know I'm really glad you've come to us
erm and you know we want to invest- [prefer] that
we're investigating this because we obviously want to
sort out your problem (.) erm as I said the x-ray
shows a shadow and I can show you the x-ray if you'd
like to see it
[01:20:04]

act: mm

can: erm (.) and (.) as I already mentioned it's difficult
for us to say what it is at this stage (.) what we'd
like to do is (.) do erm a procedure called a
bronchoscopy = [what that is] =

act: = oh that = awful thi- o::h no = that's =

can: = you how do you = know anything about it = have you
had one =

act: = o:h = my husband had that

can: oh did he

act: yes he did = it's r- horrible =

can: = he didn't enjoy = it at all

act: no he didn't it upset him for a long time

can: right

act: no I don't want to have all that

can: no

act: no I don't think it's necessary anyway

can: right well I'm sorry you feel like that
act: mm
can: erm (..) have you ever had one yourself
act: no I haven't but I mean = he was he w- =
can: = no [   ] =
act: no I don't want one thank = you =
can: = right = ok can I (.) would it be ok if I just tell
        you a little bit about it (.) because
act: well all right yes

Data Example 2 (low rated candidate: c18s1pm16)

can: good afternoon I I'm one of the doctors here seeing
        you today (.) right er (.) w- would you mind if I sat
        down had a chat with you = =
act: = = no n- not ((laughs)) (at all)
can: right
act: that's fine
can: ok (..) sor = ry I = ((indicating that he needs the
        notes))
act: = erm I've come in = for the = results =
can: = right =
act: of my chest x-ray
can: oh right ok (.) sorry about this ((reads notes very
        quickly and gives them back)) ok right erm (.) how
        did the (.) chest x-ray actually (.) go
act: well it was fine
can: it was fine
act: = yes =
can: = ok = and has an- has (.) anybody told you about er
        er what they saw or what the chest x-ray = =
act: = = no I've come in to talk to you about that
        [02:37:57]
can: sure ok (.) right erm (.) so (.) er (.) w- (.) we did
        the chest x-ray last week and erm (..) I mean wha-
        what kind of thing were you actually complaining
        about (.) before you [took the] chest x-ray
act: I was complaining about the fact er that I had a (.)
        a bit of a cough and I'd lost a little weight
can: right ok = =
act: = = and doctor green has been a very (..) kind doctor
        and looked after me very well and my husband over the
        years
can: ok
act: and erm (1.0) I came in and saw him and erm (3.0) e-
        he suggested that we had this chest x-ray as a = sort
        of =

```
can:   = sure =
act:   precautionary thing
can:   yes (.) I mean did he tell you what he thought it
       could be or (.) you know what it could be (..) this
       you know this cough = =
act:   = = well no I mean it's it's just probably bronchitis
       it's the sort of time of year and there's a lot of
       pollution and er = =
can:   = = yeah (..) ok
act:   so (.) he said a course of antibiotics should put it
       right but (.) let's be erm (..) cautious and do this
       and then we'll know what antibiotics to give you so
       that we'll give you the right ones
can:   ok
       [02:38:58]
act:   with my previous history he thought that was sensible
       and I agree
can:   sure erm from the chest x-ray (.) erm we actually
       found out that (..) erm we saw a (.) shadow on the
       lung (.) and we erm think that's this could be
       something  serious
act:   right

can:   so we would like to do more investigations to see
       exactly what this could be (3.0) I mean how do you
       feel about that
act:   not very keen ((laughs))
can:   can you tell me why you don't (.) want to go through
       more or (1.0) any concerns that you have
act:   well I (.) I (.) I don't really want to go to
       hospital again (.) you know
can:   right (.) and why's that
act:   well erm I seem to have seen a lot of (.) hospitals
       in the last few years
can:   sure (.) is it just because of the kidney problem or
act:   no my husband died about two years ago [of] cancer of
       the lung and er
can:   [oh yeah]
act:   and my kidney erm has cleared up I I've been given
       the all clear on that so
can:   right
act:   I don't feel there's anything seriously the matter
       with me so: erm
       [02:40:02]
can:     sure (.) = I mean [do you] =
act:   = makes it all a = bit of a (.) storm in a tea cup if
       you'll forgive me
```

can: mm hm would you mind me asking you know erm how did
         your husband pass away or
act: my hu- I told you my husband died of lung cancer
can: oh sorry I (..) sorry I didn't catch that (.) yeah
         erm so (.) but however (.) from the lung chest x-ray
         (.) we're very concerned that this could be something
         serious (.) we think that this could be (.) a
         recurrence from the (.) kidney problem that you have
         (3.0)
act: but I don't think it is
can: sure (.) we don't want to think it is either (..) but
         just to make sure (.) we want to do (.) a
         bronchoscopy
act: yes and I don't want you to do that
can: sure I understand (.) but er (1.5) would you want to
         know why w- w- what this (.) er mass is on the chest
         x-ray
act: well I don't think it's anything serious otherwise
         I'd be feeling ill and I'm not feeling ill (.) that
         ill = anyway =
can: = sure = (.) w- what do you think it could be apart
         from I mean =

Appendix B

Interactional Maps: Thematic, Empathetic and Retractive Features

Key:

Empathetic Style
E1 = attentive listening
E2 = joint problem-solving
E3 = contextualising and face management

Retractive Style
R1 = inappropriate responding
R2 = schema-driven progression and patient labelling
R3 = storage failure
R4 = insensitivity to patients' level of understanding

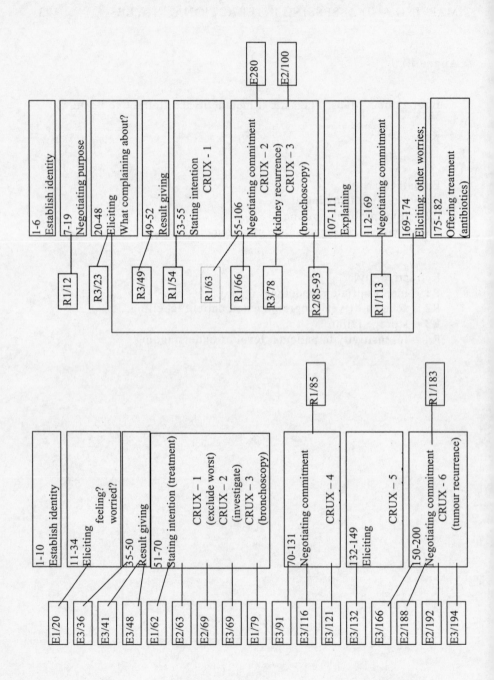

8   Distinguishing the voices of researchers and the people they research in writing qualitative research

ADRIAN HOLLIDAY

Canterbury Christ Church University College

The researcher's relationship with the social setting she investigates is always considered problematic[1]. The issue has for a long time focused around the 'observer paradox' whereby the setting is changed by the researcher's presence. In this paper I will look at how part of this problem might be addressed in qualitative research, where the interaction between the researcher and the people in the setting is particularly complex, and at how specific strategies can be employed in the writing of the research. I shall begin by characterizing a progressivist paradigm which has a more liberated view of the issue, and by describing research which I carried out on a corpus of qualitative research writing within this paradigm. I shall then demonstrate how specific writing strategies are employed in this corpus, and look at how these strategies have helped me in my own writing.

A progressivist paradigm

The discussion in this paper is based on an interdisciplinary study of qualitative research writing in a corpus of 20 published research articles, masters dissertations, PhD theses and undergraduate student assignments from health related studies, sport science, women's studies, international education and applied linguistics[2]. These were selected on the basis of being examples of 'good writing' – already published, completed with good grades or recognised as good work in progress[3]. In some cases, where the authors were colleagues or students, I was able to interview them about their writing. The purpose of the study was not so much to contribute to the understanding of genres in academic writing, but to inform myself and others about how to deal with an intensely subjective arena of action. All the examples fell within a *progressivist* paradigm (Holliday 2002: 20). I use this term as a convenient heading under which to group together a range of paradigms (critical, postmodern, constructivist, feminist etc.) which have much in common in their opposition to the more traditional, postpositivist *naturalism* (Guba and Lincoln 1994). I therefore align my approach with the now considerable progressivist, anti-naturalist literature (e.g. Denzin and Lincoln 1994, Hammersley and Atkinson 1995, Gubrium and Holstein 1997, Miller et al 1998); which presents the following argument:

a)   The naturalist position is that social reality is plain to see and can be objectively captured by a researcher who stays in the setting for a long enough period for exhaustive data collection. The researcher does however need to remain unobtrusively 'a fly on the wall' to avoid the 'observer paradox' whereby her presence will change the virgin reality of the setting.

b)   The progressivist position is that the naturalist position is naïve – that social reality is not plain to see, as it is socially constructed both by the people in it and by the researcher who looks at it. There is no such thing as a virgin setting, as any setting is always changing as it interacts with the wider world. It is thus both normal and inevitable that the researcher interacts with and changes the setting; but in so doing she needs to understand and manage this impact. Indeed, the way in which the setting responds to her presence itself illuminates the nature of the setting. Moreover, her perception of the setting will always be influenced by her own construction of it and will therefore always be highly subjective.

My aim is therefore to explore how this subjectivity can be managed in order to achieve scientific rigour, especially in writing which is an integral part of the research process. This management of subjectivity requires a subtle judicious balance between, on the one hand, a wide *diversity* of response to the exigencies of individual social settings, and, on the other hand, a *unity* of accountability, by which means the workings of the research process are shown every step of the way (Holliday 2002: 7-9).

Separation of voices

Hence the progressivist paradigm recognises that the researcher is undeniably interacting with the people in the research setting simply by being there, and that there are a complex of constructions, by her on them and by them on her. To manage this in the act of writing, she must show how this complex of relationships is managed and accounted for. One way to do this is to separate, as far as she can, her own voice from those of the people she is writing about. Thus, she addresses the major aim of being true to the worlds of the people in the setting by showing explicitly *how* and on *what basis* she is writing about those worlds, and *which* data she is using for *what* purpose. This is very different from naturalist writing, which I shall look at towards the end of this paper.

In my corpus there are several examples of how this is done. One such is the following extract from Pierson's study of how nursing assistants communicate with non-speaking demented health care residents. It demonstrates how she not only makes it clear *which* is her voice, but demarcates key aspects of her own voice in order to show exactly what she is doing:

Member's knowledge – 'It's just my common sense'

[...] Feeding residents was something that the NAs [nursing assistants] did out of their own understanding of the situation as the following comments by NAs indicate:

> 'Well, you just use your common sense, ... You can tell who needs it.'
>
> 'No one assigns you. It's just if you walk in and one is there and it looks like ... someone needs to feed them so you just do it. You use your common sense and get behind the feeding table.'
>
> 'It makes sense. I have to feed all these people so I get behind the feeding table.'

I interpreted these comments to mean that NAs were constantly assessing the situation and reacting accordingly. When a resident was not actively engaged in feeding or was known as a 'feeder', any competent NA would recognize what was needed to be done and do it. Feeding a helpless resident does not happen until the NA makes that assessment and begins the feeding. Feeding, like all other interactions is 'indexical' and 'reflexive'. Its practices are 'embodied', 'circumstantially contingent', and 'unwittingly' performed (Garfinkel, 1967; Lynch, Livingston, and Garfinkel, 1983).

Once an NA recognizes the need to feed a resident a variety of embodied, circumstantially contingent, and unwittingly performed practices are revealed, as described in the following field note:

> R., a large male NA, is standing behind the feeding table this morning attempting to feed the three most difficult feeders. I ask him what special things he does to get these residents to eat. 'Like Mr [H], you have to push his tongue down'

(Pierson 1999: 128, cited in Holliday 2002: 113-5)

The first thing to notice in this extract is the researcher's use of a thematic heading ('Member's knowledge ..), which, although emerging from the data itself, marks how she has chosen to organize the discussion. Within the rest of the extract it is clear how Pierson demarcates (a) her data (underlined), from (b) her commentary (underdotted), and (c) her argument (unmarked in the text).

There is some variation in the degree of explicitness writers employ to demarcate their data. In the extract Pierson does this particularly explicitly, and I think helpfully, by indenting it, using exactly the same referencing conventions as for quotations from literature. It is also significant that the second data extract is her own description, which is treated in exactly the same way as the verbatim data in the first data extract. By demarcating data in this way, the researcher also makes it clear that she has chosen extracts of data from a broader corpus in order to provide evidence for this part of *her* argument, which is marshalled under the thematic heading.

The commentary on the data is marked by phrases such as 'the following' and 'these comments' which specifically *point* at the data, and by 'I interpreted' and 'as described', which demonstrate *how* the data contributes to the argument. The use of the past tense here also shows that the collection of data and its subsequent interpretation took place at a specific time in the past. The use of the first person has a profound strategic role. It increases accountability by making it clear where the researcher's subjectivity lies – that *she* has chosen *these* fragments of data to support *her* interpretation and argument (Miller et al 1998: 401). It reduces the sense of abstractness found in postpositivism, naturalist writing, which 'freezes ordinary people and everyday life into a neat, coherent, timeless portrait' (Foley 1998: 11). The argument is then distinguished by more generalized language referring to the data as a whole ('any competent NA would', 'feeding [...] does not happen') and connects this with a broader set of theory ('"indexical" and "reflexive"') and literature (Garfinkel etc)[4]. The researcher is thus *telling* the reader what she believes the data extract to be saying – what she believes the data to be contributing to the argument (Golden-Biddle and Locke 1997: 58, citing Booth).

By skilfully showing the reader how she constructs her text in this way, the researcher also reveals her intent. She shows the inner workings of what Geertz calls 'an elaborate venture'. This qualitative research is not simply a naturalist reporting of what is seen and heard; 'what defines it is the kind of *intellectual effort* it is' in constructing sense of what has been seen and heard (1993: 6, his emphasis). An essential ingredient in constructing sense is the *thick description*, which displays the different and complex facets of a particular social phenomenon (Holliday 2002: 78, citing Geertz and Ryle). A good example of this is in another piece of writing in my corpus. Herrera, in her masters dissertation which reports an ethnography of a girls' school in Cairo, Egypt, tries to illuminate the 'lives, attitudes, struggles, relationships, confrontations, aspirations of ordinary teachers, students, and administrators' (1992: 79). One of the people she focuses on is the headmistress; and the thick description is constructed from a variety of interconnected data: descriptions of her dealing with a pupil, of what happens when she visits a class, of her role in the school, and of her office and its artefacts, her own account of her mission in the school, a student's account of her effect on timekeeping, and a clause on the role of the headmistress in a ministry document (Holliday 2002: 78).

The extract from Pierson's paper (above) brings accountability to this venture by showing us how a part of a thick description is actually constructed (Holliday 2002: 115). She shows us:

i.   which data, from which sources – 'the following comments by NAs' , 'the following field note'.

ii. how it interconnects within the coherence of the argument, structured by themes – 'as the following [...] indicate', 'as described in the following'

iii. what the data means – 'any competent NA would recognize what was needed to be done and do it'

iv. how each extract means what it means – 'I interpreted these comments to mean that NAs were constantly assessing the situation and reacting accordingly'

v.   relationship with theory - 'feeding, like all other interactions is "indexical" and "reflexive"'.

Textual room and ideology

By making it clear which is her voice, and how this voice is talking about the voices of the people in the research setting, the researcher is striving to protect 'textual room' both for the people she is investigating and also for herself. At one level, 'textual room' can be defined as the allowance in writing given to the identities of the different people in the text. At another level, it is creating 'textual room for counter-hegemonic narratives' (Fine and Weis 1998: 27). This implies that the researcher is not only present and influential; but that her influence is essentially ideological. Because ideology is hegemonic in the way that it pervades all aspects of perception, the researcher must define this ideology and put it in its place, *so that* she can allow textual room for people who may not share this ideology. This is extremely difficult for her to do because she is of course driven by her ideology. Nevertheless, she must do this if her writing is not going to be simply a statement of what she thought before she began the research process.

There are three necessary parts to what this involves. For her own part:

1) the researcher must come out and state her own ideological and cultural agency - by demarcating her own statements, and by acknowledging her own involvement from a position of individuality.

To protect the textual room of the people in the research setting,

2) she must apply caution and restraint in interpretation
3) she must acknowledge that what she defines as the 'setting' is only her own construction on the larger, complex world of others – and that she only understands a little of what she sees and hears (Holliday 2002: 179, 1999: 255).

(1) and part of (2) are demonstrated in the extract from Pierson's paper above, through the use of the first person and by separating comment from argument. Another aspect of (2) would be hedging (Holliday 2002: 184), which is beyond the scope of this paper. (3) can be achieved within the *conceptual framework*, which states the 'presumed relationships' within the research context and 'forces you to be explicit about what you think you are doing' (Robson 1993: 150). 'Presumed relationships' are of two interconnected types – between the researcher's ideology and current discussion and issues (e.g. in a literature review), and between her ideology and her research methodology, which in turn has a certain type of impact on the research setting in the way she sees, interacts with and treats the people involved (Holliday 2002: 52-3).

Several examples from my corpus show how this is done (Holliday 2002: 55-6). In the introduction to her short undergraduate ethnography of McDonald's, Celik (1999) comes out with a clear statement of her own ideology – that 'McDonalds has maintained cross-cultural domination'. This then leads her to state how this view will impact on how, in her approach to the research setting, she will 'have to consider how individuals are subsumed into McDonald's corporate identity'. Similarly, in the introduction to her study of gender in teenage girls' magazines, Talbot states her ideological position that 'written mass media texts construct social identities for readers' (1992: 174). This leads her, at the beginning of her discussion of methodological issues, to explain how this view will effect not only how she will see the research setting[5], but also her subsequent treatment of it:

> I will not look at the text in a traditional way as a product of a single author [...] [but as] a 'tissue of voices' [...] of characters who inhabit the text. [...] I have found it helpful to divide the 'population of characters' into three categories: interactants, characters, and subject positions. (1992: 176-7)

Note how her use of the first person enables her make this a personal statement of who she is in relation to the text. Anderson, in draft material from his PhD thesis about a professional discourse in TESOL, at the beginning of his chapter on methodological issues, uses the first person to articulate how his researcher persona interacts with his own membership within the setting, and how this impacts on how he will see and subsequently treat the people in the setting:

> I, as the researcher, am an important part of this research [...] being an insider exploring his own professional culture. [...] The way the research was conceived reflected my 'insideness' and how it evolved reflected my coming out of the inside and trying to look from the outside.

Dealing with my own ideology

These insights into how other researchers deal with their ideological impact with the research setting helped me to untangle who *I* am and what *I* am doing as a researcher. My recent study of Hong Kong university student autonomy, while on a language immersion programme in Britain (Holliday 2001), was problematic to write because I knew that the way I interpreted their behaviour was very much influenced by my own professional prejudices. I therefore found it very helpful, in my research methodology section, to be explicit about my ideology:

> I bring with me a discoursal baggage from applied linguistics and TESOL which tends to explain the behaviour of 'Asian students' (from the Asian Pacific rim) by reducing them to prescribed, 'culturist' national or regional cultural stereotypes.[6] (2001: 124)

This is both very useful in helping me to understand what I am doing in my research and also to help me develop a particular strategy to deal with my own ideological baggage, and then to rationalize the impact this would have on how I saw the Hong Kong students:

> I take steps to reduce this effect by employing *bracketing* [...].

This involves trying to see the Hong Kong students first and foremost as university students rather than 'Chinese' [...]. Whether or not 'Chinese culture' has anything to do with what I observe is thus something to be discovered last rather than considered first.[7] (2001: 124)

I then go on to clarify who I therefore am as the researcher:

I was very conscious, throughout the research [...] of being at the same time (i) a teacher who has been socialized into a particular TESOL professionalism which is pre-occupied with a 'learner autonomy' that resides in a certain type of oral participation in the classroom [...] and (ii) a researcher who is critical of this socialization. (2001: 124)

It then becomes clear what my research is really about, as I express my realization that 'the study thus becomes an account of my own attempts at liberation from the culturist preoccupations created by this discourse' (2001: 124). And of course this means that the major moral objective, of representing the students from Hong Kong as rounded, fully autonomous human beings, rather than as a reduced, prejudiced image, can be achieved far better.

Showing the sources of evidence

Moving back to the way in which Pierson (above) demarcates the different parts of her analysis, I also found this very useful as I moved from an overall understanding of how to deal with my own ideology to the practicalities of how to write my analysis of data. Using, like Pierson, the same referencing conventions as for quoting from literature, I was able to show clearly the interplay between (a) what I saw at the time and (b) my analysis of this. The following extract shows me using my observation notes from one of my own classes – in which I am trying to determine research project topics – as data to demonstrate how the autonomy of the students became more apparent as my own role in the classroom became more minimal. The extracts from the data are demarcated either by inverted commas or indentation; and bracketed references show where the data comes from:

Furthermore, my own power seemed reduced, as 'one group was between me (standing) and the 'centre' of the class. They were turning round to see me but not moving'. Then, for a while, I was once gain struggling to get attention as I tried to brainstorm [topics for] research projects – 'The first group did not seem to be listening, talking among themselves'. But when the same group came up with a very good idea, 'I then realized they had been considering this all the time, and talking about it regardless of my attempts to elicit' (class observation 3). As it became apparent that 'they certainly seemed to know exactly what to do' regardless of my eliciting, I left them to it, retiring from my 'teacher' position:

> I sat near them at the table in the only remaining space at the table, asking them if they minded me sitting there, to get on with my own work and be available, also listening in a little. Some of them asked me intelligent questions. [...] (Class observation 3)

(Holliday 2001: 130)

I hope that this extract demonstrates the complex, dialogue in my mind between (i) what 'seemed' to me to be happening, 'my own power' and 'my eliciting', and (ii) what I saw and heard my students do at the time of observation.

The value of this demarcated, open demonstration of the struggle to make sense of me looking at myself and my students might become easier to ascertain if contrasted with the next extract, from Canagarajah's description of students in a classroom in Sri Lanka:

> Ravi sat across the aisle from Rajan, who never seemed to have trouble with his English exercises. Apart from that, they had a lot in common; in particular, both detested the poverty, chaos, and corruption that surrounded them, and longed for the sort of full and purposeful life enjoyed by Peter in the story. However, only Rajan believed Mrs K [the teacher] when she said that English could give him that sort of life – an opportunity to go abroad to study or work. That's why he liked English classes best of all. (1999: 11)

The extract is part of a prologue to a complex book rather than part of a straight ethnographic tract. Nevertheless, it arguably conforms to the description of naturalism on page 126 above in that the author claims 'grounded knowledge' based on 'a comprehensive description', located in 'a clearly defined setting' (ie not researcher constructed) 'over an extended period'. He also claims an 'insider perspective' on the basis of 'participant observation' throughout this time[8]. This is in contrast to the 'fleeting images' of my own work (Canagarajah 1999: 46). It is this confidence in 'being there' and 'being part of the scene' that liberates the researcher from the need to show precisely on what basis he can claim that Ravi 'detested', 'longed for', 'believed' or 'liked'. He sees no need to demarcate what he has seen and heard from his interpretation. The absence of the first person removes the presence of the researcher as author and creates an appearance of objective truth in which 'only "the data", not researchers, "suggest" anything' (Golden-Biddle and Locke 1997: 4, also Richardson 1994: 520). I am not suggesting that Canagarajah's description is necessarily inaccurate, but that its proposed accuracy lacks accountability.

Conclusion: showing the process

I have tried in this paper to show both the impossibility and the possibility of qualitative researchers writing about other people. The reader might imagine that, in the end, all that is written about is the researcher saying what she thinks, with little room for the person of the researched to appear at all. This is indeed the danger; but it is a danger that cannot be addressed *until* the researcher has sorted out herself and her own voice. This showing of the workings is the only chance the qualitative researcher has to achieve rigour. In the subjective, shifting world in which she finds herself, the only thing that is certain is *that* she is interpreting on the basis of her own beliefs. Everything else – every assertion about what else is happening – has to be pivoted around this. I hope I have also demonstrated that writing is itself an integral part of the whole research process. Writing is itself:

> a *method of inquiry*, a way of finding out about yourself and your topic. Although we usually think about writing as a mode of 'telling' about the social world, writing is not just a mopping-up activity at the end of a research project. Writing is also a way of 'knowing' – a method of discovery and analysis. By writing in different ways, we discover new aspects of our topic and our relationship to it. (Richardson1994: 516, her italics)

Qualitative writing thus becomes very much an unfolding story in which the writer gradually makes sense, not only of her data, but of the total experience of which it is an artefact. This is an interactive process in which she tries to untangle and make reflexive sense of her own presence and role in the research. The written study thus becomes a complex train of thought within which her voice and her image of those of others are interwoven.

Examples used

Anderson, C. (in process). *The dominant discourse in British EFL: the methodological contradictions of a professional culture.* Department of Language Studies, Canterbury Christ Church University College.

Canagarajah, S. (1999). *Resisting Linguistic Imperialism.* Oxford: Oxford University Press.

Celik, N. C. (1999). *'McDonalds.'* Unpublished undergraduate assignment. Department of Language Studies, Canterbury Christ Church University College.

Herrera, L. (1992). Scenes of schooling: inside a girls' school in Cairo. *Cairo Papers in Social Science* 15, Monograph 1.

Holliday, A.R. (forthcoming). Finding social autonomy. In Bodycott, P. and Crew, V. (eds) *Language and cultural immersion: Perspectives on Short Term Study and Residence Abroad.* Hong Kong: Hong Kong Institute of Education.

Pierson, C. A. (1999). Ethnomethodologic analysis of accounts of feeding demented residents in long-term care. *Image: Journal of Nursing Scholarship.* 31/1 pp. 127-131

Talbot, M. (1992). The construction of gender in a teenage magazine. In Fairclough, N. (Ed), *Critical Language Awareness.* London: Addison Wesley Longman. pp. 175-199.

Notes

1 To avoid the ugly 'he or she' convention, I will use the feminine pronoun throughout, which, although still gender-specific, distances itself from the male-dominant discourse.

2 The discussion in this paper takes one theme from my recent book on qualitative research methodology (Holliday 2002).

3 The work in progress category relates to three doctoral research projects which had already been promoted from MPhil to PhD through the process of formal annual review by their supervisory panel.

4 It is not appropriate here for me to comment on the actual content of this extract in terms of the validity of the connections made between data, comment and argument. it would anyway be very difficult to judge on the basis of this very short extract which gives little indication as to the development of the whole article.

5 It is significant here that I am expanding the meaning of 'research setting' to encompass not only geographical locations, but also written texts, which, as Talbot's shows clearly, are as much places for social interaction as a McDonald's restaurant.

6 By 'culturism' I mean a way of thinking similarly constructed to sexism and racism, where individuals are packaged and reduced –

otherized – according to prescribed national cultural stereotypes (Holliday 1999).

7   Bracketing, taken from phenomenology, is a means for looking at the social world in a particular way to avoid easy answers and 'make the familiar strange ', by 'temporarily suspend[ing] all commonsense assumptions' in order to 'make visible the practices through which taken-for-granted realities are accomplished' (Gubrium and Holstein 1997: 40, citing Schutz, Holliday 2002: 185). Baumann (1996: 2) demonstrates how this strategy can be formulated to deal with the particular baggage the researcher brings with her. Hence, because someone with my professional socialization will take prescriptions about 'Chinese culture' as the easy answer, *for me* the more neutral stance is seeing Chinese students primarily as university students.

8   Canagarajah does talk at length about the 'tricky issues of power inherent in the relationship between the researcher and subjects' which 'he or she is necessarily objectifying', and about the impossibility of 'pure' answers (1999: 49).

References

Baumann, G. (1996). *Contesting Culture*. Cambridge: Cambridge University Press.

Denzin, N. K. and Lincoln, Y. S. (eds.) (1994). *A Handbook of Qualitative Research*. Thousand Oaks, CA: Sage.

Fine, M. and Weis, L. (1998). Writing the 'wrongs' of fieldwork: confronting our own research /writing dilemmas in urban ethnographies. In Shacklock, G. and Smyth, J. (Eds.), *Being Reflexive in Critical Educational and Social Research*. London: Falmer Press. Pp.13-35.

Foley, D. (1998). On writing reflexive realist narratives. In Shacklock, G. and Smyth, J. (Eds.), *Being Reflexive in Critical Educational and Social Research*. London: Falmer Press. Pp. 110-129.

Geertz, C. (1993) *The Interpretation of cultures: Selected essays*. London: Fontana.

Golden-Biddle, K. and Locke, K. D. (1997). *Composing Qualitative Research*. Thousand Oaks, Ca.: Sage Publications.

Guba, E. G. and Lincoln, Y. S. (1994). Competing paradigms in qualitative research. In Denzin, N.K. and Lincoln, Y. S. (eds.) *Handbook of Qualitative Research*. Thousand Oaks, CA: Sage Publications. pp.105-117.

Gubrium, J. F. and Holstein, J. A. (1997). *The New Language of Qualitative Research*. New York: Oxford University Press.

Hammersley, M. and Atkinson, P. (1995). *Ethnography: Principles in Practice*. London: Routledge.

Holliday, A. R. (1999). Small cultures *Applied Linguistics* 20/2: 237-264

Holliday, A. R. (2001). Finding social autonomy. In Bodycott, P. and Crew, V. (eds.), *Language and Cultural Immersion: perspectives on short term study and residence abroad*. pp.123-132.

Holliday, A.R. (2002). *Doing and Writing Qualitative Research*. London: Sage

Miller, S. M., Nelson, M. W. and Moore, M. T. (1998). Caught in the paradigm gap: qualitative researchers' lived experience and the politics of epistemology. *American Educational Research Journal* 35/3. pp.337-416.

Richardson, L. (1994). 'Writing: a method of enquiry.' In Denzin, N.K. and Lincoln, Y. S. (eds.) *Handbook of Qualitative Research*. Thousand Oaks, Ca.: Sage Publications. pp.516-529.

Robson, C. (1993). *Real World Research*. Oxford: Blackwell.

9 Is it a wood, or are they trees?

KEITH JOHNSON

Lancaster University

Generalization in applied linguistics: an 'immense divide'

The topic of this paper is 'generalization in applied language studies'. It is one that exercised Pit Corder not a little ('significant generalization' receives six mentions in the index to his *Introducing Applied Linguistics*). The topic was chosen partly because it relates to the unity/diversity theme of the conference – generalizations being expressions of unity or similitude - but mainly because it is an issue of considerable current importance. Three years ago Julian Edge and Keith Richards focused the debate, which has been going on for a while, in their important paper on the topic (Edge & Richards 1998). More recently there has been Dick Allwright's paper for the 8th IALS Symposium for Language Teacher Educators (Allwright 2000), together with Brumfit's inspired and inspiring book *Individual Freedom in Language Teaching* (Brumfit 2001). Both these pieces have interesting things to say on the topic.

Applied linguists are currently discussing this issue because in their practice they tend to fall on one or other side of an immense divide. On the one hand we have in our midst the positivists, or postpositivists as some would have it, living in a scientific world which seeks universal explanations, universal truths, universal generalizations. On the other are those who work within the so-called New Paradigm - the constructionists, the postmodernists. They seek context-sensitive understanding rather than universal truth. The rift is so apparently complete that it is as if an iron curtain has descended across applied language studies. Those on either side of this curtain or wall, sit and glare at each other. Maybe they meet at BAAL meetings and on Christmas Day, briefly to sing carols together before resuming hostilities, but not much more than that. This is why the issue needs attention.

The title of this paper talks about trees and woods, thus focusing attention on one small part of the bigger divide – the particular versus the general - though it should perhaps be added that the paper does in fact range – perhaps too cavalierly - over a cluster of ideas, including contextualized versus decontextualised, and hypothesis-driven versus data-driven research. But to stay with trees and woods: tree work, tree research, is highly context-sensitive. On that side of the wall is a land of case studies, life histories, stake-holder diaries. The inhabitants there are ultra aware of the dangers of transplanting from one set of circumstances to another. As a consequence of these characteristics, those on the other side of the wall criticise tree research as inconsequential, 'generalization-shy'. Tree researchers, their enemies say, see the world as a 'heap of unconnected little things' (to mutilate a phrase of Coleridge's). They gaze around at the glory of diversity and are mesmerized into inaction.

Wood research, on the other hand, sees the whole picture. The land on that side of the wall is full of experiments, questionnaires, statistics, tests. The inhabitants there attempt to reach findings that can easily be transplanted, which will grow in any soil. But their hostile neighbours on the other side regard the generalizations in one or both of two ways. Either they are false, arrivable at only by oversimplifying the issues involved. In this case the generalizations will wither and die if any attempt at transplantation is made. Or they are inconsequential, accounting for such a small part of the total behaviour as to be valueless. In that case they are regarded as weeds.

The argument to be developed here is that we need to see both trees and woods, to find ways of, Picasso-like, contemplating two different perspectives at the same time – one looking closely at individual trees, the other looking down on the wood from on high. The reasons for needing to combine these perspectives will be discussed, and ways of achieving the combination briefly considered.

The emergence of a long 'Tree Age'

In 1987, Chomsky gave a talk for the British Open University Psychological Society. In answer to a question at the end, he briefly discourses on the nature of abstractions in science. His example is taken from cellular biology and relates to the concept of the neural net. He points out that a neural net, as an assembly of neurons, will have various realizations which can be quite dramatically different from each other. They may therefore be regarded, and studied, by the scientist as quite different phenomena. But the scientist may decide to ignore the differences, to focus on what is similar in the different realizations, and hence to employ the notion of a neural net, which is essentially an abstraction. To choose an example closer to home of a choice to emphasise differences or similarities: phoneticians may analyse two sounds – an aspirated and an unaspirated version of a plosive for example. Their analysis can draw on differences – they are, after all, different sounds. Or they may wish to focus on similarities – the fact that they may both be allophones of the same phoneme. The phonetician may chose to see two trees or one wood.

What determines the choice whether to perceive similarities or dissimilarities, unity or diversity? One determinant is prevailing *Zeitgeist*. There are Wood Ages and Tree Ages. Chomsky definitely belonged to a Wood Age. He abstracts, refines, purifies, and generalizes. He talks about homogenous speech communities and ideal speaker listeners. These two concepts get him into particular trouble with those like Dell Hymes who might be seen as heralding the beginning of a long Tree Age which we are still living through. Hymes' (1970) attack on the notion of the ideal speaker listener is well known, in a world full of individuals, some with disabilities affecting language performance, all with their own idiolects, accents, dialects. Equally well known is Stern's (1983) perception that since World War 2 there is no such thing as a homogeneous speech community. Walk down any street in London, New York, Sydney - all in countries which were once regarded as monolithically 'English speaking' - and you will hear literally dozens of languages, all spoken of course by non-ideal speaker listeners.

Since the 1970s it has been one long hymn in praise of diversity, worthy of the poet Hopkins. The area of sociolinguistics is almost *based* on the notion of variation, variability, of demonstrating that what was once regarded as unified, similar, is in fact diverse, distinct. The advantages of this shift from wood to trees have been very considerable indeed, in almost every area of applied language studies. In the field of language use, we have become aware of, and even accepting of, different accents, dialects, different Englishes. By and large language planners have long since ceased trying to impose one monolithic version of English on the world. I still remember the shock I experienced in the mid 1970s when the University of Reading started one of the first pre-sessional courses, if not *the* first indeed, and it was accepted that non-native speaker teachers could teach on it. It was not shock of the 'shock horror' sort at all, but the shock of the unexpected after the firmly fixed norm that only native speakers should, where available, teach the English language. In language teaching methodology, the distinctly woody concept of 'method' has well and truly been felled. Timber! There is no *one* right method, we now accept. We further accept that generalized approaches, Communicative Language Teaching for example, cannot be exported intact around the world, like television sets or refrigerators, with the maximum required for transition being different shaped plugs for different countries. The concept of 'appropriate methodologies' has now come to fruition. In terms of research, a significant part of the research community has indeed turned away from methods which regard subjects as decontextualised rats, and has developed techniques which situate not subjects but stake holders in contexts, not laboratories. The benefits of the Age of the Tree flower all around us. They are benefits which may be accepted almost unequivocally, together with the notion that in what Brumfit calls 'socially embedded activities' (and this includes language teaching studies), approaches that fail to account in one way or another for uniqueness, context sensitivity, are lacking.

Notice that the word used earlier was 'Zeitgeist', not 'fashion'. This is because what occurs between Chomsky and now is not a mere change of fashion, but an appeal to a different tradition, the development of a different paradigm. Tree research has its roots in a broad paradigm shift, which occurs in many disciplines. We shall here briefly review the change. Crotty describes the change in terms of a movement from positivism to interpretivism, thus:

A positivist approach would follow the methods of the natural sciences and, by way of allegedly value-free, detached observation, seek to identify universal features of humanhood . The interpretivist approach, to the contrary, *looks for culturally derived and historically situated interpretations of the social life-world* Crotty (1998: 67)

Crotty further exemplifies in the terms of the late 19th century philosopher Windelband who distinguishes between the study of nature and the study of human affairs. In the case of nature, he argues, science is looking for consistencies, regularities, 'laws' (the Greek word *nomos* is used here). In the case of human affairs we are concerned with the individual case (the *idios*). So Windelband talks of natural science seeking what is *nomothetic* and the human and social sciences seeking what is *idiographic*. Another philosopher of the same age, Rickert, similarly talks of a *generalizing method* in the natural sciences, and an *individualizing method* in the social sciences. In other words, woods and trees.

The need for both approaches

So the movement from wood to trees may be accounted for in terms of '-isms'. Indeed, as Edge & Richards (1998) admit, the '-isms' on the tree side of the wall are so numerous as to cause some disarray. It is the particularly diffuse '-ism' of postmodernism that Brumfit (2001) sees as the intellectual homeland of what is here being called tree work. In his

final chapter he discusses our tree/wood debate in terms of reading the
Iliad. About the tree side he says:

> ... our grounding in culture is ... crucial. We cannot treat all
> philosophical questions as variants on a single set of deculturized
> logical premises. Reading the *Iliad* in the twentieth century's
> experience of war is different from reading it in 1910, reading it in
> Greek is different from reading it in English .... Rereading differs
> from reading ... (Brumfit 2001: 184)

Where the Old Paradigm fails to account for such context-sensitive
factors, it is inadequate. But has the New Paradigm replaced the
necessity for the old one? If we tend the trees, will the wood look after
itself? The different sides of the wall have their entrenched answers, of
course. Those of a positivist bent will argue that it is central to
academic, scientific enquiry to seek generalizations, while the
committed postmodernist will view the 'urge to generalize' as part of
the Enlightenment's unwelcome baggage, and will discard it.

But it is interesting that even among those sympathetic towards the
New Paradigm there is often a realization that generalizations will be
available and useful. Take Brumfit first. Alongside his realization of
diversity (in the quote above) there comes recognition of universality.
In relation to the *Iliad*:

> We have to account for the ways in which our experience is
> triangulated many times over: when we read, let us say, Homer,
> Virgil, or Dante, we share experiences with other humans who may
> never read them in the language we read them in, and who may
> never live at the same time as us ... If there is no universal subject,
> what happens when we read the classics, or when we talk to each
> other at all? (Brumfit 2001: 183)

This passage captures the notion that whatever *dissimilarities* occur
(between activities, experiences, ideas, entities), there are *similarities*
that can be perceived, universalities that need noting. Similar support is
available in sometimes unexpected sources. Max Weber, a sociologist
closely associated with the New Paradigm, believed that there are
general laws which may explain aspects of human behaviour. And – to
take yet another domain - in the literature on skills psychology, the
uniqueness of events is often pointed out - each tennis stroke is a
unique event, different from all other tennis strokes ever played. Yet the
point is always also made that generalizations (about tennis strokes
inter alia) are also available. As Craik (1943) puts it, skilled
performance results in 'a response which is unique on each occasion,
although it is determinate and based on constants which are, at least in

principle, discoverable'. A final example is from the applied linguistics field. Allwright's name is nowadays associated with the New Paradigm. He of all people appreciates the value of observing the particular, the local. Yet he also has concerns for the general, the global. Indeed, a major theme of his 2000 paper is the relationship between the local and the global, and he talks about 'trying to decide what the fundamental principles are behind what we are trying to achieve'. He recognizes the need for global thinking. So although there are many on the tree side who in principle have no time for the universal, this is not a view shared by all. There is a position that wants to see the wood as well as the trees.

Had this paper been written twenty years ago, a valid complaint might have been that 'we looked at the wood but ignored the trees'. This might have been exemplified by reference to a topic already mentioned, the development of Communicative Language Teaching which was exported into different contexts with little thought given to contextual appropriacy. But a more up-to-date grouch is that now 'we look at the trees but ignore the wood'. New Paradigm work that is highly context sensitive, acutely aware of the uniqueness of everything, can lead to the failure to perceive – and refusal to look for - existing and perhaps important similarities.

Edge & Richards are well aware of the 'generalization-shy' label which New Paradigm research attracts, and they move in the direction of addressing the issue by discussing a notion of 'transferability' whereby information derived from one context can be considered in relation to another context. 'We expect', they say:

> information transfer across educational contexts to be most effectively created by the reader, from richly contextualized, problematized and theorized reports and interpretations, as they are resonant with the reader's own contextualized experience. The reader understands (what is important in) his or her own situation(s). (Edge & Richards 1998: 350)

They do not, by conviction, want to go further into the wood than this. They are happy with 'information transfer' rather than 'generalizations', and with 'reader resonance' rather than anything more formal. There is something admirable in this stopping short, a kind of respect for the diversity of things. But there is also something frustrating – one is left wishing the researchers would be prepared to sift through all the available reports and interpretations, then exercise - and express - judgements as to which are likely to be of general relevance - more worthy, if nothing else, of the reader's resonance chamber. Their stance will not be enough for the positivists on the wood side of the wall, but it is at least a peep through a chink in the wall, to glimpse what lies on the other side.

Apart from the need for generalizations in the field, there is another reason why we need the two approaches together. To explore it, consider what Brumfit says before the *Iliad* quotations given earlier:

> The key point for any science is not the impossibility of shared experience, but the relationship between what can be shared and what cannot. Each of us is both universal and unique in our culture. . . . . (Brumfit 2001: 183)

We have to find ways of identifying and distinguishing what is universal and what unique, the universal being the territory of one side of the wall, the unique the territory of the other. We are here into territorial disputes. As an example of such a dispute, consider the debate on the appropriate way to study writing processes. Irmscher's (1987) position is typical of tree researchers. 'In studying the act of writing, 'he says, 'investigators should ... disrupt as little as possible the natural setting of writing with cameras, tapes, and talk-aloud protocols'. The argument is that any attempt to decontextualize writing and study it in an experimental environment means that the processes observed will not be those naturally followed when one writes normally. The wood researchers counterargue that there are cognitive processes involved in writing that will be present in *any* writing, however decontextualized (because they are not controlled by context) or experimentally induced. Trees are trees are trees, they argue, whether in a small copse, a rain forest, or a pot on the patio. In this debate one side is saying that we are dealing with universal cognitive processes which can be studied out of context, while the other argues that the processes are distorted if taken out of context. Both claim that writing processes lie on their side of the wall.

It is easy to find similar territorial disputes in applied language studies: are Foster and Skehan, or Bygate, capturing general truths about task processing in their work, or is the research deficient because it does not take contextual/educational constraints sufficiently into consideration? Does work by Doughty and Pica, Long and others on learner behaviour in information gap tasks capture general truths about human processing, or would their findings be otherwise in different, well-specified educational settings? Are SLA morpheme acquisition orders really universal[1]?

Combining the approaches

How can we answer such questions? In one area – that of problem solving – there has been context-free research, establishing possible hypotheses about general cognitive processes. There has also been context-bound work which can test the generality of the hypotheses and potentially identify context-specific parameters whose effect may lead to modifications in the generalities. Smagorinsky (1989) surveys a number of studies on problem solving that compare naturally collected data with data collected 'artificially' through concurrent verbalization. His conclusion is that 'the cumulative results of these studies suggest that the internal structure of thought processes is not disturbed when subjects utter ... verbalization'.

Whether Smagorinsky's conclusion is the right one is not the issue here, any more than it is to pass judgement on the statements about writing processes made earlier. What is relevant is the procedure for establishing what aspects of a behaviour are universal, thus solving some territorial disputes. The most important feature is that the procedure involves a combination of context-free and context-bound work; neither one is, by itself, sufficient. The wood researchers need tree research to endorse the universality of processes across contexts. Tree researchers need wood research to identify and characterise cognitive and information processing universals.

In the research I have been doing for the past year (reported in Johnson *in press*) I feel a strong need for this combination. The research has been looking at the processes task designers adopt when designing materials for class use. The data I have are sixteen two-hour long protocols of designers verbalizing concurrently as they produce a task following a given brief. The work started much more than a year ago and initially involved psychology colleagues. Certain of them were confident that experimentally-collected, decontextualised data will capture general cognitive design behaviour. Hence the laboratory-collected think-aloud protocols. One can well imagine applied linguists of a New Paradigm persuasion scowling like Beethoven when confronted by this work[2]. They would insist that data needs to be collected of individuals designing tasks 'naturally' as part of their work. My own view has three parts to it. One is that there are doubtless universal cognitive processes at work which can be initially suggested by context-free research. This is an important message to the New Paradigm – that not all research work has to involve complex tree surgery, and that context-free work has a role to play if one is dealing with aspects of behaviours which are likely to be cognitively universal. Secondly, it is likely that the data collected are far far richer than the critical tree researchers will admit. Richness is sometimes regarded as the sole prerogative of New Paradigm work, but this is not always the case. But the third part of my view is that there is a strong need to test context-free findings with context-bound, situated work, and the aim is to do this in the future. The motivation for requiring this is to be able to distinguish, as Brumfit says we should, between the universal and the unique.

If the aim is to combine the two approaches in one way or another, there are various degrees of combination that might be feasible. At one end of the spectrum is the view that one research approach will be able to encompass the two elements. This seems to have been Weber's view. As was implied earlier, he holds 'that the one scientific method . . . . should cater for nomothetic and idiographic inquiry' (Crotty 1998: 68). Woods (1996) seems to make a similar claim. His book provides a large-scale study of teacher cognitions, and he describes the model he develops as 'ethno-cognitive'. The very name suggests the fusion. Ethnographical methodology (the 'ethno' part of his label) suggests contextually-bound tree research, while the word 'cognitive' conjures up context-free wood work, to do with mental operations found throughout the human species.

How does Woods attempt to achieve this grafting together of the two approaches? Given the area he is studying, it is not surprising that he should be faced with great diversity. He has to work hard to find valid generalizations. He develops a system of analysis for his data, but claims that:

> what is crucial is not the specification of the levels of the system .
> . . . What is suggested by this study, is rather a closed set of 'patterns which connect' – the *types of relationships* between levels including goals, means and content. (Woods 1996: 115)

He seems to be saying that because of the richness and diversity of his data, conventional types of generalization (expressed in terms of levels) do not hold. If commonalities are to be found, they need to be in terms of some new entity, some new currency. This 'new currency' is, for him, the 'relationship'.

Whether or not Woods succeeds in making useful generalizations in terms of relationships is not relevant here. The point is that if we do wish to seek generalizations in complex and highly context-sensitive data, it is likely that we will have to be flexible, creative and prepared to look in new places. We will have to find new ways of defining and characterising the wood.

Another contender for a 'new currency' may be the *process* (as opposed to the *product*), and surely one reason for recent interest in process is that it makes new and potentially more powerful types of generalization available to us. It is worth observing in passing that sometimes applied linguists seem to be offering processes as a *substitute* for generalizations, whereas they are in fact a *different* type of generalization. Thus when Exploratory Practice proposes its procedures for teacher development, it would appear to be making claims about these processes, that they are something deemed exportable, something universally applicable from context to context. The claim surely needs as much caution as if what were being exported was a set of products. This issue aside, efforts to bring the two sides of the wall together are certain to involve the search for new ways of expressing similitude, of which the process may be one.

If *fusion* of the two approaches à la Weber or à la Woods is not possible, then we should seek combinations of the two. These may go in either direction – from wood to trees or vice versa. At a recent internal seminar run in Lancaster by Allwright and his colleagues in the Exploratory Practice Centre, we were discussing in groups why the impact on the established applied linguistics world of EP work undertaken by teachers is sometimes disappointing. I put forward the view that perhaps this is because the research is philosophically postmodernist - tree research which will not in principle allow its findings to be transplanted to some other wood and therefore would not appeal to audiences of wood-dwellers world-wide. One member of the group I was in eloquently pointed out the shortcomings of the alternative, overgeneralist wood approach, giving CLT again as an example of how universalist ideas need to become contextually appropriate if they are to succeed. Agreed. But, one might point out, this is indeed what has happened to a greater or lesser extent world wide, and the mediating body has been the expanding field of language teaching innovation management. Over time, monolithic, decontextualised CLT has become a series of local, contextualized CLTs. The paradigm here has been to move from universalist generalization to contextualized, situated use. It starts out with a plan for a wood and then, albeit late in the day, considers the trees. We may also expect the reverse to be equally possible. The starting point then would be pieces of context-sensitive, highly situated research which go through a process of universalization – a process which incidentally might solve the problem being discussed in the Lancaster seminar, of making research relevant to world-wide wood-dwellers. Both these paradigms involve a movement – from local to global, from particular to general, or vice versa.

Achieving 'complementary cyclical development'

We shall here finally develop the theme that however difficult, or even impossible, it is to destroy our symbolic wall, this dialectic of moving from one side to the other is crucial to applied linguistic work. To this must be added that the movement needs to be from one side to the other and back again. The point will be made in relation to various contexts, the first being the task-design procedure work mentioned earlier. The data – think-aloud protocols - are highly 'messy' in the technical sense of the word - huge mixtures of heterogeneous materials onto which it is difficult to impose any order at all. Trying to describe task designers' behaviour is like trying to landscape garden the Amazonian rainforest, and attempting to see any wood for the trees has been a daunting challenge. In the spirit of grounded theory it was decided not to start the coding from theory-driven hypothesis which would then be mapped onto the data. The procedure developed (not in any sense an original one of course, and reminiscent of grounded theory procedures) involved approaching each protocol as an individual case, at first deliberately avoiding any search for commonalities. So Protocol 1 and then Protocol 2 were coded without any attempt to find common codes (codes being the building blocks of generalizations). But then with two protocols coded began a process of searching for similarities between them. This process led to modifications in the initial coding, to capture identified similarities. Protocols were then added one by one, first being considered as individual cases, then seeking generalizations which led to modifications in all coding already done. With sixteen protocols the process was ferociously time consuming. In effect it entailed sixteen re-coding operations, each time changing codes already assigned to more and more data. But the end result has the advantage that it is sensitive to both the trees and the wood.

It is important to note that the dialectic is here two-way. The movement is from particular to general in the first place. But it then becomes from general to particular as well, as the process of generalizing over Protocols 1 and 2 for example, feed into the consideration of Protocol 3. Both perspectives enrich the other. The particular adds depth to the general; the general adds scope to the particular. This is true whichever the starting point. So, to pursue that by-now hoary example of CLT's development: its universalist origins become enriched by being made context-sensitive. The procedure does more than make the method more *appropriate* to different context, it *enriches* it, makes it more powerful as a conception. It becomes not just an 'appropriate methodology' – giving as it were something to the situation in which it is used - but an 'enriched methodology' as well. The situation gives the methodology something back.

Once this idea of 'complementary cyclical development' had been accepted, it was astonishing to see how often it made its appearance in other discussions. Allwright talks about it in his 2000 paper. His starting point is the Friends of the Earth slogan: *think globally, act locally*. He is interested in the interaction of the local and the global, and he seems also to come to the conclusion that each enriches the other.

The idea also calls to mind a paper by Scardamalia & Bereiter (1991). Their work was initially in the field of writing expertise. But this led them to consider expertise in general, culminating in a insightful book on the subject, Bereiter & Scardamalia (1993), entitled *Surpassing Ourselves: An inquiry into the nature and implications of expertise*. Scardamalia & Bereiter (1991) is mainly about writing and reading expertise, but the paper contains the beginnings of their general model of expertise, potentially applicable to all domains. The model is concerned with the 'interaction between domain knowledge and immediate cases' (p. 175). When writers compose they apply the knowledge they have accumulated (domain knowledge) to the particular writing task at hand (the immediate case). What distinguishes expert from non-expert, Scardamalia & Bereiter argue, is that with the expert but not the novice, the traffic is two-way. The expert learns from the experience of a particular writing task, and is able to feed what has been learned into general domain knowledge. So not only do experts apply what they know *in* new writing, they also increase their knowledge *by* new writing. The unifying idea of the model is, Scardamalia & Bereiter claim, 'an interaction between the general and the particular' (p. 177). Wood and trees again. Perhaps the same may be said for the expert applied linguist. Perhaps the Good Applied Linguist is the one who is able to integrate details of particular instances into general statements, unifying the diverse; looking at trees to increase knowledge about woods, and using knowledge of woods the better to understand trees.

A final expression of the complementary cyclical development idea, in a different domain, is found in a paper by the psychologist Allport (1981). The paper's title indicates its relevance to the matters we are considering. It is called *The general and the unique in psychological science*. Allport begins by discussing two sorts of statements that a psychologist 'can properly make'. These are:

(1)   The problem of human personality concerns me deeply
(2)   The problem of Bill's personality concerns me deeply

He begins by saying that (in ways we have been discussing) these two statements are 'poles apart'. His consideration of how we should relate the study of the two contains the following passage:

Why should we not start with individual behaviour as a source of hunches, ... and then seek our generalizations ..., but finally come back to the individual – not for the mechanical application of laws ..., but for a fuller, supplementary, and more accurate assessment than we are now able to give? I suspect that the reason our present assessments are now so often feeble and sometimes even ridiculous, is because we do not take this final step. We stop with our wobbly laws of personality and seldom confront them with the concrete person.' (Allport 1981: 65)

To allow for cyclical development in both directions, one might add to this paragraph another allowing the possibility of starting with general statements and then moving through individuals back to generalizations.

This paper has suggested that for a variety of reasons the two quite different research traditions we have been discussing need to be combined. Ways in which these traditions may be brought together have been considered, particularly by seeking new currencies for expressing generalizations, and by utilizing a strategy of 'complementary cyclical development'. If we manage the required combination, we will provide the field with ways of making theoretical discussion possible by means of statements which, while capturing generalizations, yet have sufficient context sensitivity to retain face validity for practitioners in the field.

Notes

1 Examples of the work referred to in this paragraph are: Foster & Skehan (1999), Bygate (1999), Doughty & Pica (1986), and Long (1983).
2 The Beethoven simile is taken from E. Annie Proulx's novel *The Shipping News* (London: Fourth Estate, 1993).

Thanks are due to two anonymous reviewers who provided feedback on a draft of this paper.

References

Allport, G. W. (1981) The general and the unique in psychological science. In Reason, P., & Rowan, J. (eds) *Human Inquiry: A sourcebook of new paradigm research* John Wiley: Chichester, 63-76

Allwright, R. L. (2000) Exploratory practice: An 'appropriate methodology' for language teacher development? Paper delivered at the 8th IALS Symposium for Language teacher Educators, Edinburgh, November 2000, unpublished manuscript

Bereiter, C., & Scardamalia, M. (1993) *Surpassing Ourselves: An inquiry into the nature and implications of expertise* Chicago: Open Court

Brumfit, C. J. (2001) *Individual Freedom in Language Teaching* Oxford: Oxford University Press

Bygate, M. (1999) Quality of language and purpose of task: patterns of learners' language on two oral communication tasks. *Language Teaching Research* 185-214

Craik, K. J. W. (1943) *The Nature of Explanation* Cambridge: Cambridge University Press

Crotty, M. (1998) *The Foundations of Social Research* London: Sage Publications

Doughty, C., & Pica, T. (1986) 'Information gap' tasks: do they facilitate second language acquisition? *TESOL Quarterly* 20, 305-25

Edge, J., & Richards, K. (1998) 'May I see your warrant, please?': justifying outcomes in qualitative research. *Applied Linguistics* 19/3: 334-356

Foster, P., & Skehan, P. (1999) The influence of source of planning and focus of planning on task-based performance. *Language Teaching Research* 3/3, 215-47

Hymes, D. (1970) On communicative competence. In Gumperz, J.J., and Hymes, D. (eds.) *Directions in Sociolinguistics* New York: Holt, Rinehart and Winston

Irmscher, W. (1987) Finding a comfortable identity. *College Composition and Communication* February, 81-7

Johnson, K. (in press) *Designing Language Teaching Tasks* Basingstoke: Palgrave Macmillan

Long, M. (1983) Native speaker/non-native speaker conversation and the negotiation of comprehensible input. *Applied Linguistics* 4: 126-41

Scardamalia, M., & Bereiter, C. (1991) Literate expertise. In Ericsson, K., A. & Smith, J. (eds) (1991 *Towards a General Theory of Expertise* Cambridge: Cambridge University Press, 172-194

Smagorinsky, P. (1989) The reliability and validity of protocol analysis. *Written Communication* 6/4: 463-79

Stern, H. H. (1983) *Fundamental Concepts of Language Teaching* Oxford: Oxford University Press

Woods, D. (1996) Teacher Cognition in Language Teaching: Beliefs, decision-making and classroom practice Cambridge: Cambridge University Press

10 Children mediating their immigrant parents' learning of L2 English: a focus on verb learning in homework interactions

PILAR DURÁN

University of Reading

Introduction

Hispanic immigrant workers in the US, as well as immigrant workers from other cultures, have been found in previous research to speak a second language (L2) using little or no verbal morphology. The immigrant workers considered here are those who, typically, are poorly educated and have a low income and socio-economic background in their home countries. They migrate to richer countries in search of work and new opportunities, remain in their own community in the target country, and hence do not normally become integrated into the target culture. Usually, they have not received formal instruction in the language of the target country. These immigrant workers' L2 production has been studied in the L2 research as representing L2 learning in untutored/naturalistic environments and they are typically called untutored learners. What researchers mean when they say that immigrant workers as untutored learners use little or no verbal morphology is that lexical verbs appear in the bare or progressive forms and the copula 'be' and auxiliaries are missing or appear in limited forms (Klein and Perdue, 1992, 1997; Lardiere, 1998; Meisel, 1997; Schumman, 1987; Vainikka and Young-Scholten, 1996). Only a few auxiliaries have been documented as occurring in untutored learners' L2, mainly 'do', 'can' and 'is'. These auxiliaries tend to be produced in the place of other auxiliaries. For example, 'do' may appear instead of 'does' and 'did'.

Another problem that US society is facing is the poor performance in school of the children of Hispanic immigrant workers. In an effort to overcome this problem, the local school officials devised school homework sharing activities. These school homework sharing activities have been argued to have a positive effect on children's literacy development (Bronfenbrenner, 1974; Henderson & Berla, 1994; Kellaghan, Sloane, Alvarez, & Bloom, 1993 as cited in Paratore, Melzi, & Krol-Sinclair, 1999). However, these activities might also be predicted to contribute to parents' L2 learning—a dimension that has yet to be investigated.

The aim of this study is to examine the interaction between the parent and the child during homework and compare it with another daily typical interaction such as that at meal-time. The input given to the L2 learning parents by their children will be studied. In addition, the parents' role in the interaction will also be explored in order to find what they do to help themselves learn English.

Input and Interaction Studies

The possible effect of input has been widely studied in both first language (L1) acquisition and second language (L2) learning. Researchers have argued for the positive effect of input in L1 (Clark, 1998; Lieven, 1994; Snow, 1994) and in L2 in classroom settings (Doughty, 1994; Ellis, 1998). By contrast, few studies have been dedicated to the study of input in untutored L2 learning, possibly because of the difficulty entailed in gathering data on this input. The main input providers in L1 and L2 in classroom settings are typically the caregivers and the teachers respectively who are generally available to the researcher. The main input provider of an immigrant worker who is learning L2 in an untutored environment is more difficult to discern, and it is not usually feasible to collect data on the input she/he receives: An immigrant worker is not to be found at a predictable place and time in the company of the input provider as is normally the case for children learning L1 and students of L2. In what follows we present a review about what has been said concerning the role of input in L1 and L2 in classroom settings. Though this study is about L2 learning, L1 research is also discussed, because the tools and research relating to L1 acquisition have always been found useful for the study of L2, and they were applied in this study of input in L2.

Two main issues have been considered in the study of input: the importance of frequency and the importance of negative evidence. The role of frequency in the input has been broadly studied in L1 acquisition. L1 researchers argue that those words and structures most common in the input are learned first and appeared most frequently in the learners' language production. Researchers such as Choi and Gopnik (1995), Goldfield (1993), Tardif, Shatz, & Naigles (1997) found that the words most used by the mothers are the ones that form the early vocabulary of the children. The frequency of morphology in the input has also been associated with the learners' production of morphology. L1 researchers claim that children's order of acquisition of verbal morphology depends on the frequency of that morphology in caregivers' input (Gathercole, Sebastián, and Soto, 1999; Shirai and Andersen, 1995). Durán (2001) also found some parallels between input and production of verbal morphology in L2 learning in untutored environments: The verbal morphology most frequent in the input (i.e., bare form 'speak', progressive form 'speaking', and the copula 'is') was the most frequent morphology produced by L2 untutored learners.

With respect to negative evidence, the debate is still open about its existence and its effectiveness in L1 acquisition. However, the presence of negative evidence in L2 in classroom settings is unquestionable since teachers typically offer instruction and/or corrective feedback. Furthermore, though some researchers (Schwartz, 1993; Schwartz and Gubala-Ryzak, 1992) question the long term effect of negative evidence, most researchers (Ellis, 1998; White, 1989) agree that negative evidence has a positive effect in L2 learning, at least in the short term.

Regarding interaction, studies of L2 learning have extensively argued for its positive effect in L2 classrooms (Chaudron, 1977; Gass and Veronique, 1994; Loschky, 1994). In those settings in which interaction occurs, the learners negotiate meaning with the input provider. Through that negotiation of meaning, it is argued that the learners may learn not only meaning but also grammar of the L2. Furthermore, interactions where the learner has to use the L2 may result in an error by the learner that may be corrected by the input provider and finally the learner has a chance to correct herself/himself.

All these findings lead us to conclude that the setting that provides input including the whole range of verbal morphology (i.e., third person –s, past –ed, progressive –ing, perfect –en, and different forms of the copula as well as auxiliaries) most frequently, will be the most advantageous setting for L2 learning. Furthermore, we assume that those settings in which input offers negative evidence most often and that derive most interaction in the L2 will be most beneficial for L2 learning. Consequently, this study starts with a general hypothesis: The input to parents from children would be quantitatively and qualitatively richer during homework than during a daily typical interaction such as that at meal-time. This general hypothesis is investigated in terms of these more specific hypotheses:

Children would speak proportionally more English during homework than at meal-time. This hypothesis is based on the prediction that as homework is typically in English, the mothers have less opportunity to avoid using English.

Children would produce relatively richer morphology during homework. Homework provides a broader range of reference for which morphology is required.

Children would provide a higher proportion of negative evidence during homework. Expectations were that children and mothers would be more likely to be in a teaching/learning mode during the school related activity. Therefore, corrections and explanations would appear more frequently during homework than at meal-time.

Being in the teaching/learning mode likely to be required in the school related activity, mothers would ask questions about the English language and would correct themselves after being corrected proportionally more often during homework than at meal-time.

A particularly innovative aspect of this study is the fact that children were considered as 'language teachers' and mothers as 'language learners', thus reversing the roles associated with traditional language acquisition studies.

Methods

Ten children and their Hispanic immigrant mothers participated in this study. The children were the L2 input providers and the mothers the L2 untutored learners. The children's age ranged from seven to ten years old. They had been attending an American school for at least two years before the onset of the study and they had been speaking English at home for a minimum of two years. At the start of the study all children were fluent speakers of English. The mothers were all untutored learners of English who had not received formal instruction in English in their home countries or in the US. Most mother/child dyads spent around seven hours per day together of which approximately half an hour was spent sharing school homework.

Two conversations were recorded for each dyad: a homework conversation and a meal-time conversation. There are two exceptions: one mother never recorded her meal-time conversation and became impossible to reach after the homework conversation; in the other case, the tape recorder of the second mother's homework conversation did not work and by the time the mother agreed to record it again, it was too long after the meal-time recording and the mother had started to attend English classes.

During the homework conversation, the child picked a book that she/he read and discussed with the mother. This was a natural activity for the children and the mothers. The schools in the area where all the participants lived had enforced school homework sharing long before the onset of this study. Therefore, the activity was natural, spontaneous, and hence ecologically valid. For the meal-time conversation, the mothers were given a tape and a tape-recorder and asked to audio-tape an ordinary conversation at dinner. Dinner was suggested because it was believed to be an ideal time for the gathering of the whole family and a time when a typical conversation would happen.

Each conversation was supposed to last thirty minutes. This was not always achieved. During homework, some children were not willing to stay focused for thirty minutes at a time. At meal-time, some mothers failed to record for as long as thirty minutes. Despite this, we collected an average of twenty minutes of conversation per dyad during homework and at meal-time. Conversations varied in the number of utterances and verbs in English. Therefore, we used percentages to control for such variations. It is important to mention here that we used percentages to investigate the quality and quantity of the English input in each conversation, homework and meal-time. However, we have to keep in mind that while the dyads spent approximately thirty minutes per day doing homework, conversations similar to that at meal-time could happen any time during the seven hours per day the mothers tended to spend with their children.

All the conversations were transcribed in CHAT format. CHAT is an international system of transcribing child language data used by the CHILDES project (MacWhinney, 1995).

The data were analysed for four features. First, the children's language choice was examined. All children's utterances were classified as spoken in English, Spanish or a mix of the two. With this, we were able to learn about the proportional quantity of English children used in the presence of their mothers during the two settings under study. Second, the children's relative frequency of verbal morphology was investigated. Morphology was studied as inflectional morphology in lexical verbs (e.g., bare form 'talk', third person singular 'talk-s'; past 'talk-ed'; progressive 'talk-ing'), as copula 'be' (e.g., 'is', and 'are'), and as auxiliary (e.g., 'do' and 'can'). The copula 'be' and primary auxiliaries (e.g., 'do', 'be' and 'have') have morphological rather than semantic meaning (unlike the modals). Furthermore, copula and auxiliaries are located in front of the subject in interrogative sentences and in front of the negative particle in negative sentences which, according to linguistic theory, are positions taken only by grammatical (not lexical) items. Therefore, the mere production of copula 'be' and auxiliaries result in the production of grammatical morphemes. We wanted to learn if the copula 'be' and auxiliaries were present in obligatory contexts and if so, what forms occurred and with what frequency. Third, we analysed the negative evidence children offered to their mothers. Negative evidence was described as utterances used to explicitly and implicitly correct the production of the mothers (e.g., Mother: she was take [% reading]; Child: taking] *and* as utterances produced to inform the mothers about any linguistic feature of the English language [e.g., Mother: was very bain [= vain]; Child: do you know what is vain? She is so beautiful,...]. Fourth, we investigated the mothers' learning techniques: What strategies the mothers used to gather information about the English language [e.g., Mother: Jim tried. Pero qué en español? [Jim tried. But what is it in Spanish] and how often the mothers corrected themselves after being corrected [e.g., Mother: the marks; Child: maths; Mother: mat mat. Homework maths].

Results

Language Choice

Language choice was examined in each utterance used by the child in the presence of the mother. Unintelligible utterances were discarded. Figure 1 shows the percentage of utterances in English spoken by the children in each setting.

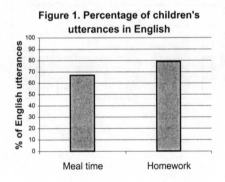

Figure 1. Percentage of children's utterances in English

In figure 1, we can observe that children spoke proportionally more English during homework than at meal-time.

Another interesting observation was that during homework children's utterances in English were mostly directed to the mothers. At meal-time, this was not necessarily the case. Many utterances in English at meal-time were addressed to the children's siblings and father. If learners need not only to hear English but also to be addressed and participate in an interaction in English, then the homework conversation offered a more beneficial setting for interaction in English.

This examination of children's language choice supported our Hypothesis 1 that during homework children would speak proportionally more English. Homework provided the mothers with a higher proportion of utterances in English than meal-time. Furthermore, during homework almost all the English used was *directly* addressed to the mothers.

Frequency of morphology

In order to examine the morphology used by the children, we first categorised all verbs in the children's data as lexical verbs with no inflection, lexical verbs with inflections, copula 'be' or auxiliaries. In auxiliaries we included all modals. Figure 2 reports the percentage out of all verb forms that were lexical verbs with no inflection (bare forms), the percentage that were lexical verbs with inflections, the percentage that were copula 'be' and the percentage that were auxiliaries. It is important to mention that since the children were fluent in English, errors in their verb forms were infrequent.

Figure 2. Percentages of all types of verbs

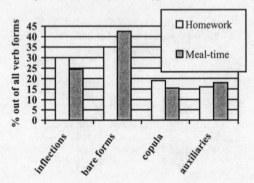

In figure 2, we can see that lexical verbs in bare forms were the most frequent verb forms for the two settings. However, at meal-time lexical verbs in bare forms were proportionally more frequent than during homework. By contrast, the proportion of lexical verbs with inflections was higher during homework than at meal-time. In fact, during homework the proportion of lexical verbs with inflections was similar to the proportion of lexical verbs in bare form. This is the first indication we have that morphology was richer during homework.

Lexical Verbs

We also wanted to learn about the forms of inflection for lexical verbs children were using in the two settings. Figure 3 shows percentage for past, third person singular, progressive and lexical verbs with no inflection. These percentages were based on the total number of lexical verbs.

Figure3. Percentage of inflections in lexical verbs

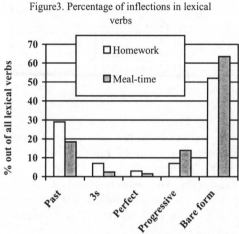

In figure 3, we can observe that progressive and bare forms, which have been reported in previous studies as the forms most frequent and first to appear in the L2 production of untutored learners, were proportionally more frequent at meal-time than during homework. By contrast, those inflectional forms that have been reported as typically missing in untutored learners' L2 (i.e., past and third person singular) were relatively more frequent during homework than at meal-time. This is a further indication that homework offers the mothers input with richer morphology.

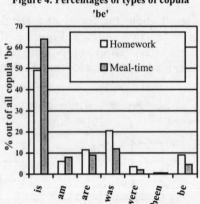

Figure 4. Percentages of types of copula 'be'

In this section, we examine the use of the copula in the input of children to their language learning mothers in the two settings under study. We wanted to learn about the forms of the copula 'be' that the children were producing and which forms were proportionally most frequent. Figure 4 reports the percentage with which children produced each form of the copula in each setting. Percentages were based on the total number of copula forms produced.

In figure 4, we can observe that although a variety of forms of the copula 'be' were present in the two settings, 'is' was relatively the most frequent form. However, the proportion of 'is' at meal-time was greater than during homework. By contrast, most of the rest of the forms, apart from 'been' which was rare, were proportionally more frequent during homework than at meal-time.

The examination of the copula in the input of children to their L2 learning mothers gives us further evidence supporting our hypothesis that input would be richer during homework. Here we showed that during homework the mothers heard a variety of forms of the copula proportionally more frequently than at meal-time.

Auxiliaries

In this section we analyse the auxiliaries (including modals) in the input offered by children to their L2 learning mothers. As with the copula, we wanted to learn which forms of auxiliaries were present and which forms were proportionally most frequent. Figure 5 shows the results for the forms of auxiliaries in percentages. The percentage for each form was based on the total number of auxiliaries.

Figure 5. Percentages of types of auxiliaries

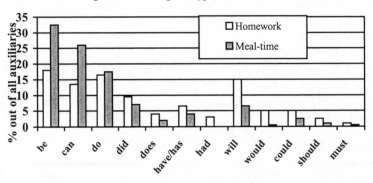

In figure 5, we can observe that 'be', 'can' and 'do' were relatively the most frequent auxiliaries produced by the children in the two settings. However, these forms of auxiliaries were proportionally more frequent at meal-time than during homework. Interestingly, these three auxiliaries have been reported in the literature to be the first to appear and the most frequent in L2 learners' production. This means that meal-time provided the mothers with those auxiliaries that they possibly already produced the most.

By contrast with meal-time, the homework input provided the mothers with a variety of auxiliaries, most of which were proportionally frequent in the data. As we can observe in figure 5, 'be', 'can', 'do' *and* 'will' were proportionally the most frequent auxiliaries during homework. However, the rest of the auxiliaries were also represented.

The examination of the use of auxiliaries in the children's input to their language learning mothers offers further indication that homework provides the mothers with morphologically richer input. In this section, we showed that the proportional frequency of a variety of auxiliaries was greater during homework than at meal-time. It must be mentioned that if what learners needed were a few forms heard at a high rate, the meal-time input could help learners with the learning of 'be', 'can' and 'do'. However, if the input at meal-time does not change as the learners progress, learners are at risk of never being exposed to the rest of auxiliaries. The input during homework offered a high percentage of occurrence for certain auxiliary forms. It also led the mothers a step further in their learning of English morphology by increasing the rate of appearance of rarer auxiliary forms.

To close this section, we can say that the original hypothesis that morphology would be richer during homework than at meal-time was supported by the data. At meal-time, only a few morphological forms were proportionally frequent and the rest appeared rarely. The forms relatively frequent at meal-time have also been observed to be first and most frequent forms in the speech of L2 learners of English. During homework the learners were exposed to a variety of morphological forms that were proportionally more frequent than at meal-time. Therefore, we can conclude that homework provides richer input that may lead the learners a step further in their development of morphology by exposing them to a higher proportion of rarer forms.

Negative Evidence

In this section, we examine the negative evidence that children offered to their L2 learning mothers in the two settings under study. Negative evidence was here described as those utterances that explicitly or implicitly corrected the mothers' production and those utterances that gave information about any feature of English. First, results were presented regarding the negative evidence in general, that is utterances that corrected or gave information about meaning, pronunciation or form. Second, special attention was given to negative evidence that related to verbs, that is those utterances that corrected or gave information about the *form* of an English verb.

Figure 6 presents the results for negative evidence in general. All the utterances produced by children were analysed to find the percentage that offered negative evidence to the mothers.

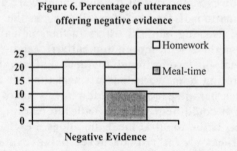

Figure 6. Percentage of utterances offering negative evidence

In figure 6, we can see that the proportion of negative evidence that children offered to their mothers was greater during homework than at meal-time. Among other forms of negative evidence, children corrected the pronunciation of their mothers, explained the meaning of words or expressions, offered words in English that the mothers did not seem to know, provided translations from English into Spanish, and from

Spanish into English. However, children produced only a few utterances containing negative evidence that targeted verb *form*. We studied these latter few utterances to investigate possible differences between the two settings under study.

Figure 7 shows the percentage of errors in the mothers' verb production that were followed by negative evidence from their children. It is relevant to mention that the number of errors the mothers made in their production of verbs was small. And the children's number of utterances containing negative evidence regarding these verb errors was even smaller. During homework, a total of 103 verb errors occurred, from which only 15 were corrected. At meal-time, a total of 43 errors were found and only 10 were corrected.

Figure 7. Percentage of all incorrect
verb forms that were followed by
negative evidence

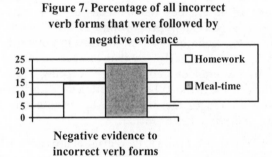

Negative evidence to
incorrect verb forms

In figure 7, we can see that the amount of negative evidence provided after a mother had produced an incorrect verb form was proportionally greater at meal-time than during homework. However, only three children contributed to the proportion at meal-time. The rest of the children did not provide this type of negative evidence at all at meal-time. By contrast, although no child produced this type of negative evidence frequently during homework, six out of the nine children used it at least once.

The examination of negative evidence in children's input to their language learning mothers suggested that hypothesis 3 that children would provide negative evidence during homework proportionally more frequently than at meal-time was partially supported by the data. When looking at negative evidence in general, the hypothesis was confirmed. When examining negative evidence offered after verb errors, the hypothesis was not supported by the data. It is important to remember that though negative evidence for verb errors was proportionally more frequent at meal-time than during homework, the amount of corrections was small in the two settings and only a few cases contributed to the higher proportion at meal-time. We can conclude that this analysis of negative evidence offers further support to the general hypothesis that input would be richer during homework since the proportion of negative evidence in general was greater during homework than at meal-time. With respect to negative evidence targeting verb forms, it is left for future research to find ways in which the school homework sharing activities might target verb errors, or more generally, form.

Mothers' Learning Techniques

After examining the input provided by the children, we wanted to learn about the mothers' part in the interaction. In particular, our interest was in the strategies the mothers used to gather information that might lead them to the learning of any linguistic feature of English. Figure 8 shows the percentage of utterances the mothers used to gather this type of information. That is the proportion of the mothers' utterances containing learning techniques out of all the utterances they produced.

In figure 8, we can clearly see that mothers tended to use a higher percentage of utterances containing learning techniques during homework than at meal-time. These utterances with learning techniques included those utterances the mothers used to gather information about meaning, pronunciation and/or form.

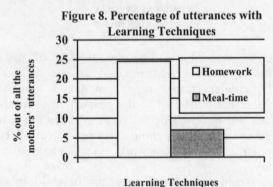

Figure 8. Percentage of utterances with Learning Techniques

Apart from these general techniques, we were interested in how the mothers reacted when offered negative evidence after a verb error. In particular, we wanted to learn if the mothers ignored the negative evidence that targeted their verb errors or if they used uptake, that is, if they tried to correct themselves with the help provided via the negative evidence. Figure 9 presents results of the percentage of negative evidence targeting verb forms after which the mothers used uptakes. Remember we mentioned that mothers' verb errors were infrequent and children's corrections of those verb errors were even more infrequent. It must be noted here that uptakes were even more infrequent than corrections. Out of 15 corrections, 4 were followed by uptake during homework. At meal time, none of the 10 corrections was followed by uptake.

Figure 9. Percentages of uptakes after negative evidence related to incorrect verb forms

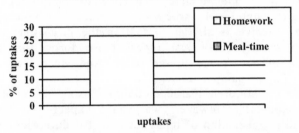

Figure 9 shows that uptakes only occurred during homework. At meal-time, no uptake happened after mothers' verb errors were corrected by children. This implies that mothers were possibly more aware of negative evidence targeting verb error production during homework than at meal-time. During homework, they used some uptake, which means that they had at least acknowledged the existence of this type of negative evidence during homework. By contrast, at meal-time mothers either ignored or did not even notice this type of negative evidence.

This examination of the mothers' learning techniques suggests that our hypothesis 4 that learning techniques would be proportionally more frequent during homework than at meal-time was supported by the data.

Conclusion

We set out to investigate the hypothesis that input during homework would be richer than during another typical daily interaction between an L2 learning mother and her child such as that at meal-time. We have seen that the quantity of English was proportionally greater during homework and that the proportion of morphology was higher during homework. Negative evidence, though not necessarily targeting form, occurred more frequently during homework. Finally, mothers' interaction techniques appeared more often during homework as well. These findings suggest that homework interactions offer a more advantageous L2 learning setting than the meal-time conversations.

With respect to the relative frequency of morphology, we found interesting parallels between the English spoken by untutored learners reported in the literature and the input provided at meal-time. That is, in the input at meal-time lexical verbs appeared in bare form or progressive form proportionally most frequently, and auxiliaries 'do', 'can' and 'be' occurred at a higher rate than the rest of auxiliaries. These verb forms have also been found to be the most frequent and the first to occur in the production of L2 untutored learners of English. After examining the relative frequency of morphology, it is less surprising that untutored learners speak without much morphology if the input they receive is similar to that in the meal-time of this study. Untutored learners may just repeat those forms that show higher proportion of occurrence in the input. And since they are not told otherwise (small amount of negative evidence was provided regarding verb forms), untutored learners continue using those forms even in incorrect contexts. However, we would expect that those learners exposed to a richer kind of input such as that during homework would eventually produce more morphology. Results in Durán (2001) pointed in this direction. Durán studied the production of the mothers in this study, and she found that the mothers produced morphology more frequently than untutored learners in previous studies. Since the mothers had been exposed to school homework sharing for a minimum of two years, it is plausible that the rich input that homework provided had helped the mothers learn morphology.

We want to propose school homework sharing as an alternative for L2 learning improvement when formal instruction in L2 is not possible or available. Homework conversations seem to provide Hispanic immigrant mothers with beneficial tools that they can use to improve their L2 learning. School homework sharing was devised by the American school system to help children coming from less privileged backgrounds to improve their literacy development. The device seems to have a side effect, that is, to aid the L2 learning by the mothers of those children. Our findings suggest, therefore, that school assignments can have far reaching benefits, not just for the child, but for the parent as well. With this knowledge, it should be possible to design interactive curricula that will help children learn school subject matter, and at the same time develop in their parents the grammatical forms of English that in the past have seemed so elusive. In the design of these curricula it should be remembered the little attention that form received in the negative evidence children provided for their mothers. It is important to point out that the children of this study were not introduced to grammar in school. Although the debate on whether or not children should be taught grammar in school is still open, an interesting question for future research is whether or not children would provide more negative evidence targeting form if they were introduced to grammar in school.

References

Chaudron, C. (1977). A descriptive model of discourse in the corrective treatment of learners' errors. *Language Learning*, 27: 29-46.

Choi, S. & Gopnik, A. (1995). Early acquisition of verbs in Korean: a cross-linguistic study. *Journal of Child Language*, 22: 497-529.

Clark, E. (1998). Constructions and conversations. *Journal of Child Language*, 25(2): 471-74.

Doughty, C. (1994). Fine-tuning of feedback by competent speakers to language learners. In J. Alatis (Ed.), *GURT 1993* (pp. 96-108). Washington, DC: Georgetown University Press.

Durán, P. (2001) *The Input Hypothesis Inverted: A comparison of the Input Given by Children to Their Hispanic Immigrant Mothers and by Teachers to Their Hispanic Immigrant Students*. Unpublished dissertation. Boston University.

Ellis, R. (1998). Teaching and research: Options in Grammar Teaching. *TESOL Quarterly*, 32/1: 39-60.

Gass, S. M. & Veronis, E. M. (1994). Input, interaction, and second language production. *Studies in Second Language Acquisition*, 16: 283-302.

Gathercole, V. C. M., Sebastián, E., & Soto, P. (1999). The early acquisition of Spanish verbal morphology: across-the-board or piecemeal knowledge? *International Journal of Bilingualism*, 2&3: 133-182.

Goldfield, B. A. (1993) Noun bias in maternal speech to one-year-olds. *Journal of Child Language*, 20: 85-99.

Klein, W., & Perdue, C. (1992). *Utterance Structure: Developing grammars again*. Amsterdam: John Benjamins Publishing Company.

Klein, W., & Perdue, C. (1997). The Basic Variety (or: Couldn't natural languages be much simpler). *Second Language Research*, 13/4: 301-347.

Lardiere, D. (1998). Dissociating syntax from morphology in a divergent L2 end-state grammar. *Second Language Research*, 14/4: 359-375.

Lieven, E. V. M. (1994). Crosslinguistic and crosscultural aspects of language addressed to children. In: C. Gallaway & B. J. Richards (Eds.), *Input and interaction in language acquisition* (pp. 56-73). Cambridge: Cambridge University Press.

Loschky, L. (1994). Comprehensible input and second language acquisition: What is the relationship? *Studies in Second Language Acquisition*, 16: 303-323.

Lyster, R. and Ranta, L. (1997). Corrective feedback and learner uptake: Negotiation of form in communicative classrooms. *Studies in Second Language Acquisition*, 19/1: 37-66.

MacWhinney, B. (1995). *The CHILDES project: Tools for analyzing talk*. (2nd ed.). Hillsdale, NJ: Erlbaum.

Meisel, J. M. (1997). The acquisition of the syntax of negation in French and German: contrasting first and second language development. *Second Language Research*, 13/3: 227-263.

Paratore, J.R., Melzi, G., & Krol-Sinclair, B. (1999). *What should we expect of family literacy? Experiences of Latino children whose parents participate in an intergenerational literacy project*. Newark: International Reading Association.

Schwartz, B. D. (1993). On explicit and negative data effecting and affecting competence and linguistic behavior. *Studies in Second Language Acquisition*, 15: 143-146.

Schwartz, B. D. & Gubala-Ryzak, M. (1992), Learnability and grammar reorganization in L2A: against negative evidence causing the unlearning of verb movement. *Second Language Research*, 8/1: 1-38.

Shirai, Y. & Andersen, R. W. (1995). The acquisition of tense-aspect morphology: a prototype account. *Language*, 71: 743-762.

Snow, C. E. (1994). Beginning from Baby Talk: twenty years of research on input in interaction. In: C. Gallaway & B. J. Richards (Eds). *Input and interaction in language acquisition* (pp. 1-12). Cambridge: Cambridge University Press.

Tardif, T., Shatz, M., & Naigles, L. (1997). Caregiver speech and children's use of nouns versus verbs: A comparison of English, Italian, and Mandarin. *Journal of Child Language*, 24: 535-565.

Vainikka, A. & Young-Scholten, M. (1996b). The early stages in adult L2 syntax: additional evidence from Romance speakers. *Second Language Research*, 12/2: 140-176.

White, L. (1989). *Universal grammar and second language acquisition*. Amsterdam: Benjamins.

11 Random association networks: a baseline measure of lexical complexity

PAUL MEARA

University of Wales Swansea

ELLEN SCHUR

The Open University, Israel

Most research in vocabulary acquisition compares the behavior of native and non-native speakers on various types of word-elicitation tasks. The performance of native speakers is considered the norm, or baseline, against which the performance of the non-native speakers is measured. This is especially apparent in research in which word association tasks have been used (cf., for instance, Kolers (1963), Riegel, Ramsey & Riegel (1967), Riegel & Zivian (1972), Meara (1978; 1983; 1992), Szalay & Deese (1978), Kruse et al. (1987) Söderman (1989), Schmitt & Meara (1997), Schmitt (1998)). The comparisons in much of this research are often very difficult to interpret because the native speaker subjects tend not to be homogeneous and to vary very much among themselves. This makes it difficult to agree on an exact point of comparison for the non-native speaker data, as there is no obvious focal point on which the L1/L2 comparisons can be based. This made us wonder whether it might make more sense to compare both native speakers and learners against a more objectively defined baseline. In this paper we ask whether **random association networks** might provide a baseline function of this sort for word association data. This is not an entirely new idea. Rapoport et al. (1966) compared L1 associations to randomly generated data, and showed that L1 association networks differed significantly from randomly generated networks in some respects. As far as we are aware, however, this approach has not been used before with L2 speakers.

In this paper we present an experiment in which computer generated random networks served as the basis of comparison for the word association networks of native speakers and non-natives speakers. We explored three questions: (1) What do randomly generated networks actually look like? (2) In what ways are these networks similar to or different from the networks produced by both native and non-native speakers? (3) Does it make sense to view the association networks of L2 speakers as mid-way between those of L1 speakers and randomly generated networks?

The Study

Subjects

The subjects were a group of 32 adult bilinguals with L1-English and L2-Hebrew, and a group of 32 11th grade high school pupils (16 or 17 year-olds) whose L1 was Hebrew and who were learning English for their 5-point matriculation exam.

Instrument

The instrument consisted of a brief questionnaire designed to elicit information about the language background of each subject, a practice exercise and a word association task. This last task comprised 50 verbs arranged alphabetically in a response box (See Appendix), and a randomly ordered list of the same 50 verbs. The fifty verbs were selected from Nation's (1986) first frequency band – i.e. they all fell within the first 1000 words of English, and thus can be considered to be part of the core vocabulary of English. Verbs were chosen to eliminate the possibility of different response patterns that might have been generated by the use of stimulus words from different parts of speech. Pilot tests indicated that the subjects at the level of proficiency being tested knew all of these verbs.

Methodology

For each word in the list, the subjects were instructed to select and write down another word from the verb box that best associated with it. They were given eight practice examples to work through and discuss before undertaking the main task. The non-native learners were given the task to do in classes by their native-speaking teachers. The native English-speakers did the task individually. No time limit was given. The native speakers completed the task in 10 to 15 minutes and regarded it as a word game. The non-native learners needed a full class period to complete the task, and, for the most part, found it quite frustrating.

In addition, we produced a set of randomly generated data using a specially designed computer program. Like the real Ss, the program made associations between the fifty verbs in the list, but it did this by selecting associations at random. The significance of this data will be explained later.

Data and Analysis

A group of 60 learners attempted the task, but not all of them completed it. It was decided to analyze the data from 32 completed questionnaires of the L2 learners. The data from 32 of the native English speakers was also analyzed, as was a selection of 32 examples of the randomly generated data-sets. At the simplest level of analysis, the data from each S consists of a set of fifty pairs, each pair comprising a stimulus word and a second word which was associated with it. Typical examples of this are: *to find ~ to discover*; *to study ~ to learn*; *to love ~ to obey*; *to dream ~ to discover*; and so on. By way of illustration, Table 1 gives a complete list of all the associations produced by each group to the stimulus word *to help*.

Table 1: the complete set of responses to stimulus: *to help*

> *Native speakers responses*: (7)
> build(1) work(1) show(1) love(2) explain(3) listen(3) assist(22)
> Learner responses: (10)
> try(1) prepare(1) earn(1) spend(1) listen(1) make(1) pay(1)
> explain(2) love(2) assist(19)
> *Random responses*: (23)
> cost(1) expect(1) learn(1) work(1) yell(1) argue(1) study(1)
> wash(1) try(1) describe(1) shout(1) obey(1) ride(1) find(1)
> measure(1) test(1) assist(2) spend(2) win(2) show(2) fly(2) cut(3)
> hear(3)

We analysed these data using a computer program which printed out each stimulus word and the responses that it generated from each of the subject groups, and the number of times each of these responses was selected. For each group, a group data matrix was then drawn up indicating the number and frequency of all the responses made to each of the stimulus words. The individual data was also analysed. Data for individual subjects was coded as a set of diagrams in which we mapped the associations among the words.

Results

The Matrices

In order to extract the critical information from the complex response matrices, the general guidelines found in Pollio (1963) were used. For each stimulus word we calculated the number of other words it elicited as a response. Each of these different responses was counted only once – that is, in this analysis, we ignore the strength of associations and focus on their variability. The full results can be seen in Table 2.

Table 2: Mean Different Responses Generated by each Stimulus Word

	L1 (n=50)	L2 (n=50)	Random (n=50)
Mean:	8.5	12.4	23.8
sd.:	2.9	2.9	1.6

This table shows that with L1 speakers, each stimulus word generated an average of 8.5 different responses; with L2 speakers, each stimulus word generated an average of 12.4 different responses; while for random data, each stimulus word generated an average of 23.8 different responses.

An analysis of variance indicated that these differences were highly significant [$F(2,49)=662$, $p<.001$]. Clearly, there is a very large difference between the random data and the others, but the difference between the L1 and L2 data is also significant ($t=12.95$, $p<.001$) with the data for L2 speakers lying between the L1 data and the random data.

We also analysed the number of idiosyncratic responses (responses produced by only one subject) and the number of common responses (responses produced by more than a single respondent). The data generated by the random group contained the highest number of idiosyncratic responses – a mean of 17.02 per stimulus word. It also generated low numbers of common responses – a mean of 6.72 per stimulus word, with no more than 3 common responses per stimulus word. In contrast, the responses generated by the native speaker group contained the lowest number of idiosyncratic responses – a mean of 4.2 per stimulus word. This group also generated a substantial number of common responses – for almost all of the stimulus words, more than 10 subjects made the same association. The non-native learners generated a mean score of 7.7 idiosyncratic responses per word, and only a small number of common responses were produced by more than 10 subjects. The responses generated by the random group were far less uniform, then, than those produced by either the native or the non-native groups. These data are shown in Table 3.

Table 3: Mean Idiosyncratic and Shared Responses Generated by each Stimulus Word

	L1 (n=50)	L2 (n=50)	Random (n=50)
Idiosyncratic responses	4.20	7.7	17.02
Common responses (n<10)	3.30	4.1	6.72
Common responses (n >10)	0.96	0.6	0

These results are consistent with the results of previous work (e.g. Postman & Keppel 1970; Riegel & Zivian 1972; Meara 1978; 1983; Szalay & Deese 1978) in which it was found that L2 learners produce more varied responses than L1 speakers on word association tasks. What is noticeable here, however, is that the L2 data is neatly sandwiched between the L1 data and the randomly generated data.

In spite of this, these findings are something of a problem for us, since they suggest that L2 association networks are "denser" than L1 association networks. "Dense" here is a reflection of the number of words each word is associated with, so that if the stimulus words generate lots of different associations, then the network for the group will be denser than if each word generates only one or two different associations. Technically, the L2 group response matrix contained more filled cells than the L1 group response matrix. Indeed, on this analysis, the random networks are typically the densest of our three groups. Almost all words are interconnected, there are many different associations for each stimulus word, and consequently there are very few empty cells in the matrix. Figures 1a-1c illustrate a small part of this data. The problem here seems to be that by looking at group data, we are masking the contribution each individual subject makes to the overall matrix. In order to explore this idea further, we constructed individual networks for each subject, and examined the properties of each of these individual networks.

Figure 1a: First 12 Words of a 50 Word Matrix -- L2 English Speakers (N=32)

Words:	1	2	3	4	5	6	7	8	9	10	11	12
1. help							1				1	
2. study												
3. scream									5	1		
4. tell	1										2	
5. expect										6		5
6. wash												
7. love					1					1	1	5
8. cost												
9. shout			9									
10. imagine					1							19
11. show	1			3			1					
12. dream					2		1			23		1

Figure 1b: First 12 Words of a 50 Word Matrix -- L2 Learners of English (N=32)

Word	1	2	3	4	5	6	7	8	9	10	11	12
1. help							2					
2. study		1										
3. scream	1		1						5			
4. tell	1			2							1	
5. expect							2		1	4		
6. wash	1											
7. love					1	1						4
8. cost												
9. shout						6						
10. imagine					1		1					19
11. show				2								
12. dream		1			1		1			18	1	

Figure 1c: First 12 Words of a 50 Word Matrix -- Random 'Subjects'
(N=32)

Word	1	2	3	4	5	6	7	8	9	10	11	12
1. help		1			1	1		1	1		1	
2. study			1	1		1	1	1		1		2
3. scream			2	1	1	2		1	1	1		
4. tell				1	1			1	1	1	1	
5. expect			2	1		3			1			
6. wash	1		1	1	1			1	1	1		1
7. love				4		2	1	1				
8. cost	1		1	1			1	1		1	1	
9. shout	1	1	1	1	1	1	1	1		1		
10. imagine						2		1		1		1
11. show		1	1	1		1	1					
12. dream		1	1	1		1	1					

Individual Data

Some representative examples of these networks for the individual L1, L2 and random data can be seen in Figures 2a, 2b and 2c respectively. In these figures, each of the numbered circles represents one of the 50 stimulus words. (It needs to be kept in mind, that these words are *both* stimuli and responses in this experiment.) Each circle is a **node** in a network generated by the subject. The nodes are linked by arrows leading from stimulus to response, i.e., an arrow going from node 5 to node 7 indicates that word 5 elicited word 7 as a response. It is immediately apparent from these figures that there is a major difference between the networks. The L1 network is largely disconnected, whereas the L2 network seems to be more interconnected, and consists of a few large **components**. These examples are typical of the data produced by L1 and L2 subjects in this experiment. On the other hand, random networks generated by the computer program typically consist of one very large component, and a handful of smaller components. Again, the L2 networks appear to fall between the L1 networks and the randomly generated networks in this respect.

Figure 2. Examples of networks

Figure 2a: Native-Speaker network

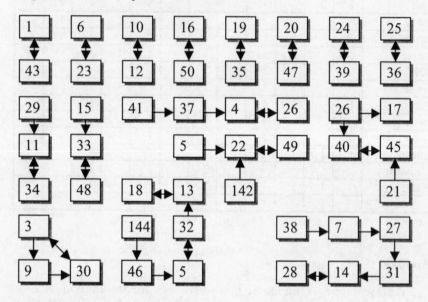

Figure 2b: L2-speaker network

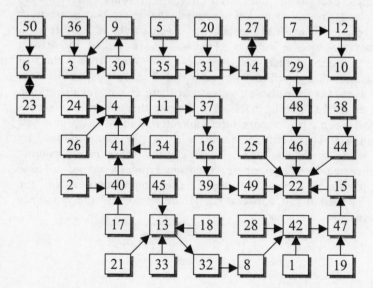

Figure 2c: Random Network

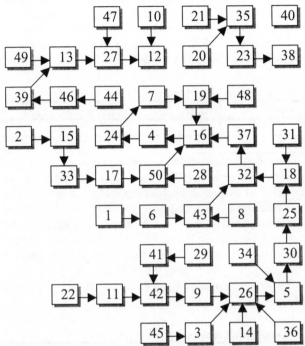

Formally, there are a number of differences between the three types of networks. The simplest analysis counts the number of network components produced by each subject. The mean number of components in the networks generated by individual subjects in each group is shown in Table 4.

Table 4: Mean Network Components for Individual Subjects

	L1 (n = 32)	L2 (n=32)	Random (n=32)
Mean:	10.6	8.9	2.4
sd.:	4.0	4.19	0.98

This table clearly indicates that the networks of native speakers contain more separate components than those of the non-native speakers, and both contain more components than the random data does. The point to note here, however, is that while the data for the real subjects is fairly varied, the data from the random networks is very homogeneous, with a tiny standard deviation.

Table 5 shows the number of network components produced by native and non-native speakers and the random group. A chi squared analysis suggests that there might be a tendency for L2 subjects to produce fewer than 8 separate network components, but this analysis is post hoc, and needs to be treated with appropriate caution since there is considerable overlap between the groups (X^2=42.06, p<.01).

Table 5: Number of Network Components for each Group

	L1 (n=32)	L2 (n=32)	Random (n=32)
7 or less	7	14	32
8 or more	25	18	0

Since there is an inverse relationship between the number of components and the number of nodes in each component, an alternative way of looking at the same data is to compute the size of the largest component in each response matrix, i.e. the number of nodes in the largest component produced by each subject. Table 6 shows that the L2 speakers produce more components of 16 or more nodes than the L1 speakers, and that the random group are more likely to produce a component containing 16 or more nodes than either of the real groups are. (X^2=62.9, p<.001).

Table 6: Size of Largest Network Component

	L1 (n=32)	L2 (n=32)	Random (n=32)
15 or fewer nodes	22	13	1
16 or more nodes	10	19	31

What is apparent from these data is that completely random networks appear to be superficially even more complex than the networks generated by either of our two subject groups. There are significantly more different responses per stimulus word in the random group matrix (as illustrated in Table 2). The number of components in the random networks is typically only one or two (Table 5) and the largest component in a random network is almost always greater than 15 nodes (Table 6).

It would seem, then, that the really significant differences are not between the L1 and the L2 networks, but between the networks produced by the real subject groups and those generated by our random virtual group. This is even more apparent if we look at the standard deviation figures for the number of network components produced and the number of different responses generated by each stimulus word. The standard deviation figures for the number of network components of both native and non-native speakers are very similar, whereas the standard deviation for the random subjects is considerably smaller (Table 4). The same holds true for the standard deviation figures for the number of different responses generated by each stimulus word (Table 2). These figures seem to indicate that the networks produced by *both* native and non-native speakers are similar in that they are both characterized by greater variation than the networks generated by the random group. However, the latter are both homogeneous and consistent, and for this reason, it seems to us that they might make an ideal baseline against which to measure both native and non-native word association patterns in future studies of this kind.

Discussion

To summarise, although there *are* differences between L1 and L2 networks, it looks very much as though the real distinction here is between the networks of L1 and L2 subjects and the random networks. For the set of stimulus words tested here, the networks of the L1 subjects have many, small, non-connected components. The random networks have few, large, and interconnected components. The L2 speakers appear to fall between these two extremes. The differences are summarized in Table 7.

Table 7: Characteristics of the Association Networks for a set of 50 Verb Stimuli

Native:	*group matrix*: least dense; smallest number of different idiosyncratic responses, large number of 10 + common responses *Individual network components*: many, consisting of fewer nodes
Non-native:	*group matrix*: denser, more different idiosyncratic responses; fewer 10 + common responses *individual network components:* fewer, consisting of more nodes
Random:	*group matrix*: the most dense, large number of different idiosyncratic responses, no 10+ common responses *individual network components*: very few, consisting of the largest number of nodes

These findings suggest that non-native speakers, for the most part, do not yet perceive vocabulary as belonging to smaller, constrained and strongly connected sets and they tend to associate words in more diverse and less predictable ways than native speakers do. The native speaker networks seem to reflect the fact that L1 speakers have a greater awareness of the semantic relations between words, and how words may fall into distinct sets. However, the networks produced by the real subject groups seem to indicate that *both* native and non-native speakers do have some degree of awareness that associations are constrained by meaning. In contrast, random networks are the most superficially complex, simply because they are connected every which way, resulting in large components, unconstrained by meaning. However, these very features mean that it is very easy to characterise what we would expect a random network to look like. This enables us to characterise L2 networks as distinct from typical random networks in ways that would not be possible if we had used typical L1 networks as a baseline.

Conclusion

This paper has explored the use of computer generated random data as a baseline for comparing the vocabulary networks of native and non-native speakers. Each of the measures discussed above (the number of network components, the number of different responses, the number of idiosyncratic and shared responses, and the number of connected nodes) can be used as an index against which the word association networks produced by native and non-native speakers, and those generated by random data can be compared. These indices may provide the basis of a more holistic measure of the L2 proficiency level of non-native speakers, as well as a clearer, more empirically based definition of the concept of 'complexity' of the mental lexicon in both native and non-native speakers.

References

Kolers, P. A. (1963) Interlingual word associations. *Journal of Verbal Learning and Verbal Behavior 2*, 291-300.

Kruse, H. J. Pankhurst & M. Sharwood Smith (1987) A multiple word association probe in second language acquisition research. *Studies in Second Language Acquisition 9*, 141-154.

Meara, P. (1978) Learners' word associations in French. *Interlanguage Studies Bulletin 2*, 192-211.

Meara, P. (1983) Word associations in a foreign language: A report on the Birkbeck Vocabulary Project. *Nottingham Linguistic Circular 11*, 29-38.

Nation, P. (1986) *Vocabulary Lists: Words, Affixes and Stems, Revised Edition*. Wellington, New Zealand: English Language Institute.

Pollio, H. (1963) A simple matrix analysis of associative structure. *Journal of Verbal Learning and Verbal Behavior, 2*, 166-169.

Postman, L. & G. Keppel (1970) *Norms of Word Association*. New York: Academic Press.

Rapoport, A., A. Rapoport, W.P. Livant & J. Boyd (1966) A study of lexical graphs. *Foundations of Language 2*, 338-376.

Riegel, K. F., R. M. Ramsey & R. Riegel (1967) A comparison of the first and second languages of American and Spanish Students. *Journal of Verbal Learning and Verbal Behavior 6*, 536-544.

Riegel, K. F. & I. W. M. Zivian (1972) A study of inter- and intralingual associations in English and German. *Language Learning 22*, 51-63.

Schmitt, N. (1998) Quantifying word association responses: What is native-like? *System*, 389-401.

Söderman, T. (1989) Word associations of foreign language learners and native speakers: A shift in response type and its relevance for a theory of language. *Scandinavian Working Papers on Bilingualism 8*, 114-121.

Szalay, L. B. & J. Deese (1978) *Subjective Meaning and Culture: An Assessment Through Word Associations*. Hillsdale, N.J.: Erlbaum.

Appendix. The Task.

Instructions:

On the next page you will see 50 verbs arranged in alphabetical order in a Verb Box. The same 50 verbs are arranged in random order in a Verb List. Read each verb in the list. Then decide which one of the verbs in the Verb Box best completes the pair for each verb in that list. Write this verb next to the appropriate verb in the list. You can use a verb from the Verb Box as many times as you need to.

Verb Box:

to argue	to drive	to help	to obey	to show
to assist	to earn	to imagine	to pay	to spend
to build	to expect	to invent	to point	to study
to buy	to explain	to learn	to prepare	to tell
to clean	to fight	to listen	to prove	to test
to cost	to find	to look	to ride	to try
to cut	to fly	to lose	to sail	to wash
to describe	to grow	to love	to see	to win
to discover	to hate	to make	to scream	to work
to dream	to hear	to measure	to shout	to yell

Verb List:

1.	to help:	26.	to describe:
2.	to study:	27.	to fly:
3.	to scream:	28.	to drive:
4.	to tell:	29.	to point:
5.	to expect:	30.	to yell:
6.	to wash:	31.	to sail:
7.	to love:	32.	to build:
8.	to cost:	33.	to fight:
9.	to shout:	34.	to prove:
10.	to imagine:	35.	to prepare:
11.	to show:	36.	to work:
12.	to dream:	37.	to explain:
13.	to invent:	38.	to hate:
14.	to ride:	39.	to see:
15	to lose:	40.	to learn:
16.	to listen:	41.	to argue:
17.	to grow:	42.	to pay:
18.	to make:	43.	to assist:
19.	to cut:	44.	to obey:
20.	to measure:	45.	to discover:
21.	to find:	46.	to try:
22.	to spend:	47.	to test:
23.	to clean:	48.	to win:
24.	to look:	49.	to buy:
25.	to earn:	50.	to hear:

12 Imposed unity, denied diversity: changing attitudes to artifice in language and learning

GUY COOK

University of Reading

Introduction

This paper is about the word *artifice*, and a change in its meaning 350 years ago. As such, it may initially seem of little relevance to contemporary Applied Linguistics. The argument, moreover, may appear digressive, with many loose ends. The aim, however, is to weave these together to suggest that the etymology of *artifice* provides insight into the ideology of current language teaching. There is also in this argument an implied critique of Applied Linguistic 'presentism', suggesting that the relocation of issues in a historical context can be a force for progress rather than reaction.

What is artifice?

Etymology

Contemporary corpus-based dictionaries privilege the most frequent current uses of a word and downgrade or ignore its etymology. Older 'traditional' dictionaries, however, had very different criteria. The 1941 edition of the Shorter Oxford English Dictionary, for example, far from prioritising current usage, lists meanings in historical order, relegating 'the ordinary sense now' to the last position rather than first. Thus its first two definitions of 'artifice' reflect the Latin roots (*arti* + *ficium*= something made from art):

> construction, workmanship

> the product of art.

These are followed by two slightly later definitions:

constructive skill

human skill,

and these by two more recent meanings

skill in expedients: address, trickery

an ingenious expedient, a manoeuvre, device, trick

this last definition being glossed as "the ordinary sense now".

The chronological nature of this list reveals a fact which would be lost in many modern dictionaries: that the earlier senses are positive (*art, constructiveness, skill*) while the later ones (*address, trickery; a manoeuvre, device, trick*) are negative. The change, judging by the examples quoted, comes in the mid seventeenth century, and is brought out nicely by this unattributed quotation from 1660

He condemned Rhetorick, as being used rather as an Artifice than an Art.

Quite how negative the word had become is illustrated by Milton's use of a derivative in *Paradise Lost* (first published in 1667) where no less of a figure than Satan is described as:

Artificer of fraud (......) the first
That practised falsehood under saintly show,
Deep malice to conceal, couched with revenge.
(Paradise Lost iv; 121)

So there was a substantial change, if not in the denotation of the word, at least in its connotations. Having once signified the skill of art and construction, it came to mean skill in the service of trickery and deception, even Satanic skill.

Collocations and semantic prosody.

These are heavy uses indeed. But what of its sense now? The COBUILD Online Sampler suggests that the commonest contemporary collocates of *artifice* (other than functors such as *of* and *was)* are: *rhetorical, theatrical, irony,* and *stage.* In contemporary usage then, the word seems less associated with dishonesty (let alone with evil) than with the transparent and socially acceptable deception of the theatre - an artifice of which most people approve (even if religious fundamentalists like Milton did not). 'Artifice' it seems has been pushed into the wings, marginalized as entertainment, cordoned off from the serious concerns of work and power. It is subterfuge, but amoral rather than moral or immoral.

Another fact revealed by a corpus search is that *artifice* in contemporary English is a word of relatively low frequency (81 occurrences in the one hundred million words of the British National Corpus) and much less frequent than two etymologically related words: *art* (15,588 in the BNC) and *artificial* (2007 in the BNC). Arguably, the word *artifice* has divided in two. *Art* has inherited its older positive semantic prosody, while *artificial* (arguably a form of the same word) inherits its negative sense. (The negative nature of *artificial* seems to me intuitively true, even though COBUILD shows the commonest collocates – such as *insemination* and *intelligence, limbs, light* – to be neutral.)

Synonyms and Antonyms.

Thus far we have explored the meaning of these words in two ways: the old fashioned way, by looking at etymology; and the modern way, by looking at collocates. A third strategy is to seek out synonyms and antonyms – something a corpus cannot easily reveal. Synonyms of *artifice* given in thesauri I have consulted (Word, WordPerfect and Roget) include *fake* and *false*, while opposites include *honesty, sincerity, candour, earnestness, frankness, openness, fidelity, integrity, probity*. Synonyms of *artificial* include *counterfeit, phoney,* and *insincere.* Opposites include *genuine, real, natural, authentic* - all words which resonate very strongly in contemporary discussions of language teaching. They are also frequent in the discourses of politics, philosophy, and religion. *Genuineness* and *honesty* have an obvious moral ring, but so too do *real* and *natural.* From Plato to the Romantics, artists, moral philosophers and political thinkers have frequently designated the *real* and the *natural* as something superior and to be sought after. It is as though, when humans, or their creations, are *real* and *natural* they are they are somehow better and truer to themselves, than when they are the opposite: *artificial.*

Why human skill?

Instinct and culture.

So *artifice* has had a strange history. It has moved from positive to negative and ended up in the theatre. But is there any continuity in this history – a denotation which persists through these changes, uniting the artistic and the artificial? In pursuit of this question, let us consider more closely one of the older definitions cited above: '*human skill*'.

To qualify *skill* as *human* implies a contrast with some other kind, presumably '*animal skill*'. To Milton's age, with its absolute confidence in the privileged position of humanity in creation[1], this clearly implied superior skill. In our own less confident times, this 'animal' versus 'human' distinction is not as straightforward. Recent linguistics and psychology has been much preoccupied with disagreements between those who wish to emphasize the continuity between animal and human life, and those who want to claim a sharp discontinuity[2]. Without necessarily becoming entangled in this debate, it seems reasonable to assume that each individual human has both a more basic 'instinctive' identity (perhaps erroneously called our 'animal' side[3]) and in addition several cultural identities. Human behaviour in other words involves the management of more than one layer of identity. Our skill – our *human skill* – is to handle these multiple roles simultaneously and to move back and forth between them.

To have got this far in this article, for example, you must have deployed some culturally acquired skills which are by no means species-specific: reading English, deploying background knowledge of linguistics, perceiving (or tolerating departure from) the conventions of academic discourse. Yet even as you read, in your highly cultural and sophisticated way, you simultaneously have more instinctive concerns. Perhaps you are feeling hungry, short of sleep, sexually frustrated, aggressive. Very likely you move backwards and forwards between these two worlds. It may even be that one feeds into the other. If you find this article boring, for example, but your eyes keep moving along the lines, you may find your mind wandering into sexual fantasy or thoughts about your next meal. If you find my argument, or my way of advancing it, annoying, this itself may be an occasion for anger. You move between your instinctive and cultural worlds quite easily.

Fantasy and fiction.

Less often mentioned in either psychology or linguistics are two further dimensions of our lives which render this human skill of moving between identities more complex still. Firstly there are fantasies (directly known, like consciousness, only introspectively). Then there are the sanctioned and externalised alternative worlds of fiction. How much adult time is spent in fantasy is hard to assess, though the available evidence suggests it is a great deal (Klinger 1971; Singer 1975); the enormous extent of fiction however is readily witnessed by our uses of the major media of communication. By far the greatest part of television schedules are taken up with drama; almost all the most profitable books and films are fictional. In the most recent medium of mass communication – the networked computer – the power of fiction is evident in the popularity of internet chat rooms, in which participants adopt fictional identities as a matter of course (James Simpson in this volume).

The choice of the word *'room'* for the virtual liaison of internet chat is significant. One of the features often remarked by theorists of games and rituals (Huizinga 1949; Cook 2000; Rampton 1999, 2001) is how they tend to take place within (literally or metaphorically) a bounded area or time. It might be a real dedicated place like a place of worship, a sports stadium, or a theatre; it may be a designated period such as 'playtime' or a carnival period; or a virtual space such as the 'chatroom'. There is a close relationship between the way we move in and out of identities, and the way we move in and out of these designated spaces. People change as they move from room to room, and the rooms help to ritualise these changes in identity. This notion of the ritual space relates (I shall develop the point later) to the importance in language teaching of 'the class*room*': a term often used metonymically to signify the very process of teaching and learning.

Whether or not this constant movement and ability to tolerate multiple identities is uniquely human it is certainly centrally human, and also the essence of artifice. Artifice *means* being two or more things at once – whether this concerns the skill of the artist, the conjuror performing a trick, the person involved in deceit, or the archangel who was also a devil – and it is this denotation which unites the historically disparate connotations of the term. When somebody acts a part on stage they are simultaneously both the character and themselves. Generally, we have no problem in being two things at once, and there is often not only tolerance of such multiple roles, but enjoyment of them. Our capacity for such movement, however, extends beyond the fiction and the game to social interaction at large. There are always other identities to those currently on show. You the reader, and I the writer, in our interaction in this article, for example, adopt a particular stance as academics – but we have other roles and identities beyond these too.

This surely applies in the language classroom – both to teachers and learners. Teachers move in and out of their roles as teachers. Learners move in and out of their roles as learners, and in and out of the two languages. When we become a language learner, we are speaking another language even though we do not have to. It is an artifice.

Language and artifice.

We all have, then, layers of identities. We inhabit simultaneously the instinctive world, the cultural world, fantasies, and fictions. We can move easily backwards and forwards between them as the occasion requires. To facilitate such movements, we have designated various areas or 'rooms' (literal or metaphoric) to ritualise the switches.

Language, of course, plays a major role in such transitions – as has long been acknowledged. From their inception, both stylistics (Crystal and Davey 1969) and register studies (Halliday, McIntosh and Strevens 1964:77-98) have been concerned with how linguistic choices mark changes in the nature of an interaction. In Hymes' functional taxonomy, the 'contextual function' is realised through brief formulaic utterances (*Let's pretend, The meeting is open etc*) which signal changes of context, without change of physical location (Hymes 1972). Goffman's notion of the 'frame' (Goffman 1974) is often realised linguistically. Not only variation within one language functions in this way, but also the selection of the language itself. For many bilingual individuals and societies, a change of language, may signal a movement into a different 'room'. This is also the case in the use of liturgical languages for worship and prayer (Glinert 1993).

Indeed, human language and dual identity seem to implicate each other. Among Hockett's 'design features of language' (Hockett 1963) there are arguably only three – structure dependence, dual structure and metalanguage – which are exclusive to language, and absent from animal communication. Each, significantly, rests upon the capacity of a stretch of language to be two things at once. Structure dependence implies that we can, albeit at a subconscious level, view a string of words as realising grammatical units and relations; dual structure implies that a string of phonemes can also be, on another level, a morpheme; metalanguage enables us to see a stretch of language both as referring to something outside itself, and simultaneously as an object to which we can refer.

In a loose way, these capacities of language to be two things at once, are related to another design feature: the capacity to lie (prevarication as Hockett rather euphemistically calls it). Whether animals lie (luring intruders away, for example, by feigning a broken wing) is a moot point, and dependent upon the degree to which we regard intentionality as constituting the act. Yet certainly there is no doubt that humans are unrivalled in their capacity for deception, and that language is the major means by which we all, in our sub-Satanic ways, are 'artificer[s] of fraud'. Children are frequently corrected for meanings but not for grammar; yet, as remarked by Roger Brown, one of the few certainties about child language development is that we all grow up to speak grammatically, and tell lies (Brown 1973). Robin Dunbar (1996) has gone so far as to suggest that the centrality of deception in human social life is one of the major causes and effects of language evolution.

Yet there is also something puritanical – Miltonic one might say – in identifying this capacity solely with dishonesty. For the human skill of producing an alternative reality need by no means only be associated with lying. The rather moralistic preoccupations of modern linguists with deceit are in this sense rather revealing. An alternative take upon the origin and function of this use of language is provided by the Russian philosopher, historian and children's writer Kornei Chukovsky, when he recounts the behaviour of his own two-year-old daughter[4].

For her, at that time, as for many other children of similar age, it was a source of great emotional and mental activity, although in itself seemingly insignificant, that a rooster cries cock-a-doodle-doo, a dog barks, a cat miaows. (........) These facts brought simultaneously clarity, order, and proportion to a world of living creatures as fascinating to her as to every other tot.

But, somehow, one day in the twenty-third month of her existence, my daughter came to me, looking mischievous and embarrassed at the same time - as if she were up to some intrigue. I had never before seen such a complex expression on her little face.

She cried to me even when she was still at some distance from where I sat:

'Daddy, 'oggie - miaow!' - that is, she reported to me the sensational and, to her, obviously incorrect news that a doggie, instead of barking, miaows. And she burst out into somewhat encouraging, somewhat artificial laughter, inviting me, too, to laugh at this invention.

But I was inclined to realism.

'No,' said I, 'the doggie bow-wows.'

''Oggie -miaow!' she repeated, laughing, and at the same time watched my facial expression which, she hoped, would show her how she should regard this erratic invention which seemed to scare her a little . (............)

It seemed to me at that point that I understood the reason for the passion that children feel for the incongruous, for the absurd, and for the severing of ties between objects and their regular functions, expressed in folklore. The key to this varied and joyful preoccupation which has so much importance to the mental and spiritual life of the child is play, but play with a special function. (Chukovsky [1928] 1963)

In this incident, and in Chukovsky's analysis of it, two important points stand out. The first is that his attitude to the child's artifice is positive rather than negative, seeing it as creativity rather than lying, and linking it to fantasy and folklore, rather than deceit. The second point, developed by Chukovksy himself in subsequent discussion, is that such distinctively human creativity is dependent upon language structure. The two-word clause which Chukovsky's daughter uses is the simplest possible: subject + predicator. In child-language development, it indicates the point at which the child may be said to first deploy adult grammar, selecting words paradigmatically and combining them syntactically. It shows also that she has acquired the essential ability to *dis*sociate the different levels of language. She sees them as independently operable, and realises that patterns at the syntactic level (in this case NP + VP) do not have to correspond with reality. Yet no sooner had Chukovsky's daughter mastered these crucial aspects of human language ability, than she uses them to create a fantastic fictional reality in which dogs miaow. Without the clause structure NP + VP, such an activity would be impossible. The human capacity for humour, deceit and the creation of imaginative realities would be severely curtailed if not made impossible altogether.

A very similar point is made by J.R.R. Tolkien in his analysis of the creative process in *Tree and Leaf* where he takes the structure of the noun phrase – *viz.* ((pre modifier) + head (+ post modifier)) – as allowing substitutions which underpin the creation of alternative realities. His example is the mixture of *the green grass* and *the yellow sun* to create *the green sun*.

Both Chukovsky and Tolkien combined philologogical erudition, scholarship in pre-Christian folklore, and talent in fiction. It is significant perhaps that we need to go back to such scholars to find serious attention to the role of language structure in facilitating artifice. The contemporary versions of the disciplines which are most concerned with human mind and language – and most inform language teaching and learning – psychology and linguistics, have little to say about the fantastic and the fictional, but focus upon what they regard as the *real* sides of human existence: the biological substrates of language, or the function of transacting information[5].

The politics of artifice.

Perhaps, as so often, these apparently objective scientific 20th century emphases are as much political in origin as scientific. There is something in the current academic and educational quests for a single reality which echoes changes in European attitudes to cultural and linguistic diversity, during – significantly – the period when the connotation of artifice underwent its change from positive to negative. Not everyone is happy with dual identity, as history testifies. Fundamentalist puritans opposed to the theatre provide one example; nationalists who can not tolerate the dual identity of ethnic minorities within their borders provide another. Language teaching approaches which want the classroom to be monolingual and 'real' – as I shall argue shortly – provide another.

Medieval carnival and Renaissance nationalism.

This is best shown by contrasting pre- with post-Renaissance Europe. In his analysis of carnival, Bakhtin ([1940] 1968) describes how in *medieval* Europe the values of the ascendant ideology of the Catholic Church were on certain feast days temporarily, and institutionally, suspended. In illustration he cites the wide circulation of bawdy parodies of the Lord's Prayer, and gives this (rather mild) example[6].

> Pater noster, tu n'ies pas foulz
> Quar tu t'ies mis en grand repos
> Qui es montes haut in celis

which might be translated – attempting to capture the mixture of colloquial and liturgical language – as follows:

> Our Father, thou art not daft;
> For thou hast given thyself a good rest,
> Who hast ascended into Heaven.

Elsewhere, Bakhtin ([1929] 1984) referred to such activity as 'double voicing', using the term (unlike words such as *duplicity* or *two-faced*) in a positive sense. In these spoof prayers it is significantly play with language – in particular the macaronic mixing of colloquial French with Latin – which effects the parody. These jokers were speakers of their own vernacular and the international language of the time – Latin. A modern equivalent would be the humorous mixing of a first language with English as a lingua franca for humorous effect (Tan 1996).

What is surprising from a modern point of view is that this apparent rebellion was not something which took place illicitly, but institutionally. These bawdy prayers were on carnival days recited in the same churches and even by the same priests whose authority they seem to overthrow. Yet this did not apparently detract from the sincerity of serious worship on other days.

The institutionalised artifice of the medieval carnival belongs to a pre-colonial Europe and hinges very much, as Bakhtin himself points out, upon the mixing of languages and a plurality of authorities. The new nation states of post-Renaissance Europe had an inability to tolerate such ambivalence, and a revulsion at the multiple identities of carnival. People were to have a single identity not a double or multiple one. The repression of duality was not only political but linguistic. The European states tried firstly to make themselves monolingual and then to try to spread that one language – as their religious missionaries spread the one true faith – throughout their empires. Roy Harris, commenting on "the rigid political divisions into autonomous nation states that are a feature of that period of European history" writes that:

'One country - one language' was the ideal to which all the major centralising monarchies aspired. Compiling dictionaries and grammars of one's mother tongue became a patriotic enterprise. In certain instances academies were established, sometimes under royal patronage, in order to give authoritative rulings on linguistic matters, so that there should be no doubt about what the proper form of the national language was. Under such regimes it became increasingly difficult to defend publicly the linguistic rights of minorities or to treat linguistic non-conformity of any kind as other than a deviation from an officially sanctioned form. (Harris 1998:31, quoted in Joseph, Love and Taylor 2001)

Examples of attempted linguistic genocide by the emerging nation states are legion. The Irish campaign of Milton's employer Oliver Cromwell, ostensibly driven by a desire to impose true (i.e. protestant) Christianity, not only reduced the population of Ireland by as much as one half through killing deportation and famine (making it an example of what in contemporary parlance would be called genocidal war) but also contributed to the ongoing decline of the Irish language (Barnard 1975: 170-180; O'Connell 2001). In Scotland, less than one hundred years later, in the aftermath of the 1745 rebellion, the English redoubled their persecution of Scottish Gaelic, making its use a criminal offence, and all but wiping it out. These are not political policies conducive to the kind of multiple identities demanded by artifice. Cultural, religious and linguistic diversity – like the carnival - were ruthlessly suppressed. It is significantly in this period – the heyday of imperial expansion and conquest – that the shift in the meaning of *artifice* occurred.

Language teaching

What, though, is the relevance of all this to language teaching? Is there any connection between the history of artifice on the grand stages of religion and politics and the ELT classroom practices of today?

Direct Method

Probably the single biggest innovation in language teaching of the last 150 years has been the Direct Method, the notion that a language can and should be taught without reference to the learners' own language(s). All subsequent successful language teaching methods have subscribed to its overarching principles, and in this sense we are still in the age of the Direct Method.

Usually, Direct Method has been portrayed as a liberation, replacing the worst excesses of Grammar Translation. Yet its progressive aura may derive more from other factors, such as its greater emphasis upon spoken communication, and from its association with the developing modern world of travel and free trade, than from its rejection of translation and first-language explanation *per se*. It can just as easily be seen, for banning students' own languages, as oppressive and totalitarian – especially in cases where the forbidden language is a minority or repressed one, or where its use is a matter of political sensitivity. It is one thing to tell Japanese or French learners of English that they cannot use their own language, quite another to tell Spanish speaking immigrants to the USA that they must not use Spanish, or Kurds that they must not use Kurdish when learning English in Turkey. Direct Method, in its early days, ruthlessly stamped out the use of other languages in the English Language Teaching classroom, often with quite severe sanctions for teacher or students who disobeyed (Howatt 1984:205). In the early Berlitz schools, teachers were monitored by classroom microphones and dismissed for using translation or for switching into the learners' language to explain.

Direct Method, by definition, denies students the opportunity to develop their skills in translation and code switching. This ban concerns more than just the appropriate means of language learning. It is also, by implication, a statement about the ends. By holding up the monolingual English native speaker as the model, it denigrates the millions of non-native speakers and teachers whose expertise is in switching between languages. It behaves as if, in any given situation, people should be one thing or another: *either* an English speaker, *or* a something-else speaker, but never both together (see Seidlhofer, this volume; Seidlhofer 2001). Moving rapidly between the two languages is not only an authentic activity and one which language learners need, it is also a supreme example of human skill in artifice. There is something sinister and repressive, surely, in a movement which denies it.

Later methodologies.

Under the umbrella of the Direct Method, there followed a series of what might – not unfairly – be called hegemonic methodologies. Recent and current language teaching theories, for all their differences, always have a single fundamentalist faith. Specific details change. Languages are to be taught and learned as habit formation, as a cognitive code, as a 'natural' progression, as notions and functions, as communicative competence, as tasks, as lexical chunks. Each successive movement has been advocated in its time with missionary single-mindedness.

Among these faiths, one constant preoccupation has been to make the classroom as real, natural, and work-oriented as possible, excluding from it any promotion of dual identity, theatricality or pretence. In the name of 'reality' the Communicative Approach and its successors have persuaded teachers to abandon any sense of the classroom as a theatre in which they perform. Exercises in which students 'speak other people's words', have been replaced by tasks in which they must be themselves, with real purposes and real objectives (Skehan 1998:95). (This is despite the implication of corpus analysis that a good deal of language knowledge is memorised ready-made – a question of following social convention and speaking other people's words.) What is needed, it has been almost universally argued, is authentic language use, not teacher dominance, or artificial classroom ritual. So teacher talk and whole class activities (choral repetition etc) have diminished. Everywhere there has been horror at any 'artificial' use of language. There must be no double layer, no stepping in and out of different perspectives. The first layer to be stripped off, by the Direct method, was the student's own language: no translation, no explanation. The second layer was the artifice which is an inherent part of learning: no breaking things down into bits, no focus on rules, no error correction, no grading, no simplifying, no learning paradigms, no artificial or invented language no classroom rituals, no rote learning, no repetition.

Yet, paradoxically, nothing could be more natural for human beings than artifice, especially in language and learning. What does the child do as she acquires a first language or languages but take on other people's words and identities? What we do when we learn an additional language but acquire yet more different roles, the ability to step in and out of new different *'rooms'*. For what could be more artificial than deliberately setting out in adult life to learn another language? When we speak it, we acquire an extra identity. We become Russian as well as English, French as well as Japanese (or whatever the pairing is). And the class*room* is the bounded designated area in which that begins to take place, with its own rituals, and roles and artificialities – a gift to the common collocate of artifice: theatricality. When freed from authoritarianism, the language classroom is a place for multiple identities.

Notes

1 See *Paradise Lost* vii: 519-550.
2 Often, in this debate, a simple opposition has been made between instinct and culture, with the degree of influence exerted by each being the subject of disagreement. For evolutionary psychologists, most of what passes for culture is regarded as instinctively driven; for constructivists, on the other hand, human cultural identity overwhelms our instinctual drives. Chomskyan linguistics occupies an ambiguous position. On the one hand it sees humans, like animals, as pre-programmed with species-specific characteristics; on the other hand it regards one particular species-specific attribute, the language faculty, as discontinuous with anything in the animal kingdom. Language is viewed as the product of an 'instinct', but one which is very different from those of other animals.
3 A blow to the simplistic view that animals are all instinct and no culture is provided by research into cultural variation between apes of the same species (Tomasello 1999, de Waal 2001) documenting the extent of their culturally transmitted and variable behaviour (such as the use of medicinal leaves).
4 For further discussion of this passage see Cook 2000: 44-6
5 Those who have found this strange are few and far between. One is the psychologist, Richard Gregory ([1974] 1977).
6 For further discussion of this passage see Cook 2000:84-86.

References:

Bakhtin, M.M. ([1934] 1981) From the prehistory of novelistic discourse. In *The Dialogic Imagination* (ed. M. Holquist. transl. M. Holquist and C. Emerson) Austin: University of Texas Press
Bakhtin, M.M. ([1929 revised 1963] 1984) *Problems of Dostoevsky's Poetics.* (transl. C. Emerson). Minneapolis: University of Minnesota Press.
Barnard, T.C. (1975) *Cromwellian Ireland.* Oxford: Oxford University Press.
Blake, William (1975) (ed. Geoffrey Keynes) *Poetry and Prose of William Blake.* London: Nonesuch.

Brown, R. (1973) *A First Language: the early stages.* Cambridge Mass.: Harvard University Press.

COBUILD Corpus and Concordance Sampler.
http://titania.cobuild.collins.co.uk/form.html

Cook, G. (2000) *Language Play, Language Learning* Oxford: Oxford University Press.

Chukovsky, K. ([1928] 1963) *From Two to Five.* (transl. and ed. Miriam Morton) Berkeley: University of California Press.

Crystal, D. and Davy, D. (1969) *Investigating English Style.* London: Longman.

Dunbar, R. (1996) *Grooming, Gossip and the Evolution of Language.* London and Boston: Faber and Faber.

Glinert, L. (1993) Language as Quasilect: Hebrew in Contemporary Anglo-Jewry in L. Glinert (ed.): *Hebrew in Ashkenaz: a language in exile.* New York: Oxford University Press.

Goffman, E. (1974) *Frame Analysis: an essay on the organization of experience.* Boston: North-eastern University Press (reprinted by Harmondsworth: Penguin.)

Gregory, R. (1977) Psychology: towards a science of fiction. In M. Meek, A. Warlow and G. Barton (eds.): *The Cool Web: the pattern of children's reading.* London: The Bodley Head.

Halliday, M.A.K., McIntosh, A., Strevens, P. (1964) *The Linguistic Sciences and Language Teaching.* London: Longman.

Harris, R. (1998) *Introduction to Integrational Linguistics.* Oxford: Pergamon Press.

Hockett, C.F. (1963) The Problem of Universals in Language. In Greenberg, J. (ed.) *Universals of Language* Cambridge Mass.: MIT press.

Howatt, A.P.R. (1984) *A History of English Language Teaching.* Oxford: Oxford University Press.

Huizinga, J. ([1944] 1949) *Homo Ludens.* London: Routledge and Kegan Paul.

Hymes, D. (1972) Models of the interaction of language and social life. In Gumperz, J. and Hymes, D. (eds.) *Directions in Sociolinguistics* New York: Holt, Rinehart and Winston: 5-71.

Joseph, J., Love, N., and Taylor, T. (2001) *Landmarks in Linguistic Thought II.* London: Routledge.

Klinger, E. (1971) *Structure and Functions of Fantasy.* New York: Wiley-Interscience.

O'Connell, J. (2001) Cherishing a Minority Language: Irish Language and National Identity Paper given at the European Language Minorities conference, University of Bath

The Shorter Oxford English Dictionary On Historical Principles. (1941) (ed. C.T.Onions) London: Oxford University Press.

Rampton, B. (1999) Dichotomies, difference and ritual in second language learning and teaching. *Applied Linguistics* 20/3: 316-341.

Rampton, B. (2001) Ritual, Cross-Disciplinarity, and Foreign Languages at School. Manuscript.

Seidlhofer, B. (2002) *Habeas Corpus* and *Divide et Impera*: 'Global English' and Applied Linguistics. This volume.

Seidlhofer, B. (2001) Closing a conceptual gap: the case for a description of English as a lingua franca. *International Journal of Applied Linguistics*, 11/2: 133-158

Simpson, J. (2002) Discourse, electronic literacy and synchronous computer mediated communication. This volume.

Singer, J. L. (1975) *Daydreaming and Fantasy*. Oxford: Oxford University Press.

Skehan, P. (1998) *A Cognitive Approach to Language Learning*. Oxford: Oxford University Press.

Tan, M. (1996) Songs in Singlish. In Maybin, J. and Mercer, N. (eds.) *Using English: from Conversation to Canon*. London: Routledge with the Open University 228-230.

Tolkien, J.R.R. (1964) On Fairy Stories. In *Tree and Leaf* London: George Allen and Unwin.

Tomasello, M. (1999) *The Cultural Origins of Human Cognition*. Cambridge, Mass.: Harvard University Press.

de Waal, F. (2001) *The Ape and the Sushi Master*. Allen Lane. The Penguin Press.

13 *Habeas corpus* and *divide et impera*: 'Global English' and applied linguistics

BARBARA SEIDLHOFER

University of Vienna

Introduction

The purpose of this paper is to present a case for a conceptualisation of English which is different from, and partly against the grain of, mainstream approaches to its description and to outline a project which seeks to describe the language from this different point of view. It seems appropriate for me to give an account of the research I am currently doing along these lines and to provide a justification for it. Of course, I am aware that not everyone reading this paper will be especially interested in descriptions of English, or their educational implications, so I intend to broaden the scope and relevance of this paper and venture to suggest what the wider significance of my particular perspective might be for other areas of linguistics and applied linguistics. I hope that this will also serve to elucidate the somewhat outlandish title I have chosen. But let me begin with a more familiar term in my title: Global English.

I think there is no need to rehearse here the usual story of the amazing global spread of English, and the facts and figures which David Graddol gave in his Pit Corder lecture last year, and which are to be found in his The Future of English? (1997). Suffice it to sketch the situation, then, in Braj Kachru's words:

> There are now at least four non-native speakers of English for every native speaker, and most of the channels of spread are especially controlled and funded by the non-native users of the language ... (Kachru 1996a:241)

McArthur (1992:355) has a more conservative estimate, namely "a 2-to-1 ratio of non-natives to natives", and to cite a voice from what Kachru calls the Expanding Circle, the German author Beneke (1991:54) adds another way of looking at this when he estimates that

80% of all communication involving the use of English as a second or foreign language does not involve any native speakers of English.

To go back to the quotation from Kachru, I have actually cut it short in a way which results in a mispresentation of what he says (not, of course an unfamiliar stratagem in academic discourse). The sentence in its entirety reads like this:

There are now at least four non-native speakers of English for every native speaker, and most of the channels of spread are especially controlled and funded by the non-native users of the language in Asia and Africa, and by agencies that they support. (Kachru 1996a:241, emphasis added)

But what of Europe? As one of the 100-200 million European non-native users of English as a lingua franca I feel left out here. I would like to be taken into account too. This, however, is not a straightforward matter, as I hope to show below.

English as a lingua franca

The fact remains that we foreigners are in the majority, and our English cannot be easily dismissed in the Fawlty Towers manner on the grounds that we are from Barcelona, or Bangkok, or Bruck an der Leitha. This situation is unique in linguistic history in terms of scale, although of course the processes involved in the development of the language are familiar ones. And when we speak of global English, what we primarily refer to, numerically speaking, is bound to be English as a lingua franca, or ELF for short. According to Juliane House,

ELF interactions are defined as interactions between members of two or more different linguacultures in English, for none of whom English is the mother tongue. Such interactions are extremely frequent now and will increase exponentially in the future. (House 1999: 74)

But it is not only a matter of numbers. The significance is social as well as statistical. As House goes on to point out,

As, moreover, they [ie these ELF interactions] often occur in 'influential networks', i.e., global business, politics, science, technology and media discourse, it seems vital to pay more attention to the nature of ELF interactions, and ask whether and how they are different from both interactions between native speakers, and interactions between native speakers and non-native speakers. An answer to this question would bring us closer to finding out whether and in what ways ELF interactions are actually sui generis. (ibid.)

Of course, we have been cognizant of all this for about two decades now, so what have we done about it? Not a lot, really.

It is true that pedagogic ideas about teaching and learning on the one hand and sociolinguistic ideas about the sovereignty and prestige of indigenized varieties of English on the other have changed quite dramatically. The empire writes back and non-native teachers assert themselves in various publications. Nevertheless, assumptions about the 'E' in TEFL have remained curiously unaffected by these momentous developments. In TEFL, what constitutes a valid target is still determined with virtually exclusive reference to native-speaker norms. So a question in urgent need of exploration is just how appropriate the 'English' is that is being taught and learnt in this emerging global era, and how it squares with the sociopolitical and socioeconomic concerns discussed in the profession, and what its relevance is for the subject taught in classrooms all over the world.

Although there is a general awareness of the need for a change in how our subject is conceived, the fact remains that, as far as linguistic models as targets for learning are concerned, these usually do not figure as a focal concern, or matter for reflection, at all. And so, whether explicitly or implicitly, native-speaker models have largely remained unquestioned. Certainly no linguistically radical proposals have been put forward which would match the thrust of the important innovations which have taken place in pedagogy. In short, no coherent and comprehensive lingua franca model has been proposed so far which does justice to these changes in terms of the actual language taught. This state of affairs allows the economic, social and symbolic power of 'native speaker English' to be reproduced (in the sense of Bourdieu & Passeron 1970) throughout ELT institutions and practices worldwide.

Inner, Outer and Expanding Circle

It must be the case that when Kachru counts "at least four non-native speakers for every native speaker" the non-natives include both what he calls Expanding Circle (English as a foreign language) as well as Outer Circle (indigenised varieties of English). Kachru's model has not been without its critics. But it has proved useful for making statements about the differences between these kinds of English, and it will be a convenient frame of reference for me to talk about the notion of Global English, for taking stock of the work on these varieties that has been done to date, and for perceiving important differences as well as lost opportunities for collaboration and cross-fertilization.

Taking World Englishes as an umbrella term for all three Circles, in the Outer Circle (ie indigenised/nativized/institutionalised varieties) important conceptual and empirical work has been undertaken, eg Kachru (1986) for Indian English and Bamgbose et al (1995) for West African Englishes. Considerable progress has been made in this area over the last twenty years or so in describing Outer Circle varieties and establishing their legitimacy in the world at large. Codification of several varieties is in progress, also due to collaboration across Circle boundaries, eg within the ICE project (the International Corpus of English, cf eg Greenbaum 1996) originating in the Inner Circle. I think it is fair to say that as far as English as an international language is concerned, the groundbreaking work has been essentially focused on, and based in, the Outer Circle.

As for the Inner Circle, in the last 15 years or so, virtually all work on the spread of English has been on the meta-level, addressing important socio-economic, ideological and ecological issues, but not the conceptualisation of English 'as a world language' as such. So a central question, for instance, has been: how do the Brits (mainly) come to terms with 'their' linguistic imperialism? How do they cope with their guilt, which, as Sinfree Makoni (1999) put it so pointedly at the last AILA World Congress, is really "their problem" and nobody else's? But not, with the important exception of Jenkins (2000), how can we describe English so that it is adequate for the roles it fulfils in the world? Interestingly, what is often termed 'international' by Inner Circle scholars, publishers etc is simply an extension from the old 'ancestral home' of English to the newer native varieties. Thus Kachru (1997), quite rightly, criticizes the Cambridge International Dictionary of English for using the term 'international' for referring to "America, Britain and Australia" (1997:70f).

And certainly, even when the term 'international English' is used, the convention seems to be that this covers the Outer Circle but is usually not taken to include Expanding Circle English (as is the case, for instance, with Todd & Hancock 1986, Trudgill & Hannah 1995). Similarly, the name ICE, for 'International Corpus of English', describing itself on its website[1] as "the first large-scale effort to study the development of English as a world language", might give rise to unwarranted expectations in somebody interested in how English is used truly globally, between New Zealand and Norway, Nigeria and Japan. Because, as Greenbaum explains,

> Its [ICE's] principal aim is to provide the resources for comparative studies of the English used in countries where it is either a majority first language ... or an official additional

language. In both language situations, English serves as a means of communication between those who live in these countries" (Greenbaum 1996:3).

Excluded from ICE is the English used in countries where it is not a medium for communication between natives of the country" (p.4).

What I find particularly intriguing, not to say astounding, in the Inner Circle is that the fantastic progress which has been made in the corpus-based description of ENL, English as a native language, of the last two decades or so has not rubbed off as it were on the description of ELF. In other words, the language has spread, but its description has not.

Whereas with the Inner and the Outer Circle you can be fairly sure where you are, namely 'In' or 'Out', things are not quite so straightforward when we come to the Expanding Circle, and here Kachru's model appears to be in need of revision. To start with, there are the terms themselves: whereas 'Inner' and 'Outer' are non-dynamic, 'Expanding', as the very verb form indicates, is different in that being progressive it is necessarily dynamic. But the irony is that it is precisely the dynamism of the Expanding Circle that is disregarded.

One of the difficulties is that Kachru's model of the Inner, Outer and Expanding Circles is somewhat skewed – and understandably so – because it is conceived of largely in historical and geographical terms: countries are described as belonging to one of these circles, but it is worth bearing in mind that what we can also be referring to when we talk about the language of the Outer or Expanding Circle is the way in which the language actually functions socially and communicatively. And from this point of view, it is obvious that English is expanding also in the Outer Circle, and even in the Inner Circle: for instance, due to new uses in new (and expanding) domains, e.g. the Internet, the lexicon is constantly being added to, so the same processes are at work in all three circles. What we have here, then, is a situation which cannot be captured directly by Kachru's nomenclature, because there are countries which previously one might have regarded as clearly Outer Circle (because of their colonial past) which now are obviously Expanding Circle too (because English is expanding in them). But it does not work the other way round – by the very definition of the terms, countries which are Expanding Circle cannot become Outer Circle and so lay claim to their own indigenised varieties of English. The problem is that since the whole model is historical and geographical, but not really sociolinguistic, it is not designed to deal with the characteristic functioning of the language in the Expanding Circle, as a lingua franca.[2] What Inner and Outer Circle have in common is that in both speakers are using English essentially as an intracommunity language, culturally intrinsic to their society and so necessarily involving matters of social identity (hence Kachru's interest in literature, cf. eg Kachru 1995). And so Kachru quite rightly points to the inequality, that the English spoken in the Inner Circle is recognized while in the Outer Circle traditionally it tended not to be. But the lingua franca in the Expanding Circle is a totally different situation – it is essentially culturally extrinsic, and the very point is that it does not belong to anybody in particular (cf Widdowson 1994). It could of course be the case that precisely because it does not make sense to lay claim to 'ownership' of a lingua franca that Expanding Circle English has fallen between two stools as it were. In fact, I am beginning to wonder whether the very power and success of Kachru's model, centred as it is on advocacy for the Outer Circle, has unintentionally contributed to the neglect of the Expanding Circle (if it is semantically possible, even in ELF, to contribute to neglect!).

If English is expanding, then knowing what we know about language it must also vary. So there is variation in the Expanding Circle English as there is in Inner and Outer Circle English. Where is the description of that variation, then? Who has taken note of it? Who has discussed the pressures that apply to this variation, that influence it? Hardly anybody – the focus has been, almost obsessively, on the Outer Circle.

More's the pity, since I find Kachru's approach to the issues raised by the global spread of English absolutely congenial for thinking about ELF, and I agree with him when he says:

> There are essentially two types of response. One is to view this overwhelming linguistic phenomenon as an age-old process of language dynamics accentuated by the complex culturally and linguistically pluralistic contexts of language acquisition, language function, language contact, and language creativity. This response demands questioning the earlier paradigms, asking new probing questions, and looking for fresh theoretical and methodological answers. The second response, from a number of active scholars, is to marginalize any questions – theoretical, methodological, and ideological – which challenge the earlier paradigms or seek answers appropriate to new global functions of English. (Kachru 1996a:242)

A conceptual gap

To sum up the situation, then, with regard to the conceptualisation of English as a Lingua Franca as defined above, all we find essentially in all three Circles is a conceptual gap – by analogy with Kachru's

(1996a:242) evocative term 'paradigm myopia' we would have to call this a 'paradigm blind spot'. To put it crudely, for most scholars in all three Circles ELF does not exist, and so 'English' has to mean either 'English as a native language' or 'English as a nativized language'. The natives are always lurking.[3]

Virtually nowhere can we see an awareness that English as a lingua franca might be what House (1999:74) calls "sui generis", a linguistic phenomenon in its own right; instead, what is still all-pervasive is a deficit view of ELF: what we have here is not a difference perspective with an acknowledgement of plurality but a tenacious deficit perspective in which variation is perceived as deviation from ENL norms and described in terms of 'errors' or 'fossilisation' – to borrow from Guy Cook's title for his paper in this volume, the picture for ELF is one of "imposed unity" and "denied diversity". This view has, of course, been successfully questioned for the Outer Circle, but no recognition is given to the fact that many of the same processes are taking place in the Expanding Circle, which is therefore still expected to conform to the Inner Circle.

This may explain why even scholars who champion the idea of linguistic human rights do not fully recognize an assertion of them in this respect. So it is that Robert Phillipson & Tove Skuttnab-Kangas (1999) talk about the Danish Prime Minister's English in terms of "errors" (p.29) rather than in terms of his legitimate, rightful appropriation of the language for his own purposes. This is also why David Crystal seems to think that his (native) English can simply be equated with the language which is "most in contention for th[e] role" of a "single world language" (Crystal 1997: viii). This also is why Peter Medgyes describes his fellow 'non-native' teachers as so self-deprecating and so much in awe of ENL and why he feels, to use his words, that they "suffer from an inferiority complex caused by glaring defects in [their] knowledge of English" (Medgyes 1994:40). Further, despite certain dissenting voices (eg Firth & Wagner 1997, Cook 1999) the non-recognition of ELF reduces virtually all SLA research to operating with a native-speaker model and to constructing non-native speakers as defective communicators. It is also one reason why practically all learner corpus research (cf. e.g. Granger 1998, Granger et al, forthcoming) is geared towards highlighting the difficulties specific L1 groups have with native English in order to make it easier for those learners to conform to ENL, and why dictionaries and grammars based on the large native-speaker corpora can lay claim to a monopoly of 'real English'.

So what we have here is a negative rather than a positive evaluation of non-conformity. Even those who assertively support the development of a continental European hybrid variety of English that does not look to Britain or America for its standards of correctness reveal a degree of schizophrenia in this respect. For example, Hoffmann (2000:19) describes the English of European learners as spanning "the whole range from non-fluent to native-like", as though fluency in English were not a possibility for those whose speech does not mimic that of a native speaker. (What about Henry Kissinger holding forth?) Similarly, van Els claims that the ownership of a lingua franca transfers from its native speakers to its non-native speakers, and yet goes on to argue paradoxically that the Dutch should not be complacent about their English because "only very few are able to achieve a level of proficiency that approximates the native or native-like level" (2000:29).

Despite the high level of scholarly activity with regard to the role and status of English in the world, then, I think that progress with respect to English as a lingua franca has been very meagre so far, in terms of both conceptualisation and description. In fact, the research and published work on contemporary English over recent years is evidence of an oddly contradictory and paradoxical situation that ultimately results in a kind of vicious circle: On the one hand, we have a very lively and prolific field of research producing extralinguistic treatments of how 'English' is – depending on the specific researcher's domain of interest and ideological orientation– being variously spread, used, forced upon, or withheld from the world at large[4], coupled with assertions of local values and the importance of intercultural communication in pedagogy. On the other hand, the rapid development in computer technology (allied, of course, with economic interests) has opened up hitherto undreamt-of possibilities in language description. The main research efforts in this area, however, are not expended on studying how English is actually used worldwide, but instead concentrate very much on how English is really spoken and written by its native speakers. We thus have an inverse relationship between perceived significance and relevance of English in the world at large and linguistic description focusing on the core native-speaker countries – one embracing pluralism, the other ignoring it.

What I find particularly fascinating is that these two contrary developments, let's call them, in a simplifying shorthand, the 'linguistic realistic' and the 'critical political', are actually interdependent and even, perversely enough, reinforce each other: the more global the use of, and perceived need for, English becomes, the greater the motivation, and of course the market, for descriptions of it, which, for historical and socioeconomic reasons, are largely provided by the 'Centre'. The more such products are on offer, the more these are regarded, quite rightly, as promoting the dominance of (L1) English, and thus the more forceful and numerous the attempts in (or on behalf of) the 'Periphery' to resist 'linguistic imperialism' (cf eg Canagarajah 1999, Pennycook 1998, Phillipson 1992, Hall & Eggington 2000). A cynic, or an economist, would say of course that this kind of dialectical escalation provides just the impetus that the book market needs.

Divide et impera

In my view, however, this state of affairs is highly unsatisfactory, and it would seem to arise mainly from a divorce of the conceptual and the empirical – a case indeed of what I perceive as a regrettable but endemic tendency in academic discourse at large: the tendency to divide up the field so as to more conveniently control it, to better cultivate your own patch - divide and rule, *divide et impera*. With regard to Global English, this means that very little work in this area is being conducted (especially in the Inner Circle particularly relevant to this conference) which has both a strong conceptual basis, ie an engagement with theory and grounding in historically-situated conceptual work, as well as a strong empirical basis. I realize that is a rather sweeping statement to make, since a) no doubt some counter-examples could be found and b) academic work does not come in pure forms, either conceptual or empirical, so obviously I am talking about strong preponderances and relative mutual neglect here. But I do not think that this would invalidate my observation of what I would call a general tendency. Let me give you a few examples. To name a couple of prominent exponents of 'critical political' work, there are Phillipson (1992), Pennycook (1994, 1999, 2001). On the 'linguistic realistic' side, we have, for instance, the British National Corpus (Aston & Burnard 1998), CANCODE (Carter & McCarthy, e.g. 1997, COBUILD (as described in Sinclair 1987). Both these areas, critical-political and linguistic-realistic, are surely relevant to Global English, but one looks in vain for any substantial common ground and cross-reference in the respective publications. I would have thought it important, for example, for Pennycook's and Phillipson's work to take into account how the language whose 'wordly' impact they discuss is actually described, with all the consequences of that description on the perception of its users, learners, and teachers. And conversely, surely it would be important for the researchers involved in the big corpus projects to constructively engage with work which critically examines the impact of the language they describe? Do not misunderstand me, I would not want to miss, or wish to criticize, the important and groundbreaking work that has been, and is being, done in both these fields, I just deplore the lack of interaction between them.

Thus Alastair Pennycook, for instance, states that we need to

...look long and hard at the wider context of our activities, and having done so, to think hard about how different macro-frameworks may be translated into the more micro-activities of classroom pedagogy, curriculum design, or textbook writing (Pennycook 1999:154)

However, I have not found any evidence of Pennycook himself following his own advice in the form of conducting analyses of curricula or textbooks that would enable him to make relevant suggestions for classroom pedagogy, let alone alternative descriptions of the language, the bread and butter of ELT practitioners worldwide. It seems that the "Applied Postlinguistic Approach" he advocates (Pennycook 2001) actually closes these avenues for him.

Conversely, when Guy Cook (1998) voices doubts about the relevance of descriptions of features of native-speaker corpora for the teaching of English as an international language, Ron Carter's reaction is:

Guy Cook is not alone in sidestepping the question of where learners are to get their models of English from, which models they might actually want, and how any such model is to be described. (Carter 1998:64)

This response illustrates precisely the problem I am trying to pinpoint: Ron Carter seems to accept that there is a case for alternative models, but at the same time he still vigorously promotes the description of native-speaker English as a kind of expediency, because this is what we now have at our disposal. I would presume to suggest that some in-depth engagement with fundamental ideas about the cultural politics of global English and cross-cultural pedagogy, combined with the very careful conceptual work of his predecessors in empirical work such as Michael West would significantly influence the way current corpus-based descriptions of ENL situate themselves *vis a vis* the complexities of ELT worldwide, and actually contribute to their strengths. If one locates this debate in its historical context, it is clear that the issues were carefully considered by people with pedagogic concerns engaging in quantitative description long before the computer appeared on the scene. It is a matter of some regret that the relationship between the pedagogic-prescriptive side of things and the descriptive side, which these predecessors were at such pains to explore, seems to be largely disregarded in current work.

Of course, Ron Carter can take up his somewhat contradictory position because there is indeed no alternative description currently available. Not yet. But this is going to change. And here, I should like to sketch briefly the research project I am currently engaged in, and then try to place this in a more general perspective. Essentially, then, I have discussed two dimensions: conceptual-empirical and descriptive-prescriptive, and have argued that there is a tendency, widespread in any academic work but nevertheless regrettable, to pursue a policy of divide and rule. After all I have said so far it will not come as a surprise that my project is one that would claim to combine rather than divide, in attempting to take into account both sides of the conceptual-empirical as well as the descriptive-prescriptive dimension.

Habeas corpus

To take my cue from Kachru again, he has long insisted that "the unprecedented functional range and social penetration globally acquired by English demands fresh theoretical and descriptive perspectives" (Kachru 1996b: 906). However, as I have tried to indicate, the suitability of the descriptive and pedagogic models we are operating with for the teaching and use of ELF has hardly been investigated at all. Hence I shall argue that it is both necessary and feasible to enquire into a description of salient features of ELF based on a large computerized data-bank. The idea, then, is to release ELF from unwarranted conceptual imprisonment, so in that sense I'd like to file an application for a writ of *habeas corpus*, or rather, *habeas ELF corpus*.[5]

Of course, this does not simply come out of the blue. I am not claiming to be coming up with something totally revolutionary and unheard-of - again, it helps to bear the historical perspective in mind. In fact a moment's reflection will reveal that obviously no empirical work can be conceptually innocent. This is driven home, for instance, in Michael Swan's review of Biber et al's Longman Grammar of Spoken and Written English (1999), in which he says:

> The analysis draws principally on data from the custom-built 40-million-word Longman corpus of written and spoken British and American English. (So corpus-based is the work, indeed, that the authors are credited by the publishers as having approached their task without 'preconceived notions of the grammar of English'. Fortunately this is not the case: the team includes several extremely well-informed grammarians.) (Swan 2000)

And so, of course, I acknowledge and build upon work that has been done before in this line. There have been various attempts in the past to come up with linguistic models for teaching English as an international language, and these pre-empt, and offer many profound insights into, many of the issues that we see ourselves confronted with today. These have either taken the shape of conceptually devised models of a reduced inventory as a first step, lightening the learning load as it were, from Ogden's Basic English, which was extremely influential in its time (eg Ogden 1930) to Quirk's Nuclear English (1982), or of empirically derived suggestions based on manual vocabulary counts, the most famous of these being West's General Service List (1953), as well as attempts to turn these to practical use, such as Palmer & Hornby's Thousand-Word English. What it is and what can be done with it. (1937). There are also contemporary speculations, such as Crystal (eg 1997), who foresees the emergence of "a new form of English – let us think of it as 'World Standard Spoken English' (WSSE)." He adds, though, that "WSSE is still in its infancy. Indeed, it has hardly been born" and yet again, there is a certain native-speaker fixation to his assumption that the variety which will be "most influential in the development of WSSE" is US English. (Crystal 1997: 136ff). But none of these various approaches to ELF fulfilled the combination of criteria that I would claim need to be met for a viable alternative to ENL in its own right, of which a very broad and substantial empirical base and a truly fresh approach in terms of independence from the dictates of ENL would seem to be the most important ones. The big opportunity which offers itself now is that it has become possible to take into account the considerable amount of conceptual work undertaken in the past and present while at the same time basing investigations on a large empirical foundation.

Eventually, such a data-base will allow us to consider what it might mean to extend claims made for the Outer Circle to the Expanding Circle, to ELF. We might even explore the possibility of a codification of ELF with a conceivable ultimate objective of making it a feasible, acceptable and respected alternative to ENL in appropriate contexts of use. As Bamgbose points out when discussing "the ambivalence between recognition and acceptance of non-native norms":

> The importance of codification is too obvious to be belaboured. ... one of the major factors militating against the emergence of **endonormative** standards in non-native Englishes is precisely the dearth of codification. Obviously, once a usage or innovation enters the dictionary as correct and acceptable usage, its status as a regular form is assured. (1998:4, emphasis added).

So in order to make it possible to investigate how ELF manifests itself, and might actually be codified, I have embarked on the compilation of a corpus of English as a Lingua Franca, at the University of Vienna – to my knowledge, the first large-scale effort to capture exclusively lingua

franca English (cf Seidlhofer 2001). In the current initial phase, this
project is supported by Oxford University Press, and therefore called
the Vienna–Oxford International Corpus of English, or VOICE. Since
the intention is to capture a wide range of variation, a corpus of spoken
ELF is the first target, at one remove from the stabilizing and
standardizing influence of writing. Another important reason for
concentrating on the spoken medium is that spoken interaction is
overtly reciprocal, which means that not only production but also
reception are captured to a degree, thus allowing for observations
regarding the mutual intelligibility of what interlocutors say. For the
time being, the focus is on unscripted (though partly pre-structured),
largely face-to-face communication among fairly fluent speakers from a
wide range of first language backgrounds whose primary and secondary
education and socialization did not take place in English. The speech
events being captured include private and public dialogues, private and
public group discussions and casual conversations, and one-to-one
interviews. Ideally, speakers will be making use of ELF in a largely
unselfconscious, instrumental (as opposed to identificatory) way –
compare Hüllen's (1992) distinction between 'Identifikationssprache'
(language of identification) and 'Kommunikationssprache' (language
for communication). At least for the first phase, I decided to operate
with a narrow definition of ELF talk. That is to say, an attempt is made
to meet the following additional criteria: no native speakers should be
involved in the interaction, and the interaction should not take place in
an environment where the predominant language is 'English', such as an
'Inner Circle', ENL country. Vienna therefore seems a good place for
this, right in the middle of Europe, and a place where many
international meetings happen.[6]

This corpus should make it possible to take stock of how the
speakers providing the data actually communicate through ELF, and to
attempt a characterisation of how they use, or rather co-construct,
'English' to do so. Essentially, the same research questions as Kennedy
(1998) regards as central to corpus-based descriptive studies of ENL
can also be addressed through the ELF corpus; he summarizes them like
this:

> What are the linguistic units, patterns, systems or processes in the
> language, genre or text and how often, when, where, why and with
> whom are they used? (Kennedy 1998: 276)

As a first research focus, it seems desirable to complement the work
already done on ELF phonology (that is, Jenkins 2000; see also Jenkins
2002) and the few initial findings about ELF pragmatics (for instance,
Firth 1996, House 1999, 2002, Lesznyak 2002, Meierkord 1996) by

concentrating on lexico-grammar and discourse. So what we are trying to establish is what (if anything), notwithstanding all the diversity, emerges as common features of ELF use, irrespective of speakers' first languages and levels of proficiency. Questions we will investigate include the following: What seem to be the most relied-upon and successfully employed grammatical constructions and lexical choices? Are there aspects which contribute especially to smooth comm.-unication? What are the factors which tend to lead to misunderstandings or even communication breakdown? Is the degree of approximation to a variety of L1 English always proportional to communicative success? Or are there commonly used constructions, lexical items and sound patterns which are ungrammatical in Standard L1 English but generally unproblematic in ELF communication? If so, can hypotheses be set up and tested concerning simplifications of L1 English which could constitute systematic features of ELF? The objective here, then, would be to establish something like an index of communicative redundancy, in the sense that many of the niceties of social behaviour associated with native-speaker models and identities might not be operable and certain native-speaker norms might be seen to be in suspense. Indeed, it may well be that situations occur in which 'unilateral' approximation to native speaker norms and expectations not shared in ELF interaction leads to communication problems, and that mutual accommodation[7] is found to have greater importance for communicative effectiveness than so-called correctness or idiomaticity in ENL terms.[8]

VOICE: some preliminary findings

Of course, it is early days yet and so far I cannot report any reliable findings based on quantitative investigations. But even a quick analysis of a few dialogues suffices to point to some hypotheses. For instance, there seems to be a tendency for particularly idiomatic speech by one participant to cause misunderstandings – a kind of 'unilateral idiomaticity' characterised by e.g. metaphorical language use, idioms, phrasal verbs and precisely the kind of fixed ENL expressions which ENL corpora are so good at revealing (but see Gavioli & Aston 2001).

　　Here is an example from my fieldnotes: In April 2000, I was involved in the following dinner conversation in southern Crete. On my left sat my English (native speaker) friend Peter; on my right, three Norwegians, users of ELF. Yiannis, the Greek waiter (and another ELF speaker) whom we know quite well, appears with several glasses of the local raki, usually complimentary after a meal, and serves it in small glasses to the Norwegians with the words "this is from the house" (maybe trying to use a phrase that Peter has taught him, but not quite getting it right). The Norwegian woman on my right, Leila, says "ja ja", nodding to Yiannis. Her response sounds like an acknowledgement that she has received some information, maybe something like "this is the house raki, we make it", but not like thanking. So my English friend Peter and I simultaneously turn to Leila to explain. Peter: "Yiannis meant that this is ON the house". But from Leila's facial expression it is clear that she does not know this phrase. So I rephrase saying "Yiannis meant that it is a PRESENT from them", upon which Leila says "Ahh!!" and, realizing that she should have thanked Yiannis, looks round to see whether he is still within earshot.

So much for native speaker idiomaticity and its usefulness for ELF. On the other hand, what also happens in my data is that typical learners' 'errors' which most English teachers would consider in urgent need of correction and remediation, and which consequently often get allotted a great deal of time and effort in EFL lessons, appear to be generally unproblematic in ELF talk, and no obstacle to communicative success. Here is another short example from my fieldnotes:

In early September 2001 on a cold and windy ferry trip in the Netherlands, Sandra, a Brazilian relative of mine, suggested having lunch, adding the expression: "Full stomach make you feel warm." Nobody in the group had the slightest problem understanding what she was saying, and indeed the only reason I noticed that there were two 'grave grammatical aberrations' in this short sentence, namely missing indefinite article and missing 3rd person –s was that I was collecting data for this talk.

The 'errors' in my data, then, include 'dropping' the third person present tense –s, 'confusing' the relative pronouns 'who' and 'which', and 'omitting' definite and indefinite articles where they are obligatory in native speaker language use are usually sanctioned in spite of the fact that they are communicatively redundant (and there are parallels with Jenkins' findings in phonology here).

My project is concerned with tracing empirical evidence of general features of ELF in my corpus, but it will clearly also need to refer to a broader conceptual framework in order to provide an explanatory dimension to the enquiry: it is one thing to say that certain features occur as data, but quite another to explain their generality. One particularly promising point of conceptual reference is social psychology, notably accommodation theory (the significance of which is demonstrated so vividly in Jenkins 2000). Another is the historical context of the essentially philosophical work on Basic English mentioned above (see also Seidlhofer 2002). In conducting further investigations on my ELF data, I will of course also continue to relate them to existing research on (native) language variation and change, nativized varieties, pidginization and creolization as well as on simplification in language pedagogy.

Conclusion

As long as 17 years ago, John Sinclair made pioneering observations about the necessity of corpus-based descriptions of English (which, of course, was assumed to be native-speaker English), and pointed out the implications of the availability of such descriptions:

> The categories and methods we use to describe English are not appropriate to the new material. We shall need to overhaul our descriptive systems. (Sinclair 1985:251).

What I am seeking to do, then, is simply to extend this claim to English as a lingua franca:

Precisely the same arguments that Sinclair is making for the description of native-speaker language, for establishing the 'real English of native speakers', apply to the requirement of establishing the "real English of ELF speakers'. It just happens to be the case that the vast new technological apparatus now available has not been used for ELF, and the reality of ELF thus not been taken into account so far, and this is what I have set out to remedy with the compilation and analysis of VOICE.

And there are some more general implications that clearly arise from a project of this kind, which I think we need to take account of, since they concern many of the basic tenets of linguistics and applied linguistics. Central to these is of course the perception of that obscure object of the linguist's and the learner's desire, the native speaker. When the status of the native speaker in linguistic description changes from holding a monopoly on relevance to being just one option of at least two, and in some cases clearly the less relevant one, this has implications for all areas of applied linguistics which make use of linguistic description. Once one questions the primacy of the native speaker, this has repercussions for a whole range of issues, some of which are addressed in this volume. These include questions about the relative communicative salience of features of the language code, the nature of authenticity in language, the relationship between learner and user competencies, and identities, and indeed the problematic concept of competence itself.

Let me repeat, I do not wish to undervalue the important work that has already been done, but we need to be aware too that there is a danger that in accounting for one linguistic reality we may pay less attention to, or even disregard, others. In short and in conclusion, to use a lingua franca of an earlier era, *habeas corpus* by all means, but let us beware of *divide et impera*.

Notes

1   ICE website: http://www.hku.hk/english/research/ice/index.htm
2   And Kachru says as much himself, cf. Kachru 1996b.
3   Cf also Bamgbose 1998:1: "In spite of the consensus on the viability of non-native Englishes, there are issues that still remain unsettled. These include the status of innovations in the nativization process, the continued use of native norms as a point of reference, the ambivalence between recognition and acceptance of non-native norms, the adequacy of pedagogical models, and the overriding need for codification. Underlying these issues is the constant pull between native and non-native English norms. Innovations in non-native Englishes are often judged not for what they are or their function within the varieties in which they occur, but rather according to how they stand in relation to the norms of native Englishes."
4   See Brutt-Griffler (2002) for a thorough discussion of these issues.
5   This translates into 'may you have the body' (of ELF texts). The purpose of a writ of *habeas corpus* originally was, of course, to liberate anyone illegally detained, a protection against arbitrary imprisonment. I assume there is no need to spell out the analogy with the arbitrary confinement of ELF.
6   The size aimed for at the first stage is approximately half a million words, ie comparable to the size of the spoken parts any of the subcorpora of ICE. The data are being transcribed orthographically and marked for speaker turns, pauses and overlaps, and provided with contextual notes and notes about paralinguistic features such as laughter. Part-of-speech tagging and some syntactic parsing may be added at a later stage, and a fairly basic system for marking for prosody is being piloted. No phonetic transcription of these texts is being untertaken, but it is hoped that sound files can be made available eventually. The VOICE homepage is currently under construction and should be up and running soon.
7   Accommodation (in the sense of Giles & Coupland 1991) seems to play a crucial role in such ELF research as is available to date (see below): accommodation was found to be an important factor in Jenkins' (2000) study, and lack of it may have contributed to the impression of "mutual dis-attention" among ELF speakers which House (1999:82) got in the analysis of her data.
8   One interesting issue which is likely to emerge, and one which of course has already given rise to some speculation, is the extent to which the adoption of English as a lingua franca will be variously influenced by the cultural and social practices associated with the speakers' own first language and the conventions of its use. A lingua franca is just as likely to vary in this respect as any naturally occurring language. The point is, however, that we need the kind of descriptive evidence that the project I am describing will yield to give substance to this speculation.

References

Aston, G. & Burnard, L. (1998) *The BNC Handbook*. Edinburgh: Edinburgh University Press.

Beneke, J. (1991) Englisch als lingua franca oder als Medium interkultureller Kommunikation. In Grebing.

Bamgbose, A. (1998) Torn between the norms: innovations in world Englishes. *World Englishes* 17/1:1-14.

Bamgbose, A., Banjo, A. & Thomas, A. (eds) (1995) *New Englishes. A West African Perspective*. Ibadan: Mosuro & The British Council.

Biber, D., Johansson, S., Leech, G., Conrad, S. & Finegan, E. (1999) *Longman Grammar of Spoken and Written English*. Harlow, Essex: Pearson.

Bourdieu, P. & Passeron, J.-C. (1970) *Reproduction in Education, Culture and Society*. transl. R. Nice, London: Sage.

Brumfit, C. (ed.) (1982) *English for International Communication*. Oxford: Pergamon.

Brutt-Griffler, J. (2002) *World English. A Study of Its Development*. Clevedon: Multilingual Matters.

Canagarajah, S. (1999) *Resisting Linguistic Imperialism in English Teaching*. Oxford: Oxford University Press.

Carter, R. (1998) Reply to Guy Cook. *ELT Journal* 52/1: 64.

Carter, R. & McCarthy, M. (1997) *Exploring Spoken English*. Cambridge: Cambridge University Press.

Cenoz, J. & Jessner, U. (eds) (2000) *English in Europe. The Acquisition of a Third Language*. Clevedon: Multilingual Matters.

Cook, G. (1998) The uses of reality: a reply to Ronald Carter. *ELT Journal* 52/1: 57-63.

Cook, G. & Seidlhofer, B. (eds) (1995) *Principle and Practice in Applied Linguistics. Studies in honour of H.G. Widdowson*. Oxford University Press.

Cook, V. (1999) Going Beyond the Native Speaker in Language Teaching. *TESOL Quarterly* 33/2: 185-209.

Crystal, D. (1997) *English as a Global Language*. Cambridge University Press.

van Els T. (2000). The European Union, its Institutions and its Languages. Public lecture given at the University of Nijmegen, the Netherlands, on 22 September 2000.

Firth, A. (1996) The discursive accomplishment of normality. On 'lingua franca' English and conversation analysis. *Journal of Pragmatics* 26/3: 237-259.

Firth, A. & Wagner, J. (1997) On discourse, communication, and (some) fundamental concepts in SLA research. *Modern Language Journal* 81: 285-300.

Gavioli, L. and G. Aston (2001) Enriching reality: language corpora in language pedagogy. *ELT Journal* 55/3: 238-246.

Giles, H. & Coupland, N. (1991) *Language: Contexts and Consequences*. Milton Keynes: Open University Press.

Gnutzmann, C. (ed.) (1999) *Teaching and Learning English as a Global Language*. Stauffenburg.

Graddol, D. (1997) *The Future of English?* London: British Council.

Granger, S. (ed.) (1998) Learner English on Computer. London: Longman.

Granger, S., Hung, J. & Petch-Tyson, S. (eds) (forthcoming) *Computer Learner Corpora, Second Language Acquisition and Foreign Language Teaching*. Amsterdam:Benjamins.

Grebing, R. (ed.) (1991) *Grenzenloses Sprachenlernen*. Berlin:Cornelsen.

Greenbaum, S. (ed.) (1996) *Comparing English Worldwide. The International Corpus of English*. Oxford: Clarendon Press.

Hall, J.K. & Eggington, E. (eds) (2000) *The Sociopolitics of English Language Teaching*. Clevedon: Multilingual Matters.

Hoffmann C. (2000) The Spread of English and the Growth of Multilingualism with English in Europe, in Cenoz & Jessner.

House, J. (1999) Misunderstanding in intercultural communication: Interactions in English as a lingua franca and the myth of mutual intelligibility. In Gnutzmann.

House, J. (2002) Developing pragmatic competence in English as a lingua franca. In Knapp & Meierkord.

Hüllen, W. (1992) Identifikationssprachen und Kommunikations-sprachen. Zeitschrift für Germanistische *Linguistik* 20/3: 298-317.

Jenkins, J. (2000) *The Phonology of English as an International Language*. Oxford University Press.

Jenkins, J. (2002) A sociolinguistically based, empirically researched pronunciation syllabus for English as an International Language. *Applied Linguistics* 23: 83-103.

Kachru, B. (1986) *The Alchemy of English: The Spread, Function and Models of Non-native Englishes*. Oxford: Pergamon. [Reprinted 1990, Urbana, IL: Univ. of Illinois Press.]

Kachru, B. (1995) Transcultural creativity in world Englishes and literary canons. In Cook & Seidlhofer.

Kachru, B. (1996a) The paradigms of marginality. *World Englishes* 15/3: 241-255.

Kachru, B. (1996b) English as lingua franca. In Goebl, H., Nelde, P., Star, Z. & Wölck, W. (eds.) *Kontaktlinguistik. Contact linguistics. Linguistique de contact*. Vol 1. Berlin: De Gruyter.

Kachru, B. (1997) World Englishes and English-using communities. *Annual Review of Applied Linguistics* 17: 66-87.

Kennedy, G. (1998) *An introduction to corpus linguistics*. London: Longman.

Knapp, K. & Meierkord, C. (eds) (2002) *Lingua Franca Communication*. Frankfurt/Main: Lang.

Lesznyak, A. (2002) From chaos to smallest common denominator. Topic management in English lingua franca communication. In Knapp & Meierkord.

Makoni, S. (1999) Contribution to Plenary Symposium and Discussion 'Applied Linguistics in the 21st Century' at AILA 12th World Congress, Tokyo, 6 August 1999.

McArthur, T. (1992) *The Oxford Companion to the English Language*. Oxford: Oxford University Press.

Medgyes, P. (1994) *The Non-Native Teacher*. London: Macmillan.

Meierkord, C. (1996) *Englisch als Medium der interkulturellen Kommunikation. Untersuchungen zum non-native-/non-native speaker - Diskurs*. Frankfurt/Main: Peter Lang.

Ogden, C. (1930) *Basic English. A general introduction with rules and grammar*. London: Kegan Paul.

Palmer, H. E. & Hornby, A.S. (1937). *Thousand-Word English. What it is and what can be done with it*. London:Harrap.

Pennycook, A. (1994) *The Cultural Politics of English as an International Language*. London: Longman.

Pennycook, A. (1998) *English and the Discourses of Colonialism*. London: Routledge.

Pennycook, A. (1999) Pedagogical implications of different frameworks for understanding the global spread of English. In Gnutzmann.

Pennycook, A. (2001) *Critical applied linguistics*. Mahwah, NJ: Lawrence Erlbaum.

Phillipson, R. (1992) *Linguistic Imperialism*. Oxford: Oxford University Press.

Phillipson, R. & Skutnabb-Kangas, T. (1999) Englishisation: one dimension of globalisation. *AILA Review* 13: 19-36.

Quirk R. (1982) International communication and the concept of Nuclear English. In Brumfit. ed

Quirk, R. & Widdowson, H.G. (1985) (eds.) *English in the World: Teaching and Learning the Languages and Literatures*. Cambridge: Cambridge University Press.

Seidlhofer, B (2001). Closing a conceptual gap: the case for a description of English as a lingua franca. International Journal of *Applied Linguistics* 11/2: 133-158.

Seidlhofer, B (2002). The Shape of Things to Come? Some Basic Questions. In Knapp & Meierkord.

Sinclair, J. (1985) Selected issues. In Quirk & Widdowson.

Sinclair, J. (ed) (1987) *Looking Up*. London: Harper Collins.

Swan, M. (2000) Review of Biber et al 1999. *International Journal of English Studies*.

Todd, L. & Hancock, I. (1986) *International English usage*. London: Croom Helm.

Trudgill, P. & Hannah, J. (eds.) (1995) *International English: a guide to varieties of standard English* 3rd. ed. London: Arnold.

West, M. (1953) *A General Service List of English Words: With semantic frequencies and a supplementary word-list for the writing of popular science and technology*. London: Longmans.

Widdowson, H.G. (1994) The Ownership of English. *TESOL Quarterly* 28/2: 377-389.

Contributors

Guy Cook (g.cook@reading.ac.uk) is Professor of Applied Linguistics at the University of Reading in England. His research interests include science communication, discourse analysis, the theory and practice of language teaching, literature teaching, and language play. His most recent books are *Language Play, Language Learning* (2000), *The Discourse of Advertising* (2001) and *Applied Linguistics* (to be published in 2003) in the series *Oxford Introductions to Language*.

Pilar Durán (p.duran@reading.ac.uk) is the Research Officer of the Vocabulary Diversity project in the School of Education at the University of Reading. She did her PhD in Applied Linguistics at Boston University, USA. From 1997 to 1999, she taught English literacy for migrant parents in a Boston based project. Her work and publications deal with issues concerning first language acquisition and the learning of a second language by migrant workers.

Julian Edge (j.edge@aston.ac.uk) works in Aston University's Language Studies Unit, where he teaches on the distance-learning MSc in TESOL, supervises doctoral research and is Convenor of the Centre for the Study of Professional Discourse and Development. He likes modern jazz and jalapeño-stuffed olives. His most recent publication (2002) is: *Continuing Cooperative Development: A Discourse Framework for Individuals as Colleagues*, published by the University of Michigan Press.

Ann Galloway (agallowa@cygnus.uwa.edu.au) is a researcher at Edith Cowan University, Western Australia, working on a project investigating literacy teaching strategies used with Indigenous students with conductive hearing loss. She is currntly completing a PhD through the Department of Linguistics, Macquarie University, researching the development of features of language use that contribute to coherence in persuasive texts written by older children.

Julia Gillen (j.gillen@open.ac.uk) is Lecturer in Applied Language Studies at the Open University. At the time of BAAL 2001 she was Senior Research Fellow at Manchester Metropolitan University. Her main research interest is the discourse of young users of technologies.

Current international projects include investigations of young children's telephone talk and a cross-cultural developmental psychology study. She is on the editorial board of the *Journal of Early Childhood Literacy*.

Adrian Holliday (arh1@cant.ac.uk) is a Reader in Applied Linguistics at Canterbury Christ Church University College where he supervises research in the critical sociology of TESOL and also directs the College-wide interdisciplinary PhD programme. In the 1980s he was a curriculum consultant at Damascus University and Ain Shams University, Cairo. He is specifically interested in discourses of professionalism and culture within TESOL.

Keith Johnson (k.johnson@lancaster.ac.uk) is Professor of Linguistics and Language Education at the University of Lancaster. He has recently completed a Leverhulme Research Fellowship during which he looked at aspects of expertise in language teacher task design. He is founder editor of the journal 'Language Teaching Research', and has published widely in the field of language education.

Claire Kramsch (ckramsch@socrates.Berkeley.EDU) is Professor of German and Foreign Language Acquisition at the University of California at Berkeley. She teaches both in the German Department and in the PhD program of the Graduate School of Education. She is the past president of AAAL and co-editor of *Applied Linguistics*.

Paul Meara (P.M.Meara@swansea.ac.uk) is Professor of Applied Linguistics at University of Wales Swansea, where he runs a research group that focusses on vocabulary acquisition in foreign languages. His current research is concerned with simulating models of vocabulary development, and the constraints that these models impose on theories about vocabulary acquisition and vocabulary loss in L2 learners. He is also Assistant Conductor of the City of Swansea Concert Band.

Celia Roberts (celiaroberts@lineone.net) is a Senior Research Fellow in the School of Education at King's College London. Her publications in the fields of urban discourse, second language socialisation and intercultural communication include: *Language and Discrimination* (Longman 1992, with Davies and Jupp), *Achieving Understanding* (Longman 1996, with Bremer et al.), *Talk, Work and Institutional Order* (Mouton 1999, with Sarangi) and *Language Learners as Ethnographers* (Multilingual Matters 2000, with Byram et al.).

Srikant Sarangi (sarangi@cf.ac.uk) is Professor of Language and Communication and Director of Health Communication Research Centre at Cardiff University. He is currently editor of *TEXT*, and Book Series Editor (with Chris Candlin) of *Communication in Public Life*; and *Advances in Applied Linguistics*. His major publications include *Language, Bureaucracy and Social Control* (with Stef Slembrouck); *Talk, Work and Institutional: Discourse in Medical, Mediation and Management Settings Order* (with Celia Roberts); *Discourse and Social Life* (with Malcolm Coulthard); and *Sociolinguistics and Social Theory* (with Nik Coupland and Chris Candlin).

Ellen Schur (ellens@oumail.openu.ac.il) is a Reading for Academic Purposes Course Coordinator and Materials Developer at the Open University, Israel. She is currently finishing up her doctorate at the University of Wales Swansea. Her main interest is Second Language Vocabulary Acquisition, specifically the structures of semantic networks in L1 and L2 mental lexicons.

Barbara Seidlhofer (barbara.seidlhofer@univie.ac.at) is Professor of English Linguistics / Applied Linguistics at Vienna University. She is the executive chair of the Austrian Association for Applied Linguistics, VerbAL and the Director of a corpus project on English as a lingua franca, supported by the Oxford University Press (VOICE: the Vienna-Oxford International Corpus of English). Her publications include *Pronunciation* (with C. Dalton), *Approaches to Summarization: Discourse Analysis and Language Education*, *Principle and Practice in Applied Linguistics* (co- edited with G. Cook), and *Language Policy and Language Education in Emerging Nations* (co-edited with R. de Beaugrande and M. Grosman). She is currently working on a book on the description and pedagogy of English as a lingua franca.

Daniela Sime (daniela.sime@stir.ac.uk) is currently a Ph.D. scholar in the Centre for English Language Teaching, University of Stirling. Her research focus is on teachers' and language learners' non-verbal behaviour in the language learning context and on participants' interpretations of bodily action during class interaction. She has an educational background in English language studies and was a teacher of English as a foreign language before starting her research career.

James Simpson (j.e.b.simpson@reading.ac.uk) is currently studying for a PhD at the University of Reading. He has worked as an English language teacher in Greece, Saudi Arabia and the UK. His research interests lie in the areas of computer-mediated communication, discourse analysis, literacy and language teaching.

Sue Wharton (s.m.wharton@aston.ac.uk) has taught on Aston University's MSc TESOL since 1993. She has worked in TESOL in France, Spain, Mexico and UK. Her research interests in written discourse analysis focus on the TESOL community, and the work reported in this paper is part of a larger project intended to assist interested masters participants and graduates to begin to publish their work.